THE STRAI

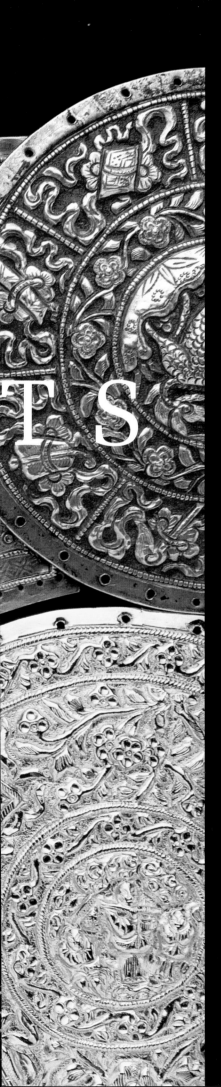

TS CHINESE

A CULTURAL HISTORY

Khoo Joo Ee

THE PEPIN PRESS
AMSTERDAM • KUALA LUMPUR

First published in 1996 by The Pepin Press B/v
Reprinted in 1998

Copyright © 1996, 1998 Pepin Van Roojen
Copyright text © Khoo Joo Ee

ISBN 90 5496 008 6

A Catalogue-in-Publication (CIP) record for this book is available from the publishers and from the Royal Dutch Library, The Hague.

The Pepin Press
POB 10349
1001 EH Amsterdam
The Netherlands
Fax (+) 31 20 4201152
Email: pepin@pepinpress.com

This book is designed and produced by The Pepin Press in Amsterdam and Kuala Lumpur

Printed and bound in Singapore

ON THE JACKET: A Penang Nyonya in formal attire of the 1920s.

PAGE 1: Decorative tiles in a shophouse in Malacca. (Courtesy Jonkers Malacca, photo H. Lin Ho)

PAGE 2—3: By the 1920s, Baba men wore western clothes. The women, however, still preferred the Malay baju panjang with a Javanese sarong. (Courtesy the Penang Museum)

PAGE 4: Silver gilt and silver decorative pillow ends. (Courtesy David Chan)

RIGHT: The Khoo Kongsi, Penang; ventilation window decorated with a legendary scene in sculptured and painted stone. (Photo Cheang Yik On)

PAGE 10: The altar in the main hall of the Khoo Kongsi, Penang. (Photo Cheang Yik On)

Contents

Contents

Acknowledgements

The author and publishers wish to thank the following persons and organizations for their assistance and contributions towards the publication of this book:

Asia House (Hong Kong), Asian Art Museum (Kuala Lumpur), Azah Aziz, The Baba Nyonya Heritage Museum (Malacca), Dorine van den Beukel, Rodney Bolt, Dr. Chan Chin Cheung, David F.C. Chan, Prof. Dr. Cheah Jin Seng, Walter Cheah, Cheang Yik On, Cheong Fatt Tze Mansion Sdn. Bhd., Audi Chung, O. Chung, H. Lin Ho, Hamidon Ali, Amy Hamidon, the late Ho Hong Seng, Ho Phaik Nooi, Jonkers (Malacca), Raymond Kam, Khoo Boo Eang, Dato' and Datin Khoo Keat Siew, Lily Khoo, King's Hotel (Singapore), Janet Kisai, Lee Siew Ee, Lim Eng Teng, Lim Kean Siew, Dato' Dr. Lim Kee Jin, Lim Lean Lee, Lim Lin Lee, Jon S.H. Lim, P.G. Lim, Datin Patricia Lim Pui Huen, Lim Suan Har, Mrs. Lim Teik Ee, Laurence Loh, George Moir, National Museum of Malaysia (Kuala Lumpur), National Museum of Singapore, Dato' Nasir Ariff, Mrs. Ong Chong Keng, Pamela Ong, Ong Siew See, Ong Siong Ngo, Penang Museum and Art Gallery, Pulau Pinang Magazine, Arend de Roever, State Chinese (Penang) Association (SCPA), Tan Joo Lan, Tan Keat Chye, Tan Kim Lan, Tan Siok Choo, Yeoh Cheng Kung, Yeoh Jin Leng.

India, China and Southeast Asia

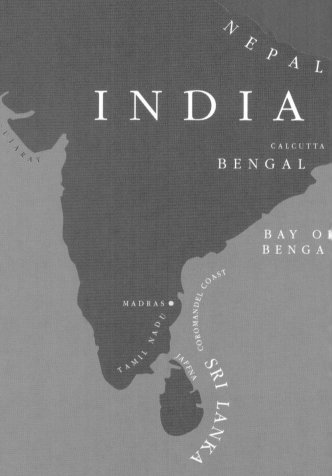

NEPAL

INDIA

GUJARAT

CALCUTTA
BENGAL

BAY OF
BENGAL

COROMANDEL COAST

MADRAS ●

TAMIL NADU

JAFFNA

SRI LANKA

INDIAN OCEAN

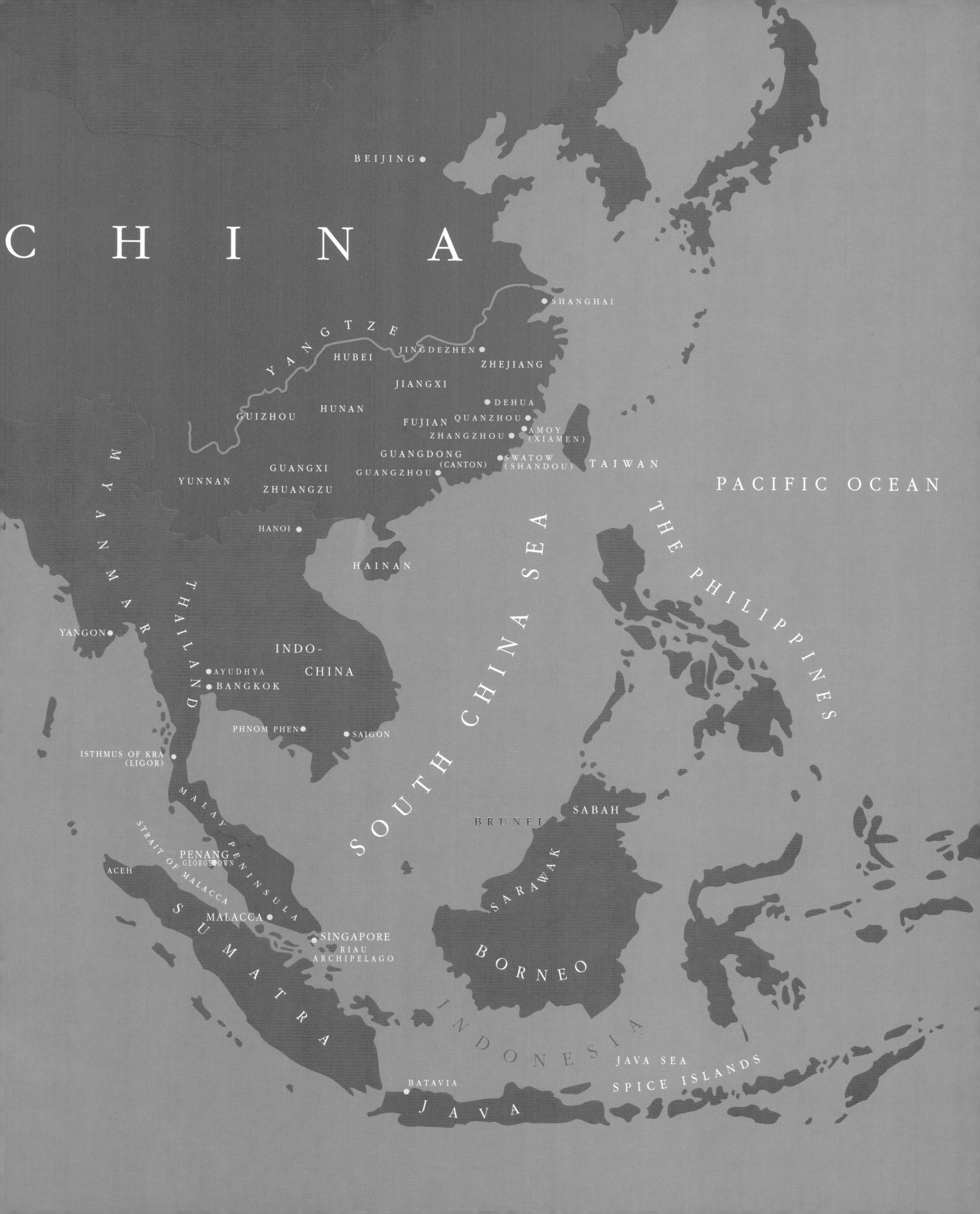

CHINA

BEIJING •

• SHANGHAI

YANGTZE

HUBEI   JINGDEZHEN •
                        ZHEJIANG
         JIANGXI

GUIZHOU   HUNAN   • DEHUA
              FUJIAN QUANZHOU •
                      • AMOY
              ZHANGZHOU • (XIAMEN)

GUANGXI   GUANGDONG   • SWATOW
               (CANTON)   (SHANDOU)   TAIWAN
YUNNAN   GUANGZHOU •
         ZHUANGZU

                                              PACIFIC OCEAN

HANOI •

M
Y
A
N
M
A
R   HAINAN

                                                        THE PHILIPPINES

T
H
A
I
L
A
N
D

YANGON •   INDO-
                        CHINA

        • AYUDHYA
        • BANGKOK

        • PHNOM PHEN   • SAIGON

ISTHMUS OF KRA •
(LIGOR)

                                    SOUTH CHINA SEA

MALAY PENINSULA

                                        BRUNEI   SABAH

STRAIT OF MALACCA

PENANG
GEORGETOWN

ACEH   SARAWAK

S
U
M
A
T
R
A   MALACCA •

            • SINGAPORE   BORNEO
              RIAU
              ARCHIPELAGO

                              INDONESIA

                                    JAVA SEA
                                    SPICE ISLANDS
        • BATAVIA

J A V A

Malaysia
and
Indonesia

MALAY PENINSULA

PROVINCE
WELLESLEY
GEORGETOWN •
PENANG
○ TAIPING
LARUT ○ IPOH

ACEH

S U M A T R A

○ MEDAN

SELANGOR
○ KUALA LUMPUR
NEGERI SEMBILAN
MALACCA ●
MALACCA

JOHOR

○ JOHOR BARU
● SINGAPORE

RIAU ARCHIPELAGO

MINANGKABAU

JAMBI ○

PALEMBANG ○

LAMPUNG

MALAYSIA

SABAH

BRUNEI

SARAWAK

KALIMANTAN

INDONESIA

PASISIR

●BATAVIA
CIREBON●
●PEKALONGAN
●SURAKARTA
●JOGYAKARTA

JAVA

Introduction

Sailing ships and luxury goods

Prior to the fifth century AD, Chinese records contain few references to the *Nanyang*, the Southern Ocean, which was the general term used to refer to the Southeast Asian region. The foreign trade desired in China was in luxury items from West Asia, which the Chinese called the 'Persian trade'. Before the fifth century, these goods were carried overland from West Asia to northern parts of China, and only subsequently did the 'Persian trade' begin to use the sea route. From the fifth century onwards, the increased use of the sea to transport goods between West Asia and China via India led to the rise of ports in the Malay Archipelago. Thus, the exotic marine and jungle produce of the Malay Archipelago was drawn into the international trade of early Asia. The Archipelago is linked with these two great markets of the early Asian world by the monsoon wind system.

The Straits of Malacca are geographically at the 'end of the monsoons' where ships had to await the change of winds to continue further, or return homeward. The channel is so sheltered that it has been frequently compared to an inland lake. Malacca, founded in about 1380 and flourishing in the fifteenth century, was equipped with warehouses where merchants could store their goods while awaiting incoming cargoes. Such storage facilities were necessary, it being impossible for the traders from India, China and the Eastern Archipelago to arrive at the same time, since all sea traffic was governed by the monsoon winds. At the time the Malacca Sultanate also had the allegiance of the *orang laut* or sea people, i.e. pirates. As an entrepôt, Malacca collected spices from East Indonesian islands and redistributed Indian textiles from Gujarat, Coromandel, Malabar and Bengal. Malacca, according to Tomé Pires writing around 1515, was 'of such importance and profit that it seems to me it has no equal in the world'. He reported that every year four or five thousand Gujarati mariners sailed to Malacca, where nearly one thousand Gujarati merchants conducted business. They carried goods in substantial quantities to the Malaccan emporium and returned with exotic merchandise from the Spice Islands and China.

The first phase of Chinese immigration into the *Nanyang* was by traders and merchants from China's south coast. Beginning with the march of Han Chinese towards the tropics (Weins, 1967), the southern provinces had always been considered 'rebellious' in the eyes of the northern capital. The final sinization of southerners was dur-

OPPOSITE PAGE: The interior of the Chan House in Malacca. (Courtesy the Baba Nyonya Heritage Museum, Malacca, photo H. Lin Ho)

17

ing China's golden age, the Tang Dynasty (AD 618-906), and for this reason, southern Chinese have traditionally referred to themselves as Tang Chinese (Fujian: *T'ng Lang*, Cantonese: *T'ong Yen*). The province of Fujian held out against northern Han Chinese expansion till the fourteenth century. It is somewhat ironical that the famous anti-Manchu Ming loyalist Koxinga was Fujianese, or Hokkien in Malaysian parlance. The Manchu ruling China under the Qing Dynasty (1644-1911), were particularly unpopular in the southern provinces, whose traditional maritime activities were persistently disrupted. The traders from China's southern provinces who came to Malacca in the late 1300s were an established class by 1400. Emperor Yongle (1403-1424) of the Ming Dynasty (1368-1644), in expanding Chinese trade overseas, selected Malacca as a convenient trading centre in the Straits at the 'end of the monsoons'. His Admiral, Cheng Ho (Zheng He), visited the Malay Peninsula in 1409 and again in 1411. After that Chinese settlers could be found sporadically along the west coast of the Peninsula. Around 1462, however, some five hundred Chinese moved to Malacca. *Bukit Cina* or Chinese Hill, which is a cemetery, is believed to be their resting place. Except for the settlers in Malacca, it was only after the arrival of the British that the Chinese population of the Peninsula increased significantly.

Originally, Portugal like other European kingdoms, had been receiving its Asian spices from the Venetians, who had obtained them from the Muslim Mamluk Empire in Egypt and Syria. Fifteenth century Portugal was blessed with peace and prosperity, and her rulers, beginning with Infante Dom Enrique or Prince Henry the Navigator (1394-1460), embarked on land and sea expeditions. One of the objectives was to collect spices directly from the Spice Islands. An expedition led by Albuquerque himself captured Malacca town on 10 August 1511. The conquest was not surprising since, apart from the superiority of Portuguese firearms, Malacca itself was divided by palace factions; it fell after a siege of just over a month.

It is interesting to note that early Portuguese maps of Malacca show that there was a *Kampung Cina* or Chinese village, as far back as the sixteenth century.

The Dutch East India Company was formed in 1602, and Batavia (modern Jakarta) became the company's headquarters in Asia in 1611. Malacca, captured from the Portuguese in 1641, was the company's outpost in the Malay Peninsula.

The drink of China was served in china: tea in porcelain. This was part of the chinoiserie that swept through Europe in the eighteenth century. Chinese porcelain stuffed with Chinese tea formed the bulk of the cargo that the Dutch East India Company carried to Europe. From the *Nanyang*, China herself desired forest and marine products. Malay rulers held monopolies on goods ranging from rattan to edible birds' nests, a delicacy in Chinese cuisine. The Malay Archipelago was an important trans-shipment area in the valuable China Trade which flourished between 1600 and 1860. Chinese merchants, however, did not want the goods Europe could offer. Payment in silver was a heavy drain on British reserves of bullion. In order to secure the China Trade, the English East India Company, founded in 1600 and based in India, resorted to shipping Indian cloth and opium to the Malay Peninsula. In exchange they got tin and spices which China also wanted, besides the exotic forest and marine products of the South Seas.

Anglo-Dutch rivalry in the Archipelago over the Spice and China Trades worsened with the increasing number of private English 'country traders'. Country trade meant 'port hopping', trading from port to port within East Asia, i.e. east of the Cape of

Good Hope. It was localized in contrast to the long haul from Europe to East Asia via the Cape. Both private country traders and the English East India Company participated in country trading. British private country traders in the eighteenth century were more numerous than other European ones. They were well financed and professionally organized. They even cultivated good relations with Malay courts. These traders outnumbered and overshadowed the official English East India Company itself.

By about the middle of the eighteenth century, the English East India Company had gained control over the cloth-producing and poppy-growing areas of India. As a result, they controlled the supply of opium to Southeast Asia and China, although even before then, it had been available in the Archipelago, where it was smoked mixed with tobacco. Added to these advantages in trading, the British Navy was moving ahead of that of other European nations in the fields of cartography and shipbuilding. The East Indiamen, built in India in the eighteenth century, were big ships for their time, capable of carrying very substantial cargoes.

Siam in the first half of the sixteenth century was always a threat to the Malay Peninsula. At that time, the Thai state of Ayudhya was, in fact, the most powerful state in Southeast Asia. It demanded tribute. This submission, known as *bunga mas dan perak* or 'gold and silver flowers', was made every third year. The 'gold and silver flowers' were actually more like trees, about a metre high, and were accompanied by offerings of slaves, weapons and cloth. Ayudhya's main administrative centre in the south was Ligor. It also demanded burdensome tributary gifts, as well as corvée labour. When the Thai general Chakri, later known as Rama I (1782-1809), seized the throne in 1782 he renewed aggression on the Thais' traditional enemy, Burma. Malay vassals from the Peninsula sent their share of weapons and fighting men. Malay rulers of the border states made personal tribute to Siam.

The Sultan of Kedah, being pressured by both Burmese and Siamese, offered to lease the island of Penang to the English East India Company. In return he expected protection against possible attacks from either Burma or Siam, and also from any future uprisings in his own palace.

A country trader named Francis Light entered into negotiations with the Sultan, following which, in 1786, he took formal possession of Penang Island in the name of King George III of England. Penang became an outpost for the English East India Company in the trade of goods such as pepper, gambier, nutmeg, betel nut, edible birds' nests, copra, gum arabic and tapioca from the Malay Peninsula and the Sumatran coast. Penang Island, known as the Pearl of the Orient, also later had her own spice plantations. British mercantile free-trade policy, expounded by the government of the English East India Company, attracted nearby Sumatran, southern Indian and southern Chinese petty traders and merchants to Georgetown, the pioneer town of Penang Island. In 1807, the British set up a Charter of Justice to ensure cultural and religious freedom for all immigrants. This attracted further settlers to the island. Each of these groups maintained its own traditions and identity within a competitive milieu. The island, located at the northern entry to the Straits of Malacca, has a spacious, sheltered natural harbour which is surrounded by the deep waters of the Indian Ocean. The setting up of this outpost for the China Trade and the Spice Trade is said to have been undertaken by natives, who cleared the jungle in search of coins fired from ships' cannon.

Convicts from India were sent to Penang in 1790 and in 1796 by the English East India

Company. The Andaman Islands in the Bay of Bengal had been India's penal station, and this was transferred to Penang. Singapore became a British settlement in 1819, and Indian convicts were also sent there in the 1840s. Penang remained as a penal station until 1857. Bencoolen, in Sumatra, was also a British penal station for convicts from India. They were not taken back to India when Bencoolen was ceded to the Dutch after the Napoleonic Wars (1795-1815); but were sent to Singapore. The British also brought Indian artisans and labourers into Penang.

When the English East India Company set up its port in Penang, only a few Chinese were living there. However, in time, more probably came across from the mainland of the Peninsula, and soon many more came from China. By the early nineteenth century, about one fifth of the population of the island was Chinese, three-quarters of them from Fujian province. From Penang they traded with the Southeast Asian mainland and India, as well as nearby Sumatra. Francis Light and other British residents also traded in Mergui, Burma. This would explain the colony of Burmese in Penang, where there is a Burmese pagoda dating from 1803. Trade in Penang flourished, although it did not draw shipping from all over the Archipelago.

A strip of land on the mainland opposite Penang Island was leased by the ruler of Kedah to the English East India Company in 1800, in return for an additional pension. The mainland territory was named Province Wellesley.

The English East India Company took temporary possession (British Interregnum) of Dutch colonies in Asia during the Napoleonic Wars (1795-1815). Malacca was included in this strategy, intended to prevent Dutch possessions from falling into French hands: Holland was conquered by Napoleon in 1795. After the Napoleonic Wars, Britain returned the colonies she had occupied to Holland, and exchanged Bencoolen for Malacca. These arrangements were provided for in the Anglo-Dutch Treaty of 1824, which was also meant to keep other European nations away from the Archipelago. The Treaty used the Straits of Malacca as the dividing line between Dutch and English colonies in South-East Asia. To this day it remains the boundary between Indonesia and Malaysia except, of course, in Borneo.

Singapore was better sited than Penang. Although Penang was founded, like Singapore, on the principles of free trade, it could not sustain a pan-Asian trade because it was not on one of the major routes between China and West Asia. In 1819, when Sir Stamford Raffles arrived in Singapore, there were fewer than fifty Chinese on the island who, we assume, went there from Malacca or the nearby island of Riau. Only five years later, the Chinese formed a third of the total population. Within three decades the Chinese had formed a well-established community. Early Singapore, like Penang, encouraged settlers. Early Chinese traders who went to Singapore still looked for the marine and forest goods which the British called 'Straits produce'. These included edible birds' nests, camphor, seaweed and dragon's blood, which is a reddish gum from the rattan palm. The very nature of these goods meant that the supply was intermittent and unreliable. The middleman needed to cultivate a personal relationship with the collector. So it followed that agriculturalists were encouraged.

The policy of the English East India Company was to let settlers own as much land as they could clear. Penang, an example of this type of early settlement, attracted a large cosmopolitan population including the British themselves, Arabs, Armenians, Bugis, Burmese, Chinese, Indians, Javanese, Malays and Siamese. The Straits Settlements, comprising Penang, Singapore and Malacca as one administrative unit, was established in 1826 with Penang as the capital. This move coincided with expanding trade in all three ports. In 1832 the capital was shifted to Singapore, and in 1867 the administration of the Straits Settlements was transferred from India to the Colonial Office in London. This followed the closing down of the English East India Company in 1858. The Company had already lost its monopoly of the China Trade in 1833. The Straits Settlements enjoyed a trade boom with Europe and East Asia towards the end of the nineteenth century because of the introduction of steamships and the opening of the Suez Canal.

The Straits Chinese 1

The Babas and early economic activities

Originally, only Chinese traders set up trading posts in the same manner as the European East India Companies, though on an individual basis. Leaving China with the northeast monsoon at the end of the year, they sailed back there with the southwest monsoon in the middle of the year. They therefore spent about five months a year in each port. After a while, they set up second homes in Malacca, with local wives who looked after their businesses when they returned annually to China. Pioneering immigrants did not, as a rule, bring their womenfolk on hazardous journeys to faraway lands. Indeed, virtually no Chinese women came to Malaya until the mid-nineteenth century. In present-day Malaysia, the marriage of a Chinese man to a Malay woman would necessitate his becoming a Muslim. In bygone days it is likely that this rule was not always observed, especially in Malacca, where, moreover, there would have been ethnic Malays, including potential wives for Chinese husbands, who were not Muslims.

In most cases, the offspring of such inter-marriages would marry among themselves. Alternatively, the daughters were married to Chinese males who had newly arrived, and had demonstrated great industry and promise. Family records would not show details of the lineage of females. At most, only their names would be known. This is in line with the preoccupation of the Chinese, and other patrilineal groups, with male heirs. Male offspring of these early Malacca marriages were sent back to China for education while the daughters remained in Malacca with their local mothers. When Chinese emigrants settled for good in the Straits, their descendants, who continued to form the merchant communities, tended to group together in certain parts of town. A large majority of the members of these communities in the Straits Settlements were from Fujian province.

Straits Chinese, Straits-born Chinese, Baba Chinese or simply Baba, and *Peranakan* are terms which have been used interchangeably by the people themselves and by people describing them. Their womenfolk are called Nyonya. The Straits Settlements, comprising Penang, Malacca and Singapore, formed a historical political unit which no longer exists. Throughout the period when it did exist, not all the Chinese living in the Straits Settlements were born there. Therefore, strictly, a distinction should be made between a Straits Chinese and a Straits-born Chinese. The latter, however, used

OPPOSITE PAGE: *Kapitan Cina* Chung Keng Kwee (c. 1821-1901) in a Mandarin robe of the Second Rank and a Manchu cap; his Mandarin square features the golden pheasant. (Courtesy Asia House, Hong Kong)

the term Straits Chinese as a contraction, so that now there is no distinction between the two terms. However, those born in the Straits during the time when the Straits Settlements existed, regarded this as the only essential qualification needed to be termed Straits Chinese. The expression which the Straits-born Chinese used for those not born in the Straits was *Sinkhek* or newcomers. The expression Straits (-born) Chinese has always meant those of the historical Straits Settlements, and does not include Chinese in other states which also border the Straits of Malacca.

The etymology of the term 'Baba' has provoked much discussion. The term travelled to the Malay Peninsula when the English East India company extended its trade influence from its stronghold in India to the Straits of Malacca. The word itself appears to originate from India, and ultimately from West Asia. In northern India, where the Hindustani language is greatly influenced by Persian, Baba is a general title of respect; a Pakistani wife addresses her husband as 'Baba'. The honorific Baba in time came to refer primarily to Straits Chinese men. The word 'Nyonya' for Straits Chinese women is less exclusive, being applied also to the women of Sumatra and Java. In fact, Nyonya, and its variants *Nyonyah*, *Nonya* and *Nona* are traditional Malay forms of address for non-Malay married ladies of some standing: they can probably be traced to the Portuguese word for 'grandmother'.

Descendants of immigrants who were born in Malaya and Indonesia are called *Peranakan*, a Malay word that applies to those who are native by birth. The term is from the Malay root word *anak* for child or children. By definition, the *Peranakan* community encompasses all local-born Indians, Eurasians and Chinese, including those born in communities outside the former Straits Settlements, such as the Indonesian Chinese. (There are also important coastal Chinese settlements in Java and Sumatra.) Thus, a Baba is a *Peranakan* but not all *Peranakan* are Babas.

In much earlier literature there is the assumption of a homogeneous Baba culture throughout the former Straits Settlements. The earliest members of these communities were from Malacca. These Malacca Babas were linguistically assimilated, speaking a form of Malay patois termed Baba Malay (see Everyday Life). By and large, Singapore's Baba community was an extension of that of Malacca.

The Babas of Penang, Malacca and Singapore, while being distinct groups within the Chinese population, exist at various levels of assimilation with the culture of the local Malays. Offspring of later Chinese immigrants, who have been acculturated to the Babas but who do not speak the Baba patois, form the next largest group within the Straits Chinese community.

In order to accommodate both the China Trade and other markets in Europe, entrepreneurs extended their activities beyond exotic products, and ventured into commercial agriculture. Early Baba traders and shopkeepers were among these entrepreneurs. Europeans and Chinese provided the capital and initiative while the former also contributed technology. The early Chinese cultivated pepper, gambier, nutmeg, sago, pineapple, and vegetables, besides being fishermen. Tapioca, which was cultivated especially in Malacca, yielded quick returns because of its relatively short life cycle. Early Malacca produced sago, and this too was controlled by Chinese planters; they also pioneered sugar planting in Province Wellesley.

In the 1820s, Aceh in Sumatra was the chief producer of pepper. By the 1850s, when the trade reached its height, other new pepper ports on the east coast of Sumatra sprang up. Towards the end of the nineteenth century, Penang started planting pepper

Three Chinese with hair queues. The queue is a misconstrued Chinese tradition: it was imposed by the Manchus. (Courtesy Penang Museum)

and competing with Aceh. The crop is seasonal and relatively slow to mature, but it was usually combined with gambier, which was harvested the year round; the gambier acted as a cover for the pepper, helping to reduce erosion. Its leaves were processed by boiling and the residue was used as fertilizer for the pepper vines. By the third decade of the nineteenth century, the Chinese, especially in Singapore, had established extensive pepper and gambier estates. The products were originally meant for the China Trade, but their usefulness in Europe later proved even more profitable. Before the invention of plastics, natural products like leather were used more extensively. Gambier was used to tan leather, although in the Straits area itself it was used mainly for making medicine.

These commercial agricultural enterprises were often plantations outside the Straits Settlements. Later, the merchants, who soon became landowners, ventured into shipping and banking or became general traders in rice, cotton and tea. They also ran shops and warehouses, and were government agents, or farmers of public revenue, especially of taxes on tobacco and opium. Their later enterprises included the supply of indentured labour for mines and rubber plantations.

The Babas, being descendants of pioneers, and proud of their established position in the British colony, called themselves local-born or *Peranakan*, thus setting themselves apart from recent immigrants from China. The Nyonya adopted Malay dress and developed a spicy Malay-influenced cuisine. The Babas, partially assimilated into Malay culture, also began to embrace the European ways and mores of colonial society. However, they remained Chinese in their religious beliefs and ceremonies. The identity of the Babas, like their speech, tended to be a cultural blend of Chinese, Malay and European. The observation made by Viraphol (1972:30) about Bangkok Chinese could very well be applied to the Babas: 'Their unique social structure was based on Chinese habits; but without renewal from China, great modifications by indigenous and foreign forces produced a distinct culture'. A Baba then had little incentive to visit China; he identified with the place of his birth, where the luxury he enjoyed was a product of his unceasing industry.

The Babas were an urban white-collar community who consciously allied themselves with the British government and sent their children to schools where English was the medium of instruction. In their evolution into the trading élite, they developed a rapport with Europeans, which resulted in their adopting westernized habits and business procedures. The western culture that the Babas met with was that of a ruling class, and early indications of taking to British ways were ostentatious displays of wealth, such as big houses, carriages and collections of *objets d'art* — all material possessions of the ruling class which could be acquired relatively easily.

After graduating from school, the younger Babas often opted for an apprenticeship with a western business firm instead of joining their fathers' enterprises. Their training period was likely to be six to ten years. They emerged from it equipped with a certain competitive edge: they had learnt modern western business practices besides gaining an insight into the colonial bureaucracy. Furthermore, they would have cultivated personal contacts with western capitalists. The Babas opted for English education because of their lead in business, not because they were being edged out by more industrious *Sinkhek*. In fact, it could be surmised that the business leaders, Babas or not, sent their sons to English schools to gain familiarity with modern western commercial and financial management as well as to obtain technical know-how.

The period from around the mid-eighteenth to the mid-nineteenth century could be said to be the heyday of the wealthy Baba élite and entrepreneurs. It was then that they became westernized. This was the period during which the already wealthy Malacca Babas, most of them merchants and landed gentry, expanded their business network to Singapore. These urban, Malay and English-speaking Chinese began to be on the committees of all sorts of organizations. This did not mean that they were regarded by all Chinese as leaders of the community, but in a society where the official language was English they were at an advantage. When an organization was run by a western-style committee which had been formally elected, the westernized English-speaking Babas were prominent. Many of them were appointed as leaders by the Government. Publicly, they were leaders in organizations which included both English-speaking and Chinese-speaking members, but it did not follow that they controlled policy.

European entrepreneurs, together with Chinese merchants, were the *nouveau riche* of the time and their opulent mansions were statements of rank. Their wealth was acquired from trading profits, land speculation and from being revenue farmers (collectors of taxes for the Straits Government). While some used their wealth and influence to obtain tenders for the liquor, opium and gambling farms, others simply worked incessantly in trade to amass capital. Some of the better-educated, however, formed the an anti-opium movement.

The Babas' elaborate material possessions demonstrated how different they were from other Straits Chinese, and they began feeling their distance from the newcomers. They even had clubs where *Sinkhek* were barred. This distance was accentuated when the Straits Settlements became a Crown colony in 1867, and the Babas became British subjects. Later there was a Straits Settlements Society which was quasi-political. It was formed in 1905 as a branch of a London-based body representing the interests of British subjects.

The Babas' self-importance derived from their early arrival, and rested, therefore, on the same basis as that of other aristocracies. The flowering of Baba culture coincided with British rule in the Straits. Although many Babas were segregating themselves by the end of the nineteenth century with their own network of social clubs, they also remained in certain associations which cut across all sectors of Chinese society. This was especially so with the Penang Babas. The Babas in Penang and Singapore were by then English-speaking and westernized, but their womenfolk, the Nyonya, were comparatively more assimilated into Malay culture.

Within the Baba community, there were distinctions among language groups. Hokkien Babas who called themselves 'true Babas', tended to deride Teochew, Cantonese, Hakka, and Hainanese Babas since these groups were more socially and culturally Chinese. The Hokkien Babas in Penang were already a distinct social group before the 1860s when Vaughan (1879) wrote about them. However, they interacted more than some other Babas with non-Baba Chinese and because of this interaction in fact reaffirmed their 'Babaness'.

Generally, the Baba lifestyle can be said to have consisted of: Chinese religion, customs and practices; Chinese and European (including Anglo-Indian) architecture; Malay language, customs and cuisine. Their lifestyle of cultivated gentility was syncretic, being a fusion of mainly Hokkien Chinese, Malay and British elements. Old families having arrived in high society, flaunted their cultivated gentility and displayed

a certain haughty arrogance. As mentioned earlier, the Baba community in Singapore was similar to that of Malacca, although it emerged later. In Penang, however, a community of less assimilated Chinese developed, acculturated to a lesser degree with indigenous life. The daughter of a Sumatran *Kapitan Cina*, Queeny Chang, visited Penang in the early 1900s, and remarked in her memoir, on the high life of Penang's Chinese. (Chang 1981:51-52). In Medan and other Sumatran towns, the rich Chinese *Peranakan* élite were more restrained in public displays of wealth, never matching the flamboyant, gay élite of Singapore and Penang. Penang's dominant Hokkien group had built up a network of business and kinship ties, with marriage connections that reached Borneo, Sumatra, Burma and Siam. Their business interests ranged from Calcutta to Hong Kong.

As the nineteenth century advanced, Baba numbers increased with the assimilation of immigrant men. As soon as an immigrant from China had saved enough money, he often started a small shop in a Malay village, where he learned to make himself understood in colloquial Malay. When he was ready to start a family, he asked for a girl from a poorer Baba family or a daughter of one of the concubines of the wealthy. Such Nyonyas are to be found today in rural areas, married to small shopkeepers, and their children are Babas.

There is a tendency to equate the Babas with the élite. This is because, inevitably,

A Straits Chinese family of the early nineteenth century. The men are still in Chinese clothes, while the women are already in Malay costume. (Courtesy Penang Museum)

A bridal couple on the twelfth
day of their wedding. (Courtesy
Tan Keat Chye)

accounts of Baba lifestyle tend to record the cultural monopoly of the rich and their more visible and memorable style, and they had, after all, dominated trade and social life in the Straits Settlements into the early decades of the twentieth century. This is not to say that the rural Babas made no impact on chroniclers: they have their share of documentation.

One of the differences between the élite urban Babas and their country cousins was the degree of borrowing from the Malay and British cultures. The three cultural influences — Chinese, Malay and Western — all operated, and the balance between them was related to social circumstances, and could change with social mobility, but generally the rural Babas were more acculturated to the Malays and the urban Babas, who represented the upper social stratum of their community, were more anglicized.

In the 1930s many of the Babas who owned extensive rubber estates suffered greatly because of the Depression. During the Second World War and the Japanese Occupation of Malaya the Babas shared wartime hardships with other Chinese: the landowners had to abandon their homes and their property, while the Nyonyas sold their jewellery to buy food.

The non-Babas, accustomed to hard work, managed to recover from the effects of the war, but not so the majority of rich Babas, who had been born with the proverbial silver spoons in their mouths and were used to luxury. After the war they underwent a period of deprivation and decline, and some of them sank into genteel poverty. For many of them it became difficult or impossible to maintain their former lifestyles. They could no longer afford to import crockery from China, and there was no more made-to-order furniture or silverware.

In these circumstances, the highly developed culture began to disintegrate. Moreover the identity of the Baba community became blurred, partly as a result of the changed structure of society, and partly because of the conversion of many Babas to Christianity.

In the early days, local birth — being a *Peranakan* — was a distinguishing feature of the Babas. It became irrelevant within the larger Chinese community as more and more Chinese were born in the country. Also, the post-war financial decline among the Babas coincided with the growing tendency of Baba sons and daughters to marry Chinese of more recent immigrant origin. Possibly this, more than anything else, helped to erode the differences between the Baba and other Chinese communities.

Traditional associations

Immigrants bring with them their cultural baggage. In it is their speech, and the customs and forms of social organization that have conditioned them. Clan associations are normally formed voluntarily on the basis of blood ties. Among overseas Chinese, however, members of the same clan are those with common surnames, although not necessarily with common ancestry. Another type of grouping is according to place of origin in China, which may mean anything from a small village to a province. Overseas Chinese invariably group themselves according to smaller territorial units. Most overseas Chinese are from two southern provinces only, Fujian and Guangdong, but two associations would not have been enough for the whole community. Besides associations based on surnames or places, there were others based on language or dialect. Finally, artisans, merchants and professionals formed themselves into guilds to protect their occupations. Of all these co-operative systems, which are unfettered by political boundaries, the clan association or *Kongsi* is especially effective. It can develop into a bureaucracy with a network all over South-East Asia, of district branches each manned by a hierarchy of managerial, clerical and menial staff which functions to maintain a 'secretariat' which is also its clan temple. Clan associations, which were formally structured by the beginning of the nineteenth century, still operate in the same way today.

The *Kongsi*, in looking after the welfare of the clan, dispenses cash, educational aid and daily living expenses to poor and aged clansmen without families. A *Kongsi's* property is used to provide homes for the aged and disabled. Although the records of a clan do not include female lineage, spinsters and widows come under its welfare scheme. Marriage ceremonies are often held at the *Kongsi's* premises, which are equipped for such functions. A *Kongsi's* property includes burial grounds and the *Kongsi* is responsible for burying clansmen who have no relatives. In the past, the funeral procession of a deceased member would be accompanied by bearers carrying the banners and lanterns of the clan association: clan members who did not attend would be penalized. However, nowadays, besides clan organizations, other bodies also cater for marriages and funerals. Originally, a clan association also managed internal clan problems; the clan would lose face if a British magistrate arbitrated in disputes among clan members.

A *Kongsi* may be a company with business interests in the nature of a co-operative. Clan leaders are often businessmen, men of wealth and influence, or both. A clan may even be a semi-political league. Thus the incentives to become a clan member are business connections and mutual protection. At least one of these bodies has even instituted a provident fund for its members. Clan associations also function as banks for their members.

Kongsis of the same speech group may unite, as in Penang where the so-called 'big five surnames' formed a corporate Hokkien group *Kongsi* in 1800. These big five surnames, Cheah, Khoo, Lim, Tan and Yeoh, were, in fact, those of close neighbours in the same county in the province of Fujian. There is in Penang a sort of personalized clan temple built by a *Kapitan Cina* for himself (see Architecture). Besides an ancestral hall, it housed, at one time, a family school.

The main manifestation of lineage was filial piety. To sustain this family tree, when there was no male issue, adoption was resorted to. Within the immediate family, unmarried brothers and sisters were the charges of the eldest or only son after the parents' death. He would have been expected to continue to live with his parents after marriage.

Both in China and Malaya, different Chinese language groups tended to regard each other almost as foreigners, and often became involved in feuds. In Malaya, until the early twentieth century, they acquired more understanding of British values than they did of each others' languages and customs. Turnbull (1972:35) noted that the Hokkien Chinese in Malaya were historically the most prosperous and 'settled' of any Chinese in the country. The bulk of the trading and shopkeeping classes in the towns were Hokkien. Initially, these were their main occupations; later they diversified into agriculture. Hokkiens are reputed to keep their daughters and not allow them to move far away after marriage. This is contrary to general Chinese practice and may be related to the vestiges of a matriarchial system.

Nine Nonyas in full festive attire assemble for a formal photo.
(Courtesy Tan Keat Chye)

The clan has its 'secretariat' —
a *Kongsi* building — many of
which are most elaborate; it also
functions as a collective ancestral temple. This is the façade of
the Khoo *Kongsi* in Penang
which looks not too different
from a temple. The 'top-heavy'
structure emphasizes the roof,
which is heavily embellished.
Its ground floor gives the
impression of a decorative
plinth; it is in fact an enclosed
space with masonry pillars
supporting the temple proper.
(Photo Cheang Yik On)

Individuals may be of the same surname or clan but speak different languages. They
then normally gravitate to their own dialect group, but this is not always so. The
Teochew dialect is akin to Hokkien and both groups have closely related occupations
and customs, but the affinity was undermined because the Hokkien community was
originally more influential and urban, and therefore tended to be more westernized.
Teochew people, most numerous in early Singapore, originated from Swatow, a city at
the mouth of the Han River in Guangdong Province. The Cantonese dominated mining, but they were also craftsmen and artisans excelling in carpentry and black-
smithing. Hailam people from the island of Hainan excelled in running food establish-
ments, while their original role was as domestic servants.

Generally, Hokkien-speaking Chinese predominated in the Straits Settlements while
the Cantonese were more numerous in the Malay states of the Peninsula. Competition
for control of labour in the tin mines, and later in the rubber estates, accentuated
rivalry between the Cantonese and another Guangdong group, the Hakka (or Khek).
Towards the end of the nineteenth century, the two main speech groups, Hokkien and
Cantonese, managed to come together. In Penang, this was achieved by the establishment of a common organization for the two groups in 1880. Further moves for unity
were made by temples: for instance the temple of the Goddess of Mercy in Penang
arbitrated between feuding speech groups and factions. Finally, pan-Chinese associations were formed.

Secret societies

One of the organizations nineteenth century overseas Chinese brought with them was
the secret society. It provided the individual with a social background of mutual aid,
protection, assistance and a sense of kinship in a foreign land. An example of mutual
help was the Pauper Hospital in Penang built by a secret society leader in 1854. It
was renamed the District Hospital in 1906 by the British Government. A community

leader in the mid seventeenth century bought a whole hill and donated it as a cemetery for the Chinese community in Malacca. In fact, the secret society was a major social, commercial and even political organization, and a powerful and pervading system in Chinese communal life. British administrative control did not reach into the Chinese community until late in the nineteenth century.

In Malacca, the Dutch started the system of having a *Kapitan Cina* or Chinese Captain, i.e. headman: the expression does not refer to ships or the army. These community leaders were often rewarded with grants of state revenue farms if they helped keep peace and order. As rules of succession to the post were not defined, the system itself generated quarrels between different factions of the Chinese community because of the economic rewards involved. Usually the *Kapitan Cina* himself was a leading member of a secret society. It was an especially demanding position, considering his obligations to the society itself, compounded by the host of competing interests of the other Chinese organizations. Few *Kapitan Cina* could have managed to exert their authority over all Chinese in their area.

For the employee, it was impossible not to belong to the society in control of his place of employment. This was not always bad, as the network of secret societies was the most important organization within the Chinese community throughout most of the nineteenth century, encompassing the entire Chinese population. It was sometimes difficult, however, to distinguish between secret societies and clan associations which were welfare societies. These latter bodies also had large memberships and likewise exercised considerable influence over their members. Thus, a secret society was often almost synonymous with a clan association and was wealthy because the members included successful businessmen. Sometimes a society was controlled by one speech group, or even a clan. With the passage of time, there were naturally changes in leadership. The composition of groups was changeable, so that splinter societies arose in some cases while amalgamations occurred in others: at any given time a society might have several branches for different speech groups.

The secret societies were generally drawn from one group, probably because a language group had the monopoly on both the original and newly imported labour and its placement in jobs. Thus the *Sinkhek* had to join the respective groups that controlled them: this sort of control of labour was usual in the economy of the time. While some societies were exclusive and small, others were big and more open, with even Malay, Portuguese and Indian members. Dutch Malacca strictly controlled these societies, limiting their activities to mutual aid and rituals related to ancestor worship.

By the 1830s, there were three main societies in the Straits Settlements: the *Ghee Hin*, the *Ho Seng* and the *Hai San*. However, there were in fact only two main rival alliance groups: these developed according to dialect. Alliance to these groups spread throughout the Straits Settlements and the Malay Peninsula. The Cantonese *Ghee Hin* was the largest group and had a wide sphere of influence. The *Ho Seng* are believed to have been a splinter group of the *Ghee Hin* and were also Cantonese, but they were based in Penang. The common rival of these two groups was the *Hai San* (whose members were mainly Hakka Chinese), and their allies the Hokkien-dominated *Khian Teik* of Penang. The protracted struggle was for control of lucrative trade and franchises from the Government. The *Khian Teik* secret society has often been erroneously referred to as the *Tua Pek Kong* or sometimes *Tokong*, which are names for the generic God of good fortune worshipped by all overseas Chinese. Vaughan

The Chew Jetty *Kongsi* in Penang. (Photo Khoo Joo Ee)

(1879;1971:103) observed that the *Khian Teik*, which he also erroneously called *Tua Pek Kong*, were chiefly Hokkiens and Babas. The *Ghee Hin* were fishermen, labourers and artisans. The *Khian Teik* on the other hand, were prominent and prosperous traders in opium and firearms.

The existence of these societies was not secret: only their initiation rites, oaths and rituals were. In Malacca the societies were more like exclusive clubs with élite members. The much larger Chinese communities in Penang and Singapore, where there were shorter traditions of leadership, had more conflicts.

The members of the Penang societies ranged from the *Sinkhek* to the oldest and best established businessmen. Both China-born and locally born members battled for control of labour, the basic commodity of early primary industry. In Penang's Georgetown, each of the two main societies had both Indian-Muslim and Malay allies. The *Jawi Peranakan* community, consisting of descendants of marriages between Indians and local Malay women was, and still is, substantial in Penang and Province Wellesley. These *Peranakan* also formed two secret protection societies of their own on the Chinese model, going by the names of Red Flag and White Flag. The flag societies were racially mixed: their members included Hindu Indians, Malays, Javanese and Achinese. By the second half of the nineteenth century, the *Jawi Peranakan* societies had aligned themselves with rival Chinese societies. They even went through the special initiation ceremony (Blythe 1969:130). The *Ghee Hin* were allied with the White Flag while the *Khian Teik* teamed up with the Red Flag society. Thus, the underlying cause of secret society conflicts was not racial. There were class divisions within a society: especially for those in the front line during gang fights, there were arrangements for pensions and gratuities; such amenities were needed less by members who did not risk their lives during such fights (*Penang Riots*, 1867:6).

The Malacca and Penang societies began to extend their activities into the Malay states in the 1820s. From Penang, the Cantonese *Ghee Hin*, in particular, branched into the Peninsula during the second half of the nineteenth century. This group concentrated on economic development, especially in the state of Perak. A district would be simultaneously ruled by the Malay and the Chinese factions which were allied. As elsewhere, the Malay and Indian Muslims in Perak were divided, aligning themselves with either the Penang White Flag or Red Flag.

One Malay State Councillor for Perak, the *Orang Kaya Temenggong*, was probably a member of the Red Flag society, and another of the State's Councillors, Raja Idris, sympathized with the White Flag; both served on the first State Council formed by the British Resident Hugh Low in 1877.

In Singapore, there were also non-Cantonese divisions of the *Ghee Hin* society but, unlike the Penang societies, which included non-Chinese members, the Singapore ones were confined to Chinese speech groups. The Singapore *Ghee Hin*, with its five sub-divisions corresponding to the major southern Chinese languages, each of which was further split along clan lines, illustrates the multiplication of sub-divisions in the secret society network. Thus Chinese from the same area and speech group might very well be divided by different allegiances.

In Southeast China, secret societies began as mutual aid organizations with some religious overtones. As early as the seventeenth century, however, they took on a political function. In Guangdong and Fujian provinces they purported to have the noble objective of overthrowing the Manchus and restoring a Chinese dynasty, but in fact they represented the division between the influential rich and the weak poor. Because most of their members were poor, they were secretly disaffected with the state.

Secret societies and clan rivalries became embroiled with Malay politics in the nineteenth century. Feuding Malay chiefs were unable to pool enough funds to extract tin from deeper veins as surface deposits were gradually exhausted. In 1848, the Malay territorial chief of the district of Larut in Perak invited Chinese miners to develop the tin deposits there. Larut had been uninhabited before 1850 (Purcell 1978:103); it is separated from the state of Perak proper by a range of hills. When settlers did move in, *Hai San* supporters formed the majority in the district. Fighting broke out in 1861 when a group of *Ghee Hin* supporters tried to gain control of a waterway serving the mines of both factions. This quarrel could not be confined to Larut because each group had strong ties to societies and business interests in Penang. In addition, many Larut Chinese claimed to be British subjects from the Straits Settlements. Penang merchants were anxious to influence the outcome of the dispute; their reward would have been control of the opium trade around the tin mines in Larut. Up till then the Straits Chinese merchants had been financing mining operations in Perak.

In 1867, the very same year that the group of Straits Settlements was transferred to the Colonial Office, there were secret society riots in Penang. The reason for the quarrel was competition for control of the tin mines on the mainland. The riots were the culmination of a gang war between the *Khian Teik*, the *Hai San* and their allies, the Malay Red Flag, on the one hand, and the *Ghee Hin* and its supporters, the Malay White Flag, on the other. Since non-Chinese allies participated on both sides in the riots, they were seen as secret society conflicts, not as ethnic clashes. The town was in a state of siege for ten days, but there was no real victor. However, the *Khian Teik* leader, Khoo Thean Teik, a trader who also controlled immigrant labour, together with the leader of the *Hai San*, Chung Keng Kwee, extended trade monopolies for the two groups into the neighbouring state of Perak. Together, they controlled the sale of tobacco, liquor, and opium, and ran gambling farms. These farms had trade rights or franchises leased (or 'farmed out') by the colonial government.

Numerically, the *Ghee Hin* along with the White Flag society were far superior; but the *Khian Teik* were fully prepared for a fight to the finish (Blythe, 1969:131). Being wealthy merchants and shop-keepers, they possessed firearms and ammunition (*Penang Riots*, 1867:6), giving them a distinct advantage during the riots.

Blythe (1969:238) observed that secret societies were more deep-rooted in the life of Penang than elsewhere. All secret societies in Malaya had headquarters in Penang but the *Ghee Hin* and *Hai San* were strong in the mining Kinta district of Perak. In records of secret societies registered in 1879 in the Straits Settlements, Blythe (1969:208) lists ten societies in Singapore, six in Penang and five in Malacca. The number of members was highest in Penang, being 39,267. In Singapore there were 23,858 society members, while in Malacca there were only 3,500.

Although the *Hai San* formed an alliance with two other societies, the Penang-based Hokkien *Khian Teik* and the *Ho Seng*, another conflict in 1872-3 went unresolved. Impending quarrels about succession in the Malay states soon became deeply entangled with the society fights in Perak. In 1896 it was estimated that almost fifteen thousand workers were members of a society, which was about three-quarters of the Chinese mining population.

The 1860s saw the culmination of this protracted struggle to control Chinese society and the economy in Malaya. The Larut Wars between *Ghee Hin* and *Hai San*, which dragged on from 1862 to 1874, reached an explosive level in the Penang Riots in 1867. In this fierce conflict the *Ghee Hin* fought it out with the *Khian Teik*, who were allied to the *Hai San*. In Singapore in 1863 the *Ghee Hin* were engaged in battles with the *Ghee Hock*, a mainly Teochew group originating in Singapore and with an affiliate in Penang. At the same time the commercial community in the Straits Settlements was certain that the disturbances in the Malay states endangered not only trade and capital investment, but that they also inhibited future economic development. At this stage, Chinese clans and societies were supplying money and fighting men at the request of Malay leaders.

Through public meetings, the press, petitions and personal connections, the interest groups in the Straits Settlements argued that Britain must take steps in the Malay States to create a climate more conducive to investment and trade: there were continual petitions and memoranda to this effect from the Straits merchant community.

Besides disputes between Chinese secret societies, and palace disturbances among Malay princes, there were pirates off the coast of Sumatra. Financial backing for some of the warring factions came from the Straits Settlements and was supplied not only by Chinese merchants but also by British entrepreneurs. The 1860s and early 1870s saw the Straits Government being bombarded by various lobbies as the fighting became more widespread. The parties involved ranged from individual merchants and shareholders of big companies, to English legal firms representing Chinese secret societies. There were two zones of operation; societies originating in Penang influenced the whole of the north of the Peninsula, especially Kedah, Perak and coastal Selangor, while Singaporean societies extended their activities into the states of Johor, Malacca, Negri Sembilan and parts of Selangor.

Secret society power began to be eroded during the last quarter of the nineteenth century. A Chinese Protectorate was set up in Singapore in 1877. Stricter laws were introduced and Hong Kong administrators, who would have had experience with secret societies, replaced those from India. The British Government had superior arms power and with the help of the formidable Sikh police brought society-based riots under control. Following this, the societies were no longer in control of the labour force which was dubbed the 'pigling trade'. Chinese sailing junks were inferior to the European steamships which took over the coolie trade in the late nineteenth century. The strategy of the British Government was to make a division between the China-born from the Straits-born, the latter being British subjects by birth and therefore unbanishable.

In reality, the societies did not disappear, but their activities were diverted to more socially acceptable forms. In the late nineteenth century dialect associations and mutual aid societies mushroomed, taking the place of the disappearing secret societies. When secret societies were banned in 1890, their assets were transferred to institutions such as temples. One such association in Penang enshrines that generic god of prosperity *Tua Pek Kong (Da Bo Gong)*, patron saint of overseas Chinese and merchants in particular. An annual flame divination, which was originally held by mercantile communities and had continued through the days of the secret society, is still carried out in our own day (see Religion), and beside the main *Tua Pek Kong* hall, there is an altar for the ancestral tablets of early leaders of the *Khian Teik* society. By 1881, having amassed wealth and consequently gained respect, the leader of the society had become a philanthropist and was a founder of the Penang Chinese Town Hall. Thus the powerful secret societies in Malaya sometimes made their leaders eligible for honours from the British Crown.

The secret societies in nineteenth century Malaya were effectively political organizations run by influential capitalists for economic advantage, and with little respect for the colonial administration. When, in 1858, a Hokkien leader was arrested by the colonial Government for engaging in gang warfare, the Hokkien community went on strike to obtain his release. The secret societies were really a major problem for the Government with the street fights between rival groups and the rioting which often broke out when some unpopular law was introduced. In the nineteenth century, the secret societies were the major organizations within the Chinese community, and it was difficult for individuals to avoid becoming members. The sinister aspects of the activities of the societies were blackmail and extortion; they also ran gambling dens and brothels. Potential criminals, therefore, operated within their influence. Societies earned their disrepute because of these undesirable elements.

When new prostitutes arrived in the 1930s, the street they moved into would be called New Street; even the Malays called it Street of New Ladies. Similarly, when a street had new brothels with Japanese prostitutes, it was called New Japanese Street. Streets where brothels were located were given the name of the race or place of origin of the prostitutes, for example, 'Japanese Street' and 'Teochew Street'.

After Teochew merchants in the Straits Settlements made representations to the Chinese Government in the late 1800s, China prohibited migration from Swatow, from where the Teochew originate. In 1921, an imperial edict in Japan outlawed prostitution. Many of the women who were originally labourers working to pay for their passage from China or Japan eventually became prostitutes. Some became addicted to gambling or opium, thus incurring even more debts. The higher-class prostitutes were dubbed *'cheongsam ladies'*, probably because they dressed in *cheongsam*, 'long dress' in Chinese) and they catered to wealthy merchants and white-collar office workers. These women often became secondary wives or concubines to rich businessmen. Sometimes the Chinese Protectorate or some philanthropic association arranged marriages. Warren (1993) pointed out that such a marriage was cheaper than getting a bride from China. The *Po Leung Kuk* is the name of an institution in Penang, started in 1888, meaning the Preservation of Virtue. The virtue protected was that of women and girls. It was a sanctuary for women who had just arrived from China, in cases where the honest employment promised by recruiting agents was not available.

The *Sinkhek* and tin

Straits merchants contended that 'Straits produce' alone could not service both the China Trade and the growing markets in Europe; alternatives were commercial agriculture and tin mining. The supply of tin had already decreased during the time of Portuguese rule, having been disrupted by disputes and by intruders from northern Sumatra at the beginning of the seventeenth century. There was a further decrease in production during Dutch rule. The nineteenth century revival of tin mining coincided with the growth of British interest in the Peninsula. At the same time, there was an increase in demand for the metal. Until around the mid-nineteenth century, tin from the Malay Peninsula was sent to India and China. The British tin plate industry and the accompanying repeal in 1853 of duties on imported tin, led to a jump in sales. They were further stimulated by the opening of the Suez Canal in 1869, which shortened the journey to Europe. The initial capital for tin mining came from Malacca and Penang Babas who had by then acquired wealth through trading, land speculation and revenue farming. Chinese entrepreneurs had access to the capital necessary for development on a substantial scale. Besides an efficient network of business organizations and capital to buffer temporary losses, they also had access to a ready pool of labour. From the middle of the nineteenth century, a second phase of Chinese immigration occurred, filling the need for a labour force in tin mining, and later in the production of rubber. Unsettled conditions in South China, and especially the outbreak of the Taiping Rebellion in 1851, acted as a stimulus to migration. Although men emigrated from southern China, women were not allowed to do so. Port officials expected that married men would return to visit their families. Single men took their savings back to China with them in order to marry. Because of the strength of Confucian sentiment, another reason for men to return to visit China was to pay their respects to their ancestors and finally to be buried with those ancestors. The Manchu port authorities could therefore extract 'presents' from these men to permit them to re-enter. Some emigrants paid their own passage and bribed officials in order to leave their home country, so that either way the port authorities profited from bribes.

The majority of emigrants came under the notorious credit ticket system, whereby the *Sinkbek*, voluntarily or involuntarily, bound himself to an employer in return for his passage from China. These men formed the labour force in the urban centres, the agricultural estates and the tin mines of the Peninsula. The workers had to be willing to undergo back-breaking labour if they went to the mines. The lives of the tin miners were controlled by the secret societies, which ran gambling and opium farms as well as brothels. The ticket system resulted in the exploitation of the labourers. They lived and worked under appalling conditions and visits to the dubious amenities just mentioned were their only form of recreation. Sickness and death were common among these wretched indentured labourers, as was poverty and a cycle of indebtedness under the ticket system. These men had escaped from political upheavals and famine in South China to seek a new livelihood. As we have seen they were referred to as *Sinkbek* by members of the longer established Chinese community, who called themselves *Laokbek* or old(er) people. The *Sinkbek*, however, referred to themselves simply as overseas Chinese. At least one *Laokbek* sympathized publicly with the plight of the *Sinkbek*: 'The institution of man-hunting crimps (persons engaged in forcible recruiting), the sight of the barricaded coolie-depots, the spectacle of innocent ignorant coolies, guarded by Sikhs, parading through the streets, are repugnant to every liberty-loving mind.' (*The Straits Chinese Magazine*, June 1903,7 #2:45). Survivors with a determination to succeed had to have a competitive spirit. A classic example is the famous Hoo Ah Kay, known as Whampoa after his birthplace, who arrived in Singapore in 1830 as a youth of fifteen, and went on to make his fortune in land speculation.

By the beginning of the 1860s, Penang businessmen were financing the working of the tin fields (Wong 1963:70). Hugh Low, the Perak state administrator, encouraged the local-born Penang Hokkien to finance mining in the state. In return, he offered them tax-farming monopolies. For three years, the *Khian Teik-Hai San* financial corporation, which was already prospering in Penang, dominated government monopolies and mining throughout most of Perak. Tin mining in Perak gave a big boost to Penang's flagging economy during the last quarter of the nineteenth century.

Because of numerous vested interests, any Malay disputes in the tin producing states had far-reaching repercussions. Civil wars over succession and territorial rights were rife in the Peninsular states in the nineteenth century. As Malay chiefs fought for political control, mining groups and Straits merchants were keen that the victorious Malay faction should favour their particular interests. Straits merchants, as financial backers, became involved in Peninsular affairs. Chinese merchants in Malacca advanced capital for the development of mines in return for a share of the profits. A symbiotic arrangement arose, where Malay princes established good relations with Straits merchants and officials and in return received a share of the profits.

The territories which were later to become the Federated Malay States were brought under British jurisdiction from 1874, following which an economic boom led to acute labour shortages. The coolies were inspired with self-determination, feeling less intimidated because of increased British strictness with the secret societies, whose influence began to be curbed at the beginning of the 1870s. A Chinese Protectorate was established by the British in 1877, as we have seen; this superseded the *Kapitan Cina* system as a means of governing the Chinese. The Protectorate also monitored the treatment of coolies, and the ticket system was abolished.

An influx of miners during the last two decades of the nineteenth century led to an imbalance between the sexes in the Chinese population. It was only towards the end of the century that large numbers of Chinese women emigrated. The social life of these Straits Chinese was therefore somewhat unnatural. The rich man who had worked for his position might eventually have a wife and one or more concubines, but the majority of *Sinkhek* were condemned to celibacy. With this newly arrived group being unable to fit in with the existing population, fresh social conflicts arose within the Chinese and the Malay societies. A distinct division existed between the westernized Babas (and their 'Malayified' Nyonya) and the *Sinkhek*, who were still steeped in their southern Chinese heritage.

The earlier Chinese migrants had been traders or shopkeepers, but the emphasis during this later period was on commercial agriculture and mining. Many of those who began as labourers in the plantations had, within a year or so, worked off the passage money they owed and ventured into agriculture on their own. Within a decade or so the miners became shop-owners and even comfortable middle-class traders. By the turn of the century, many of the *Sinkhek* who had come to work in the tin mines had already caught up with the Babas in terms of wealth. Some assimilated into the existing Baba lifestyle and their womenfolk adopted Nyonya dress. This section of Straits culture was far more 'Chinese' than the Baba culture, although it was definitely a modification of Chinese culture as practised in China. It was not long before the Baba Chinese were challenged by these successful later immigrants.

A new wealthy class emerged in the 1930s. It consisted of Chinese-speaking businessmen who overshadowed those in the Baba community, who were English-speaking. In Penang, the *Sinkhek* overwhelmed the Babas in such numbers that the Hokkien language prevailed. The situation in Penang differed from that in Malacca and Singapore, since the larger Chinese community had absorbed the Babas long before the British left. By the 1940s, two-thirds of Malayan Chinese were China-born, i.e. could be classified as *Sinkhek*.

Occupational niches

BELOW LEFT: The extended family, all under one roof, posed for a formal commemorative photograph on such occasions as Chinese New Year or the sixtieth (and successively seventieth and eightieth) birthday of the matriarch and patriarch. This gathering was on the lawn of a typical Anglo-Indian bungalow.
BELOW RIGHT: The widowed matriarch took precedence over her sons. This Chinese New Year reunion photo was on the 'five-foot way' arcade of the terrace house.

The Baba sector of the Straits Chinese gradually moved from more enterprising undertakings in trade to the security of office jobs, particularly in the civil service. With white-collar status, they became complacent; Purcell (1947:125) even described them as having approached a condition of moral decay. In the municipal services and local Government, Eurasians were preferred, especially in the Education Department, because their mother tongue was English. They formed half of the local intake. However, general clerical staff made up the largest single professional group and many of them were Chinese. Junior technicians, teachers and doctors formed a smaller group. Locals were not considered for senior civil service posts.

Private commercial firms also showed a preference for Eurasians because of their command of the English language. The Chinese, however, became the largest group in commercial clerical employment. Generally, and by contrast with the Government service, European and Chinese commercial firms employed few Indians. The western-trained Chinese lawyer should have had a special role to play in a society where English law prevailed, but locals reasoned that it would be more beneficial to engage the services of an English lawyer since the Government was British, the judges were

British and the courts of law were conducted in English. Only matters which could be easily settled out of court were dealt with by Chinese lawyers. The British colonial Government itself had a similar attitude. Although Chinese lawyers were appointed to the Straits Chinese Consultative Committee and the Chinese Advisory Board, which were dominated by businessmen, none were on the *Po Leung Kuk* Committee which was responsible for the protection of Chinese women and girls.

The most important, even indispensable, Chinese were the businessmen, who form a majority in the records of appointments as Justices of the Peace. While Chambers of Commerce were formed along communal lines, there was co-operation on issues of common interest. The Association of Chinese Chambers of Commerce in British Malaya held a conference in 1925 to discuss the Straits civil service. The feeling was that because locals were sharing in the defence of the colony as volunteers, the Government should admit them to the civil service if they were professionals and British subjects. Outside business, the banking profession was almost the only other sector in which the Chinese could hold their own with regard to white-collar jobs. Since the economy was nowhere near industrialized, members of the technical professions were not appreciated at all.

BELOW: Four generations meet to celebrate the eightieth birthday of the patriarch whose widowed sister in the centre was almost a centurian. (She pounded her own *sirih* leaves for her toothless bite)

21st. JUNE 1952

The entrance portico of Chung
Keng Kwee's personal temple.
The roof ornamentation is of the
Shiwan style of sculpture.
(Courtesy Asia House, Hong
Kong, photo Cheang Yik On)

Enclaves

Certain streets were dominated by one profession or trade, and this is often reflected in street names. The inevitable social and class divisions which commonly segregate people into enclaves also applied to the Straits Chinese. (The first local-born generation very often stayed on in the family home and clung to its parents' lifestyle.) Just as the early Chinese merchants in Malacca were close to the river or seafront, the first trading firms in Penang built warehouses and offices along the waterfront. The road where these imposing buildings still are, is accordingly called Beach Street. Simple houses on stilts over the shallow waters of the shoreline formed clan enclaves. Today, because of reclamation, large areas of these 'water villages' are on dry land, with only jetties projecting out to sea.

Georgetown, originally rectangular in Captain Francis Light's plans, grew into a typical Chinese town. In inner Georgetown, within the Hokkien-dominated enclave, members of the secret societies could move unobserved between clan complexes and temples, which were separated only by low walls. There was sometimes a secret passageway through terrace houses situated between these complexes. The northern beach of Penang Island was the area where Francis Light and his associates chose to live, and during the first decades of the nineteenth century wealthy Chinese merchants also resided here, when they had achieved a stature qualifying them for occupation of this oldest enclave of stately homes, dubbed 'millionaires' row'. The construction further inland, in 1888, of the abode of the Resident Councillor led to a shift of the élite residential suburb. In the neighbourhood of this new mansion, called The Residency, are the polo club, racecourse and sports club. In the early twentieth century, the Chinese moved into an older enclave, originally populated by Europeans and Eurasians, between the north beach and The Residency.

In Singapore too, the earliest settlements were along the coast and the rivers. The Chinese quarter was on the marshy southwest bank of the Singapore River. The commercial sector was along the eastern seacoast but early in the nineteenth century it was moved to the west bank, where the Chinese were already established. Chinatown developed in the area west of the river adjacent to this commercial quarter, while the Government retained the east bank. Around the middle of the nineteenth century, in the wake of their increased prosperity, extended families who had each been living under one roof, began to move outward from the town's central area to the suburbs. Villas and mansions of this era still stand.

Interracial and intraracial relations

The anglicized Babas pursued western pastimes and recreations, but generally they did so among themselves. Very few joined the Europeans, who led an exclusive social life. The European community was wealthy, and its members were also often staid, snobbish and Victorian. On the other hand, the Chinese businessmen could be parochial and clannish. So these two segments of the upper crust only met on their evening drives along promenades, exchanging brief social pleasantries. By the end of the nineteenth century, the European community was already substantial. This meant that its members were no longer forced to associate with non-Europeans for recreation or entertainment, and they set up clubs that were exclusively for whites. With this development, the wealthy Chinese with whom the Europeans had been associating, were excluded. Past favours were no longer continued. The practice of farming out revenue was ended in 1909: instead the Government itself collected taxes. Western-educated Straits Chinese who had acquired a belief in equality through western education were disappointed and became resentful. As a result, they formed their own exclusive clubs. Being westernized themselves, they modelled their clubs on the European ones.

Within the Chinese community itself there was, and still is, segregation. Divisions by speech groups, clans and commercial interests are common in traditional organizations. The secret societies especially were torn apart by feuds and open warfare. The Babas themselves had social clubs which did not admit *Sinkhek* (Vaughan 1879-1971:2-3). Even with English-speaking *Sinkhek* there was little social mixing. The majority of members of the Chinese Chambers of Commerce were non-English speaking. The Baba Straits Chinese with white-collar jobs recognized that where investing capital and risk-taking were concerned, they were no match for the Chinese-educated. So a Baba did not initiate policy in the Chambers of Commerce, he only helped to implement it. The English-speaking and non-English-speaking Chinese continue to be separate communities, although this fact is not always formally admitted. The British Government regarded both groups as one until the formation of Straits Chinese British Associations by Babas. In fact, each of the two groups regarded the other with a tinge of disdain. Even English-educated Chinese who know written and spoken Chinese and Chinese history are not totally accepted in Chinese-speaking circles.

The influx of *Sinkhek* Chinese immigrants in the late nineteenth century led to the re-

Opium smoking was not confined to labourers; it was widespread and the élite indulged in it on luxurious opium-beds, such as this one from blackwood with marble slabs and mother-of-pearl inset. (Courtesy P.G. Lim, photo The Pepin Press)

sinization of the longer-established but smaller Straits Chinese community. This influx also happened in other European colonies: for example in Indonesia the Chinese *Peranakan* also underwent the same process vis-à-vis the *Totok*, who are effectively the counterpart of the *Sinkhek*.

The League of Helping Friends (*Hu Yew Seah*) in Penang was a society which brought the races together. Besides holding classes to teach the Chinese national language, it was active in Chinese affairs. Malay teachers taught in its Literary Section, while the distinguished Indian poet Rabindranath Tagore laid the foundation stone of its new building in 1927. In Penang there was also a group calling itself 'The Lost Souls', comprising Malays, Chinese, Indians and Eurasians. These Lost Souls took as their model the art of discussion over coffee. Dr Samuel Johnson had shown that such a cultivated art form required high intellect and perceptiveness. Membership of this select body was determined by the ability to discuss matters of interest, and the Lost Souls limited its numbers to only nine, chosen regardless of race and religion.

Early Malacca may have had interracial integration, if the presence of an unusually dark member of a Baba family is an indication of intermarriage with one of the Indian *Peranakan* known as *Chitties*. Conversely, the modern *Chitties*, though still Hindus, often look remarkably Chinese. There is another cross-cultural group of Portuguese Nyonyas who are, of course, Eurasians. Princes in the Malay States sometimes had business partnerships with Government officials and Straits merchants, thus promoting good relations.

The inner part of Georgetown on Penang Island has a multiracial quarter where a symbiotic socio-economic situation grew out of a convergence of cosmopolitan traders. There are Hindu, Chinese and Muslim communities here; there is no hard and fast dividing line demarcating the end of one group and the beginning of another. The Chinese here cannot and do not distinguish between a Tamil trader and a Bengal merchant; all Indians are classified as '*Kling*' (derived from Kalinga in south India, since south Indians are in the majority). 'Under the palms' is the name of a street once lined with palms. Along it are four religious buildings, namely St George's Church, a Temple of the Goddess of Mercy, the Sri Mariamann Temple and the Kapitan Kling Mosque. These represent the major religions of modern Malaysia. Jewellers and money-changers also line this street of worship.

Further details of cultural mixing can be traced historically. Arabs, particularly those from the Hadramaut, traded extensively in the Archipelago. Both Chinese and Muslim tombstones were made by Chinese masons. In Penang in the mid-nineteenth century, the leader of the Malay Red Flag Society, dubbed *Kepala Kongsi*, (clan leader), one Syed Al-Atas, married the daughter of a wealthy Chinese merchant, Khoo Tiang Poh. In these early Straits entrepôts where Achinese, Armenians, Arabs, Chinese, Indians and Malays carved mercantile niches for themselves, there must have been reasonable tolerance as they co-existed side by side and occasionally integrated. We can conclude that such historic enclaves, which still exist, like the multiracial quarter of Georgetown, made the Straits Settlements a melting pot.

While each group maintained its own value system, they all benefited from interaction with the others. However, although Malays, Chinese, Indians and Eurasians were friends in little enclaves, individually they could be indifferent to each other.

Nevertheless, among the wealthy and well-educated, multicommunal societies did exist. Among them were The Lost Souls already mentioned, the Hospital and Prisons

Visitation Committee and the Poppy Day Appeal Committee. Although recreation clubs provided opportunities for the meeting of different communal groups, on the whole communal organizations were more important than intercommunal ones.

Like Penang, Singapore has several major buildings of different religious persuasions within an area of a few square miles.

The Thai connection with Penang has been analysed by Cushman (1990) as a lineage which may even amount to a 'dynasty' as an enterprising Straits Chinese family established a business empire straddling the Malay-Thai border. This 'lineage' lasted for one and a half centuries, during which time the family, in establishing relations with the Thai court, even had members who held governorships in southern Thai provinces. The bulk of the business was in tin mining, where up-to-date Australian technology was employed. The early establishment of Thai connections with this northern Straits Settlement is indicated by the presence in Penang of a Thai temple dating from 1845.

When the *Kek Lok Si* temple (see page 60) was built in 1905, Chinese from Sumatra and Thailand made donations for its construction. There were Sumatran traders in all three Straits Settlements. North Sumatra, especially, was a hinterland supplying the three entrepôts. Sumatran pepper and rice continued to be shipped from Penang to India and Europe even after Singapore became the chief port for the China Trade.

Some Penang Babas had their tertiary education in Calcutta, and when they later ventured into business had branches there, and in Rangoon and Mandalay. Rice was the main commodity traded. The Burmese involvement in trade was partly because of clan connections.

The China connection

Male offspring of early traders who set up house with local women were repatriated to China for their education. Both civilian and military titles of honour, of various ranks, were purchased by many wealthy Chinese to enhance their social status. In China itself, mandarin squares were purchased for the deceased to wear to keep them from being disturbed by evil spirits. Mandarin squares were made of embroidered silk and were worn on the robes of Chinese officials of the last two dynasties to indicate rank.

There were Straits Chinese who even after an extended sojourn did not consider the Straits Settlements as their homeland. A good example is the legendary rags-to-riches Whampoa, alias Hoo Ah Kay who, in spite of the prestige which led to his being fully accepted in colonial circles, chose to be buried in China. He was not the only one who returned to the 'motherland' either on retirement or for burial.

In 1881, three clans in Penang, the *Cheah*, *Khoo* and *Yeoh*, formed a society to manage donations solicited by their clansmen in China to alleviate a disaster. The committee still exists today but its funds are no longer sent to China; instead they are used locally as scholarships for the children of members. In rotation, each clan association undertakes the project for three years.

One successful entrepreneur from Java, well-connected with Dutch officials, Thio Thiau Siat or Chang Pi Shih or Cheong Fatt Tze (pronunciation differs with dialect), moved to northeast Sumatra and thence to Penang between 1877 and 1879. This millionaire, (see Architecture, Cheong mansion), whose trading, agricultural, shipping and tin-mining enterprises had made him the wealthiest Chinese businessman in

The Medan connection. Daughter of a *Kapitan Cina* or Chinese headman, the Nyonya wore a batik sarong with a tunic called *baju panjang* (Malay: long dress) of fine batik, covered with small floral motifs. On her feet she wore stub-toed slippers embroidered with metallic thread, variously called *kasut tongkang* (bum-boat shoes), or *kasut kodok* (frog slippers). (Courtesy Yeoh Jin Leng)

OPPOSITE PAGE TOP: 'Woodville' in
the French chateau style was
constructed in 1925. Its main
entrance is sheltered by a roof
canopy with oyster glass panes.
OPPOSITE PAGE MIDDLE: A building
erected about the middle of this
century, but using Art Deco style
of the 30s. Dutch influence is
evident in the roof and gable
ends.
OPPOSITE PAGE BOTTOM: A
Bauhaus-inspired, streamlined
building on Millionaires' Row.
(Photos Cheang Yik On)

BELOW: An Italianate villa named
'Homestead' built in 1919. Its
symmetrical façade has a
columned portico flanked by
two identical towers.
(Photo Cheang Yik On)

Sumatra and one of the wealthiest in the *Nanyang*, was invited into the service of the Chinese Government. Besides being appointed special trade commissioner in Southeast Asia to attract merchant capital from overseas Chinese, he was the first Chinese Vice-Consul in Penang, and subsequently Consul-General in Singapore. There was no consular representative in the Dutch East Indies at the time, so the Singapore office was also responsible for protecting the interests of the overseas Chinese in Java and Sumatra, as well as in British Malaya. Cheong's generous contributions to various causes such as the establishment of technical schools and flood relief in China, eventually reached the attention of the Empress Dowager in 1903. By 1905, Cheong was promoted to the position of a top-order Mandarin.

When the Guomintang were active in Malaya, the loyalty of the Straits Chinese came under scrutiny and the British Government was prompted to exert greater vigilance over the Chinese. A Chinese doctor from Penang internationally acclaimed as a pneumonic plague-fighter, Dr. Wu Lien Teh (Gnoh Lean Tuck), opted to give his allegiance to China. He even urged the Straits Chinese to go to China and witness for themselves the modernization programmes there. Sun Yat-sen's revolutionary activities found support among some Chinese organizations, which received his charter and were fronts for his movement. However, when he visited Penang in 1910, an English language newspaper, while publishing the text of his speech, commented adversely on it. Sun Yat-sen had tried to solicit donations from the *Nanyang* capitalists. An unpublicized role of the Chamber of Commerce was effectively that of a Kuomintang consulate.

Both English-speaking and Chinese-speaking Straits Chinese staged public talks. The

English-speaking group pointed out that the Straits-born already considered the Straits Settlements their home, and that there should be no dual loyalties. The Chinese-speaking, on the other hand, contended that their critics were only thriving on borrowed culture.

Sympathy with China was not only shown in times of natural disaster. In 1927 for example, after Rabindranath Tagore's visit to Penang, public-spirited Chinese leaders formed a committee to endow Tagore's University in Calcutta with a chair of Chinese literature, philosophy and civilization. They even celebrated China's national day on a big scale in 1928.

Political involvement

By the end of the nineteenth century English-educated Babas became more outspoken about their position in the light of social and political reforms going on elsewhere. They sought recognition as a political entity and were vocal about the matter. The *Sinkhek*, not being British subjects, had no political status. Chinese nationalism in China became an issue. The Qing Government was wooing the *Nanyang* capitalists (Godley, 1981). Three Straits Chinese scholars — Song Ong Siang, Dr. Lim Boon Keng of Singapore and Dr. Wu Lieu Teh — started the *Straits Chinese Magazine* in 1897 and public debates revolved around Confucianism, Baba identity, allegiance and loyalty. By then the colonial Government, which had been 'working hand in glove' with the Babas in the administration of tax farms and the commercial running of tin mines, was watching the Straits Chinese very closely — was their allegiance with the Kuomintang and Sun Yat-sen or were they loyal British subjects? The Baba community was caught up in this historical development. Their articulate leaders had in effect declared that loyalty to the Straits Government, expressed by regarding it as a mother country, was limited to a minority which included the Malays, Eurasians and Straits-born Chinese. This was especially so in Penang which had just encountered an influx of *Sinkhek*.

Because the Baba leaders were absorbed into Government and quasi-Government bodies, their early clamour for 'political rights' was centred on senior civil service positions, not a political question in the common sense — and they were not an organized political party. The Straits Settlements Society, which complemented the Municipal Commission, was a quasi-political institution. Taking their status as British subjects seriously, its members lobbied for social reforms. In Penang, however, the disagreements between the English-speaking, who were represented by the Straits Chinese British Association, and the Mandarin-speaking, who found a voice through the Chinese Town Hall and the Chinese Chamber of Commerce, undermined the public movement for reform. Thus the northern Babas were comparatively less active in agitating for reforms. The Penang Straits Chinese British Association was formed twenty years after that of Singapore. By the end of the nineteenth century and in the early decade of this century, the colonial government, because of overseas Chinese sympathy with the brewing revolution in China, was more and more pro-Malay.

In 1926, however, a Malacca Baba statesman, Tan Cheng Lock, headed a move to press for more participation in the government. He began by attempting to unite all Chinese, but he communicated with them about things Chinese in the Malay language. Having effectively rallied the Chinese into a political party, which he presided over, he proceeded to hold talks with Indian and Malay parties. Thus a Baba was instrumental in setting up negotiations and co-operation between the ethnic-political blocs whose coalition still rules modern Malaysia.

The Penang secession movement

When the Federation of Malaya was formed in 1948, absorbing the Straits Settlements except Singapore, groups which had flourished under British rule felt threatened. In the aftermath of the Japanese Occupation (1941-45), a terrorist insurgency which had begun in June 1948 also generated a feeling of insecurity. A committee representing professional and mercantile bodies in Penang decided to secede from the Federation. Besides the Straits-born Chinese, Indians and Eurasians supported the move. The reso-

Cheong's courtyard mansion (1896-1904) was in keeping with the Mandarin status conferred on him by the Empress Dowager. (Courtesy Cheong Fatt Tze Mansion Sdn. Bhd., photo Cheang Yik On)

46

lution was passed on 23 December 1948. Obviously, the Straits Chinese wanted the Straits Settlements to continue as a political entity because within that framework, they had played a prominent part in government; inclusion in a Malayan state would reduce them to a minority group (Sopiee 1976:57). A more important underlying fear was for the loss of their rights; they felt that their privileges had been earned, not merely handed out.

In 1946 trade regulations passed by the administration in Kuala Lumpur prohibited Penang merchants from exporting to their traditional markets, Sumatra and Siam, because Penang's free port status, conferred in 1877, had been revoked. However, it was the denial of *jus soli* which finally fired seething resentment. The underlying aim of the secessionists was also to have the same rights as the Malays. For them this was much more important than ending colonialism and fighting for indepence 'hand in hand' with the Malays, which was what Tan Cheng Lock stood for. The Singapore Straits Chinese British Association was in favour of restoring the Straits Settlements and this encouraged the Penang secessionists. However, they finally realized that they were powerless against the surging tide of Malay nationalism in the states of the Peninsula and the secession movement collapsed. It had received no encouragement from the British, and its supporters felt let down by this.

Hardwicke, an English-style stately home built at the end of the nineteenth century on Penang's north coast. The ground floor Gothic windows surmount a coat of arms while English lions, also bearing coat of arms sit on the balcony. Among the stone sculptures in the garden are a pair of Chinese lions (from the family's earlier country house).
(Courtesy Lim Kean Siew, photos Cheang Yik On)

Religion, Customs and Festivals 2

Chinese 'religion' and customs

Many people need to identify with a group. This is especially so when they are faced with a new environment and need to retain their cultural values. Hence immigrants often provide themselves with reassurance in the form of rituals and religious ceremonies. It is not uncommon for them to bring actual effigies of their gods to their new home. In the Straits Settlements there was a high degree of religious tolerance, so the Chinese community undertook the building of temples and never forgot its commitment to religious and festive celebrations as statements of its identity.

Whatever the phrase 'Chinese religion' may mean, it undoubtedly encompasses reverence for ancestors. There are, however, very few temples built exclusively for one purpose such as the worship of ancestors, or Taoist (Daoist) or Buddhist deities. Chinese religion, as practised by the Straits Chinese, is an inclusive system in which the dominant belief accommodates other cults and deities. Thus, it is not unusual to find that local or popular deities co-exist with spirits, Buddhist deities and Taoist heroes; Confucian maxims can also be revered. The Chinese, especially their womenfolk, occasionally visit sites of legendary Malay supernatural power to pay reverence. This is not necessarily because they believe in the alternative customs represented there: it is merely a sign of their desire to gain the favour of all forms of supernatural entities.

Personalities of local folk tradition or notable figures from imperial China may be revered for their virtue and other qualities. For example, the three-star eunuch Admiral Cheng Ho, who visited Malacca in 1409 and 1411, is honoured with a shrine near *Bukit Cina*. This imperial admiral has also been deified elsewhere by Southeast Asian Chinese, so that he has had supernatural powers thrust upon him. Memory fades without written records, and in Malacca there is confusion about a Sultan's well at the foot of *Bukit Cina*. The Chinese admiral was supposed to have drunk from it, causing the water to be perennial and pure. This claim pays no regard to the chronology of the admiral's visit which occurred long before the well was dug.

Fear of the unknown generates superstition which, when habitually practised, establishes itself as a custom. As is universally the case, some of the superstitious practices of the Straits Chinese stem from lack of understanding. Even Christianity cannot erase some deep-rooted customs. One example of this concerns *kong teik* — papercraft

OPPOSITE PAGE: A Penang bridal couple and their pages outside the bride's family home, indicated by the two cylindrical lanterns flanking the central hexagonal one to heaven. (Courtesy SCPA)

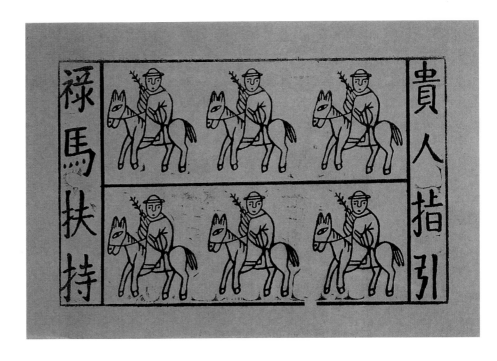

fashioned for the dead — which, because of a long-standing taboo, is never allowed to enter a Chinese house. A true Christian, who is presumably less superstitious, ought perhaps to allow *kong teik* into the house, but in practice he may not do so. Another belief is that ritual cleansing can divert contamination by an illness; such contamination can in turn be reversed by exorcism. Ritual cleansing is especially needed for the protection of a mother during confinement (which customarily includes a period of some weeks after delivery). She is very susceptible to all kinds of evil influences after having had her womb 'opened' during delivery. Among a whole host of taboos and rituals, a new mother believes that even after a ritual bath she must rub her fingertips with onions to prevent evil wind from entering her body. This peculiar practice is different from other traditional preventative measures against flatulence.

It is customary not to wash containers in which food for an auspicious occasion has been presented; the luck they hold would be washed away. Therefore, after emptying a container, it is refilled with some token gift so as not to wish the giver ill by not reciprocating: an empty container is a portent of poverty. The Chinese also believe that personal mirrors should be sheathed, because if one's image is unwittingly reflected, an evil spirit may do it harm; the spirit may even snatch away the image which is thought to be one's soul. Perhaps this is also a means to ensure that vanity and displays of wealth are discouraged. (It is widely believed that the ostentatious Khoo clan temple in Penang was originally even more pretentious. It was mysteriously gutted by fire, presumably because its palatial dimensions incurred Heaven's wrath.)

A popular form of divination involves the use of a pair of kidney-shaped wooden blocks about the size of the palm of the hand. They are dropped on the floor in a similar fashion to tossing coins. The deity's approval or assurance is indicated by the flat side of one block and the convex side of the other facing upwards. Another ancient divination rite, the flame-watching ritual which is conducted by a Baba association, is still practised in Penang. The ceremony is held on the fourteenth night of the Chinese New Year at the seaside temple of the deity *Tua Pek Kong.* The purpose of

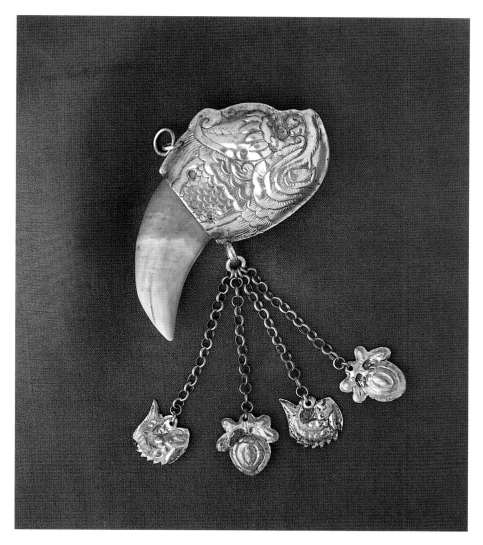

ABOVE LEFT: A *hoo leng* (Hokkien
for 'fish-dragon') amulet worn
by children. The tiger claw adds
potency to the amulet. Silvergilt.
(Photo H. Lin Ho)
ABOVE: A pageboy wearing a *hoo
leng* amulet.

the ritual is to try to predict fortunes for the coming year. The ceremony starts just
before midnight, and the tide must be rising. The association's patron deity *Tua Pek
Kong* and his urn containing burning joss-sticks are carried in a ceremonial procession
to his earlier home shrine by the sea. As the embers in the urn are fanned, lights in
the temple are switched off. In a similar fashion to the waves beating and leaping up
against the retaining wall of the temple, the flame leaps up in the darkness in a dramatic arc. The height of the flame, which flares up from the urn of *Tua Pek Kong*,
who is known as the god of prosperity, is an indication of fortunes to come. Early the
next morning the deity's urn is returned to his abode in town in a procession through
the streets of Penang. (See also Architecture, geomancy.)

Ancestor worship

The belief in a life after death sometimes influences the behaviour of the Chinese in
this life. They feel that money donated for religious purposes is a form of investment
for the afterlife. Apart from actual funds required for religious ceremonies, they invest
mainly through their offspring. While it is the responsibility and right of the eldest son
to conduct rites and rituals, in practice it is the womenfolk who attend to the logistics.

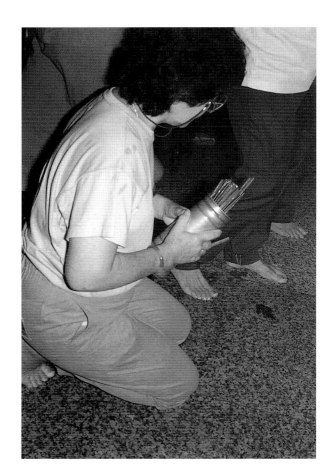

The filial male sustains the family's lineage by performing ancestor rites on the first and fifteenth of every lunar month as these days mark the new and full moon respectively.

Temples also display and maintain ancestral tablets. The family cult inculcated by Confucius has been devotedly sustained for generations, especially through the extended family. In very old family homes ancestral tablets arrayed on the altar may span as many as four generations. Although previously it was normally only the poorer families who were likely to lodge their ancestral tablets in temples, nowadays modernization, and the relative instability of both the extended and immediate family, may cause more affluent families to do the same.

While full-scale secondary burial after cremation was not practised by the Straits Chinese, it was and still is customary for a token collection of bones to be obtained after cremation and stored in an urn. The reason for doing this is that bones and tablets are opposite and complementary parts of the cult of the ancestors, the former being ying and the latter yang (Aijmer 1968). The essential features of the cult, therefore, are tending to these two aspects — body and soul — of a dead person (rather than 'worshipping' him, as the western term 'ancestor worship' suggests).

It was, ironically enough, during the heyday of the Babas that a period of seeming extremism occurred. This happened around the beginning of this century and took the form of Confucianism being consciously revived. The initiative came from Singapore, where the first Confucian school was founded. Following that, other schools and associations sprang up, not only in the Straits Settlements, but also in the Malay States. The Straits Chinese Magazine, published in English, was the vehicle for disseminating Confucian thinking. The isolation of the Babas from Chinese literature because of their inability to read and write Chinese prompted them to re-examine and re-evaluate Confucian ethics.

Other manifestations of ancestor worship are posthumous ceremonies and the erection of commemorative structures (see Architecture). Ancestors are also credited with earthly powers. Qingming, (Hokkien: cheng beng) literally meaning clear and bright, is the spring equinox, the time for sowing rice. The rice seeds are offered to the ancestors, to whom the worshipper kneels and prays. The rice shoots are regarded as presents returned by the ancestors. The seed offering is similar to food laid on a grave. *Cheng beng* is observed universally by the Chinese and falls on either the fourth or fifth of April, according to the Gregorian calendar. Alternatively, the festival is celebrated on the third day of the third moon according to the lunar year. This visit to the grave during the sowing period of the agricultural cycle is believed to be returned by ancestors visiting their living progeny at Chinese New Year.

Cheng beng is also a celebration of the end of the dormancy of winter. People travel to the countryside to see and feel the beauty of nature. The significance concerns rebirth. The departed, enshrined in tombs, are beseeched to participate in the rejuvenation of the earth. Both the tomb and the area around it are tidied. Although in ancient China family members placed yellow ribbons weighted down by stones on top of tombs, the Straits Chinese put paper lanterns and replicas of paper money on the graves. In either case, the purpose is to ward off evil spirits and to replenish the wealth of the entombed.

The ceremony at the graveside begins with the burning of joss-sticks and candles. After paying homage to the departed, the ritual is concluded by a libation of rice wine poured on to an additional stack of burning paper money. The wine is part of the food offerings. In ancient times the *cheng beng* festival also included kite-flying.

Rice is harvested at different times of year depending on its type. The twenty-second or twenty-third day of the ninth month of the solar calendar (about the ninth day of the ninth lunar month) is the autumn equinox in the northern hemisphere; it is harvest time in the southeast provinces of China. People climb mountains or ascend hills on this special day because ancestors are believed to reside in the mountains; striving upwards is a token of thanksgiving either to them or to Heaven for a good harvest. The Straits Chinese in Penang, but not those in Malacca and Singapore, perform a pilgrimage to a hill temple dedicated to the Taoist Queen of Heaven (see Popular Buddhism) as manifested in her nine sons during the ninth day of the ninth lunar month. Because this exercise is simply described as paying homage to Heaven it has become a nondescript all-purpose ritual with no apparent relationship to ancestor worship. The same harvest thanksgiving in China is also characterized by ceremonial kite-flying, which symbolizes striving upwards, but Straits Chinese boys play with kites with absolutely no vestiges of religious ceremonial.

In the Taoist temple, the God of Heaven, or Jade Emperor, is the highest entity. *Kuan Kong (Guan Gong)*, the God of War and Justice, is popular with the Hokkiens. Confucius and his teachings are also represented in the temple, being no less important than the Buddhist Eighteen *Lohan*, disciples. The host of gods and godlings may vary slightly among language groups, but the methods of interaction between deities and devotees are more or less the same. All dialect groups believe in sending gods back to their abodes after their annual visit to earth, and they are ceremonially sent home in notional sedan chairs or on horses. Images of these vehicles are featured on token papers which are burnt. The ritual also includes a token offering of thanks in the form of a replica of paper money which is believed to have even more influence when folded into the shape of a gold ingot.

A god who may be an invention of overseas South-East Asian Chinese is *Tua Pek Kong*; he is sometimes referred to as the household god of the earth. From the various attributes that have been conferred on *Tua Pek Kong*, he appears to be a deified cultural hero who bestows success and good fortune. In Penang, his original shrine, built in 1799, is on the northeast coast, which was once the landing place of immigrant

Spirit or token paper money, usually made of newsprint, is stamped with gold or silver paint. The folding is decorative, and at the same time creates air-space in between the sheets so that they burn easily. (Photo Khoo Joo Ee)

traders travelling by sea. The dried oyster porridge served in the fire-divination ceremony in this seaside shrine is symbolic, the oyster being obtained from the seashore. Other smaller shrines to *Tua Pek Kong* in houses, beside graves, or by the roadside are more homely and personalized.

Religious syncretism

Popular Buddhism

A schism in Buddhism developed soon after the death of its founder Siddartha Gautama (c. 566-486 BC). The group who believed in maintaining the original Buddhist Order, as propounded by the historical Buddha Gautama, called themselves *Sthaviravadin* (Sanskrit: 'Believers in the Teaching of the Elders') which in Pali is *Theravadi*; hence this sect's form of Buddhism is called *Theravada* Buddhism. (Pali was the dialect of Western India, and is still used in Buddhist monasteries.)

Around the first and second centuries AD, another very important sect, the *Sarvastivadin* was powerful in Northwest India where many new ideas were advanced. This led to the major division of Buddhism into the 'Great Vehicle' and the 'Lesser Vehicle'; *Mahayana* and *Hinayana* respectively, vehicle being the means to salvation. As new sects of *Mahayana* grew in popularity in many parts of India, the earlier Lesser Vehicle took refuge in Sri Lanka from where it spread to Southeast Asia.

RIGHT: While some censers are made of pewter, as in the Hai Kee Chan temple, ceramic ones, often decorated with colourful opaque enamel, are also quite common. This cylindrical censer has a salmon-coloured scalloped ogival panel featuring two phoenixes, one in flight and one perched on rocks. Height (excluding stand) 12.5 cm, diameter 16.5 cm. (Courtesy Madam Ong Siew See, photo H. Lin Ho)

BELOW: A pair of ceramic candlesticks of bell-shaped bases and deep cup-shaped drip-pans. The decoration on the bases is dominated by two ogival panels in pink against a green background between an upper border of *ruyi* lappets and a lower border of lotus panels. The peonies on the drip-pans are also against a green background. Height 21 cm. (Courtesy Prof. Dr. Cheah Jin Seng, photo H. Lin Ho)

The *Theravada* sect of *Hinayana* is particularly prevalent in Sri Lanka, Burma and Thailand.

The 'Great Vehicle' or *Mahayana* itself also divided into various sects as it spread to China and Japan. By around the eighth century a third 'vehicle', *Vajrayana*, 'The Vehicle of the Thunderbolt' arose in Eastern India.

The forms of Buddhism which filtered into the Straits Settlements were syncretic of all three 'Vehicles', although *Mahayana* was, and still is, predominant. Even the Sri Lankan, Burmese and Thai *Theravada* forms have strong *Mahayana* influence.

Without a sophisticated level of education in the community, it would have been futile to expound the subtle differences between the various schools of Buddhist thought. Two *Theravada* schools of *Hinayana* Buddhism effectively reached the Straits Chinese from Thailand and Sri Lanka. The relatively clean-cut Thai *Theravada* appeals to the layman; its statuary adds visual appeal. Singhalese monks' command of English gives them a particular advantage, although very often Buddhist priests speak to the laity in Malay. Thai priests may teach in Hokkien, which is very similar to the

Teochew dialect which predominates amongst the Chinese of Bangkok. There are occasional classes in Pali and for the study of *Theravada* Buddhism, although the various types of Buddhism practised are syncretic versions of *Mahayana*, as we have just seen. Rituals like burning joss-sticks and paper artefacts, which actually have nothing to do with Buddhism, are also undertaken during visits to a Buddhist temple.

Associations and societies are usually affiliated to, or even have their premises in, a temple. Penang seems to be the centre of Buddhist activities, possibly because of its proximity to mainland Southeast Asia. Thus the only Burmese temple in the whole of the Peninsula is in Penang. (There is a group of Buddhist countries in mainland Southeast Asia, while island Southeast Asia is largely Muslim: Islam is, of course, the official religion of Malaysia.)

Variance in Buddhism exists because of the differences between *Hinayana* and *Mahayana*. The *Mahayana* pantheon has many *Bodhisattva* (personified entities possessing 'Buddha qualities') who remain in waiting as Buddhas-to-be for the rest of the world to work out its salvation. *Hinayana* states that each individual works out his or her own salvation, or rather world-view, without the help of earthly gods, so that, theoretically, there are no *Bodhisattva* in *Theravada*. (*Vajrayana* expounds a 'short-cut' to enlightenment by acquiring magical powers.)

Kuan Im (*Guan Yin*) is the most popular of the *Mahayana Bodhisattva*. This figure appears in slightly different forms in different Buddhist countries and was first seen in India, where the deity was embodied as a man. By the time it reached China, it was for a while asexual, but soon became female. The female *Kannon* is Japan's version. *Kuan Im* is also called the Goddess of Mercy because she is merciful and compassionate. There are no images of Buddha in a *Kuan Im* temple.

Of the many Buddhist temples in Penang, the most impressive is the *Kek Lok Si* which was built in 1880. It stands on a hill and the entire complex spreads over twenty acres of land. This temple has the honour of being the only one outside China with an imperial sanction, which was bestowed in 1904 by Emperor Kuang Hsu (Guangxu); he also presented the temple with a set of *sutra*, Buddhist scriptures. A gigantic statue of

ABOVE: The oldest temple to the Compassionate *Bodhisattva* Kuan Im in Penang. (Photo Cheang Yik On)

BELOW LEFT: The earliest shrine in Penang to *Tua Pek Kong*, on the northeast beach of the island, a favourable landing place for a sailing ship. (Photo Cheang Yik On)

BELOW: A unique feature of the Straits Chinese (and other Southeast Asian Chinese) graves — a little shrine to *Tua Pek Kong* (Da Bo Gong), literally Eldest Grand Uncle in the precints of the grave. (Photo Khoo Joo Ee)

RIGHT: A water sprinkler. Sprinkling water is a widespread ritual, practised by Brahmins, Hindus, Buddhists and Muslims. It continues to be familiar to Straits Chinese. Gilt silver, height 35 cm, 400 mg. (Courtesy Dr. Chan Chin Cheung, photo H. Lin Ho)

OPPOSITE PAGE: The Buddha in his manifestation as the Laughing Buddha almost only peripherally admitted into the precincts of a clan temple, where a patron saint, deified ancestors and Chinese legends take places of honour within the temple; the image of the Buddha sits on a low column at the foot of the staircase. (Photo Cheang Yik On)

The Kek Lok Si temple and its
eclectic pagoda on the slope
of Penang Hill. (Photo Cheang
Yik On)

Kuan Im located on the hill beyond the temple is visible from afar. Seafarers worship a female deity, the Queen of Heaven. This Taoist goddess, who is known by several names — *Sheng Mu, Matsu, Tian Hou, or Mah Chor Poh* — appears to have been conflated with the Goddess of Mercy, *Kuan Im.*

When the earliest Hokkien and Cantonese of Penang joined forces to build a temple to the Goddess of Mercy, they tried to buy land along the seafront for the purpose, although the *Mahayana Kuan Im* is normally associated with mountains rather than the sea. However, the aim of building a temple as a shrine for a goddess was duly accomplished and although the original dedication was to the Taoist seafarers' goddess, as shown in temple records, today the popularity of *Kuan Im* has overshadowed *Mah Chor Poh* altogether.

Hungry ghosts

The seventh lunar month is not very providential because the restless souls of the departed who were not properly cared for are believed to roam the earth. Their living relatives, therefore, would do well to make amends with these neglected spirits who cannot rest in peace. The Hungry Ghosts' Festival was celebrated in the past, especially in Penang, but it then became less important until there was a revival of interest in the 1970s. In Penang, both the main language groups, the Hokkien and the Cantonese, celebrate the festival in a big way, although the Cantonese proceed in a more private manner, with individuals offering prayers and burning paper replicas of clothes and money.

The ghosts at large are all represented by effigies, although former practice was to venerate them with an inscribed tablet. Large amounts of food are laid out on makeshift altars as offerings to the ghosts. Temporary shrines and canopied shelters are erected in open spaces and temple compounds, or just by the roadside. Large flags and rows of giant joss-sticks are further signs of the site of the celebration, which lasts for about a week. The festival is organized by neighbourhood or clan groups, and hawker and market associations. During the period the temporary festival sites and permanent amusement parks feature Chinese operas to entertain both the roving spirits and the devout. At the makeshift shrines, a vigil is kept. Needless to say, during the night-long watch when time hangs heavy, gambling, especially at *mah-jong*, is prevalent.

BELOW LEFT: One of a pair of dragons, composed of cupcakes, flanking (and guarding) the King of Hungry Ghosts.
BELOW: A long-tongued Hokkien King of Hungry Ghosts. (Courtesy *Pulau Pinang Magazine*)

The effigy representing the roaming spirits is named the King of Ghosts. He is not usually alone but accompanied iconographically by four minor acolytes who are personages from Hell, namely 'Big Uncle', 'Second Uncle', 'Regional Officer' and 'Secretary'. Besides these officials from Hades, the Ghost King is guarded by a pair of dragon effigies in the form of colourful cup-sized muffins. A Taoist priest 'initiates' and 'animates' the ghost effigies by daubing red paint on various parts of them: then the spirits can see, hear and even move. These spirits are also offered paper replicas of money and other material goods, very much like *kong teik* in funeral ceremonies. On the last day of the rite, effigies, money and papercraft go up in a roaring bonfire. These effigies used to be sent out to sea in a boat provided with coins and food.

Burning and cremation are sure signs of the Buddhist influence in Chinese religion. The influence of Taoist and pre-Buddhist practices results in the mixed character of the Hungry Ghosts' festival. The fearsome King of Hungry Ghosts, animated by a Taoist priest, carries on his headdress a little image of *Kuan Im*, the Goddess of Mercy, the most revered *Bodhisattva* of *Mahayana* Buddhism. This compassionate Buddha-to-be, in order to save the hungry ghosts, assumes human form, but actual depiction of the awesome spirit varies in detail. Hokkien Kings of Ghosts have long protruding tongues which hang down, whereas Cantonese personifications are tongueless. The tongued icon has ancient folk symbolism.

The Buddhist retreat of three summer months coincides with the lunar month's full moon or fifteenth day of the fourth to sixth month. Thus one legend has it that the mother of one of the Buddha's disciples was a hungry ghost. In order for his mother to be saved, he had to prepare a feast of one hundred dishes for the monks at the end of their fast. The emphasis in this parable is on filial piety, which falls right in line with Confucianism. The inclusion of a mother in religious parables appeals to popular sentiment. Such parables referring to family and society were later introduced into popular Buddhism since they were of universal appeal. The original Buddhist renunciation of society in search of void cannot be accepted by the Chinese, who have such a high regard for the importance of lineage. In the same way, many practices had to be adapted to fit in with opposing beliefs. A good example of this is the nature of the offerings in the Hungry Ghosts' Festival. The 'three meats' were considered by Confucius to be the greatest form of offering to ancestors. They were originally beef, mutton and pork. Disregarding the Buddhist preference for vegetarianism and modifying the advice of Confucius, Penang Chinese offer their ancestors pork, chicken and seafood.

Christianity

Generally, there is no antagonism among the Chinese towards Christian denominations. There is, however, the occasional adverse reaction to some aspect of Christianity, even from those who have attended Christian schools. Among the reasons for this is that Christianity sometimes clashes with Chinese customs; and there were persecutions within individual families. It is clear that Christianity did not have a very great impact on the Chinese, as most of their own traditions have survived. It did, however, cause a rift in some families when some of the members were converted and others were not. In such cases, the convert is relieved of the expenses of maintaining the family altar with its regular offerings. Posthumous ceremonies are dispensed with because homage to ancestors is abandoned, and there is no necessity for an elaborate funeral. However, many Chinese Christians still mourn for their elders, sometimes for long periods, and the maintenance of the family grave is still important for everyone. (Buddhist cremation, it may be noted, has the edge over Christian burial in respect of expense.)

Because of the number of Chinese who have converted to Christianity, there has been a change of attitude towards some traditional rituals, although Chinese New Year is still celebrated by almost all Chinese Christians. Changes in marriage and funeral styles came about through modernization and because of economic hardship rather than because of the influence of Christianity. Non-Christian Baba and other Straits Chinese took to the reformed style of wedding especially after the Depression.

Nineteenth century printing in Southeast Asia was largely a Protestant missionary activity for the instruction of converts in the region. Missionary publications were in Chinese and other languages. Agents of the London Missionary Society set up printing presses in Malacca, Penang, Singapore and Batavia (Jakarta). Both the American missionaries and the London Missionary Society had, in fact, stayed in the Straits Settlements and Batavia, because of the large Chinese population in these places. However, they were only temporary bases, and when the ban on missionary work in China was lifted with the Treaty of Nanking in 1842, thus opening up the country, the missionaries left for China.

Nowadays, while the congregation of the Methodist Church in Penang is English-speaking, those of St.George's Anglican Church and the Catholic Church of Our Lady of Seven Sorrows may not be so. Similarly, religious services for Chinese *Peranakan* are conducted in Malay as well as English, and Christian hymns have been translated into Malay. As with Indian converts, most of whom were, and still are, estate workers and rubber tappers, the earliest Chinese Christians were non-English-speaking. The records of St. George's Church show that most of the Chinese converts were from the working classes.

Common origins

Although the appearance of dark-skinned Chinese may suggest mixed marriage with Malays or Indonesians, some southern Chinese are in fact as dark as some Southeast Asians, and there has never been a homogeneous Chinese ethnic type. The physical and cultural division between North and South China, which is akin to the differences between North and South India, is often overlooked. 'Golden lilies', the poetic name for the bound feet of Chinese women, while appreciated in northern China, were not popular in the south, especially in the isolated province of Fujian, which generally had greater independence. Sinization of southern China by the northern Han Chinese had been resisted until as late as the fourteenth century, and the folk traditions of the region were not so much Chinese as Southeast Asian. One Chinese stereotype, '*Fumanchu*', was a western creation; it was, however, in a light vein and was a sort of spin-off from the China Trade and chinoiserie in Europe.

There is evidence of cultural affinity between South China and Southeast Asia in similarities in their languages, and in the fact that bamboo, rice and betel are native to both regions. While women of both regions use the sarong, a cylindrical piece of cloth worn in various styles, Chinese men have their version of the Malay head cloth, which they tie in a variety of ways.

Southeast Asia is part of a larger cultural region which sometimes features, among other traits, a matriarchy with female rulers. Because of this, women, and therefore goddesses, priestesses and female shamans or exorcists, have prominent roles. Another cultural trait of maritime peoples in the region is the soul-boat, or ship of the dead, which is often depicted in other media, especially textiles. Perhaps there is a connection between the boatloads of people on Chinese temple tops and those seen on the so-called ship cloths (textiles with ship motif) of southern Sumatra. Kingdoms in the Lower Yangtze shared maritime affinities with Southeast Asia and a type of dragon boat is depicted on ancient bronze drums from Vietnam.

The Dragon Boat Race

This well-known festival takes place on the fifth day of the fifth lunar month, the 'double fifth', at the Summer Solstice. The symbolism of the Dragon Boat Festival was forgotten long ago, even by the earliest Straits Chinese traders, who had travelled from afar, and had decided to make Malacca their home. In Penang, however, the festival is still celebrated, although the only vestige of the original ceremony which remains the same is the competitiveness of the racing. In ancient times the race also involved sacrificial ceremonies for hunters engaged in tribal warfare.

People who lived by rivers worshipped the River God and it was believed that a dragon in the river controlled the water needed for agriculture. This dragon received offerings just before the coming of the rainy season. The dragon became a deity and a good luck symbol for both the northern and the southern Chinese.

Annual crops depend on the regularity of the seasons and one of the ancient practices of agrarian communities is to try to control the seasons to ensure a good harvest. Canoe racing seems to be a ritual aimed at magically controlling the rain essential for agriculture. The Dragon Boat Race was, and still is, ceremonial. The boat simulates the dragon and Man handles and manipulates it. Through sympathetic magic, by controlling the dragon which is the boat, one controls the waters. This was the practice of peoples designated Wu and Yue of eastern and southern China who had traits in common with 'pre-Chinese' peoples. The rite of rain-making, i.e. having water when necessary for agriculture, is certainly of pre-Chinese origin. It seems likely that this ceremony used to be accompanied by a human sacrifice, with the victim being drowned to appease the river deity.

In China, the dragon boats are very narrow and can be up to thirty metres long, with a carved wooden dragon head at the prow. There are ten to fifteen oarsmen. They either sit, using short oars or stand, using long oars. Two men stand in the middle, one beating a gong and the other a drum. A man at the prow chants working songs as he waves a small red flag to keep the beat for the oarsmen. In some parts of China, the Dragon Boat Race, which was also related to the ancestor cult, was held at the time of transplanting the rice seedlings. During this interruption of growth, the rice plants were believed to have lost their souls or vegetative potential. Only the deceased ancestors would have the power to recall the escaped souls of the rice, thus restoring growth.

Chinese accounts dating from the third century, mention similar boats coming from Fu-nan (roughly the area occupied by modern Cambodia with part of Vietnam). A carved fish's head and tail were at the bow and stern respectively. The boats were propelled by means of paddles, not sails, and carried crews of about a hundred men. Different varieties of the shape and style of the boat are found over a very wide geographical area, from the whole of Southeast Asia to southern China and Japan.

In a more practical style in South China, boat racing was a means of training the navy. At the same time battles were fought in these dragon boat canoes against the northern Chinese. Pirates, smugglers and the water police of southern Chinese coastal regions utilized boats of this type until well into the nineteenth century. These war boats are the same ones used in Southeast Asia, where they also functioned as symbols to preserve the state's safety. Today, in some Southeast Asian states, dragon boats are retained as ceremonial decorative barges.

The dragon boat (deriving ultimately from a dug-out tree trunk) is carved in such a way that the ends are elevated, sometimes as high as five or six feet above the water. The bow and stern are decorated with a detachable dragon head and tail respectively. Alternatively the bow may carry some form of dog head or the head of an aquatic creature, for example the Malay egret (*bangau*) or the Arakan Burmese crocodile. The finished boat is lacquered, oiled and waxed. The long narrow canoe has no sails: men seated two abreast paddle it. The number of crew members ranges from twenty to a hundred, according to the length of the boat.

A ceremonial launching imbues the craft with magical powers and in this sense it becomes a dragon, crocodile or some such animal. In Vietnam, Cambodia and Laos, boats of this type are decorated inside with red lacquer and outside in black and gold. Siamese craft were hollowed from a single tree trunk and the ends were greatly elevated. They were gigantic dug-outs, often well over a hundred feet long, with crews of as many as a hundred-and-fifty men. The Siamese royal barge of today is a hundred-and-fifty feet long by eleven feet wide with a gilt pavilion amidships as the place of honour. It is the most evolved form of the dragon boat.

The original appeasement, or attempted control, of the river dragon later became a festival to honour Qu Yuan, the great poet and patriotic political figure (of the Warring States period, 475-221 BC) who drowned himself on the fifth day of the fifth moon. He died in southern China while under banishment. This virtuous statesman, who had been unjustly disgraced, became a martyr, and the search for his body developed into an established custom to commemorate him. This legend seems to have been created long after the demise of ritual canoe racing.

A special food (called *chang*), a steamed glutinous rice dumpling wrapped in leaves and with a variety of fillings, is associated with the Dragon Boat Festival. Various types of palm leaves are used to wrap the dumpling in a pyramid shape. The Straits Chinese use bamboo leaves, those from China being preferred because they are larger. Again, the story of the statesman who drowned himself lies behind the preparation of this rice dumpling. Legend has it that rice which had been steamed in bamboo sections was offered to his soul in the river. (Rice cooked in this way is still common among China's minorities, and the style is a traditional method of cooking for Southeast Asians.) The river dragon, however, got to the rice before the statesman's spirit and it then instructed the people to wrap the dumpling in leaves.

The betel

Chewing the leaves of the betel plant is alien only to urban Chinese. The habit has long been prevalent throughout India, Southeast Asia and southern China and is still practised in these regions today, especially in rural areas. The elderly often pound all the ingredients in a compact tube-shaped mortar and pestle. Tobacco chewing went together with betel chewing and was an important part of Southeast Asian material

Betel chewing set of brass and woven cane. (Courtesy Lim Lean Lee, photo The Pepin Press)

ABOVE LEFT: Betel chewing set of Burmese lacquer from Penang. Height 10 cm, diameter 7.2 cm. (Courtesy Tan Joo Lan, photo The Pepin Press)

LEFT: A rectangular silver betel chewing set with all four sides decorated with the phoenix; the small containers have floral designs. 24 x 14.3 cm, 1.3 kg, Ta Hing shopmark. (Courtesy Dr. Chan Chin Cheung, photo H. Lin Ho)

RIGHT: An unusual betel-chewing set, including home-rolled cigarettes of tobacco in palm leaves. Smoking and chewing shredded tobacco, together with betel chewing, is not uncommon among the older generation of Straits Chinese. Two whole areca nuts *(Areca catechu)* await husking and slicing. The smoking and chewing ingredients are served in a brass pedestal bowl decorated with overlapping triangular motifs in repoussé. (Collection Muzium Negara, Kuala Lumpur, photo The Pepin Press)

OPPOSITE PAGE: A Penang *sirih* set with Thai influence in its design. Gilt silver. Tray height 6 cm, diameter 20 cm, 600 gm. (Courtesy Dr. Chan Chin Cheung, photo H. Lin Ho)

BELOW RIGHT: A silver *sirih* set of finely worked repoussé. It includes a conical betel-leaf container and a mortar and pestle. (Collection Muzium Negara, Kuala Lumpur, photo The Pepin Press)

68

RIGHT: A ceramic spittoon in the form of a jar with wide mouth and high shoulders. It is portable and can be placed on a table. (Courtesy Penang Museum, photo Cheang Yik On)

ABOVE LEFT: Brass spittoon, to be placed on the floor under tea-tables. Height 36 cm. (Courtesy Tan Joo Lan, photo The Pepin Press)

ABOVE MIDDLE: Brass spittoon, of Indian manufacture, with chase-work and fluting. Heights 60.5 cm and 39 cm. (Courtesy Dato' Khoo Keat Siew, photo Cheang Yik On)

ABOVE RIGHT: A pair of Nyonya-ware spittoons, decorated with phoenixes in flight in mirror image. (Courtesy Penang Museum, photo Cheang Yik On)

culture. Betel chewing sets are made in a variety of materials, including precious metals, wood, cane and plaited or matted plant fibres. Offering a person betel leaf, as a small prepared package (quid), or offering a betel chewing set itself, is an invitation, an act of friendliness or a token that an agreeement, such as a bethrothal, has been made. Offering betel was also a sign that a favour had been asked for or granted. It said more than the social cup of coffee or glass of wine. The betel set was an important item in a wedding ceremony. A displeased mother-in-law, when suspicious that the bride was not a virgin, would topple the set as a sign of her anger. Wedding invitations were termed 'sending the betel'.

Rites of passage

Full moon and childhood

The birth of a child and its attainment of a full month of being alive are about the only two occasions for celebration during the child's life. *Mua Guek* means full moon, signifying the new-born babe's attainment of a full month's survival in good health, which calls for celebration. This takes the form of distributing turmeric-coloured glutinous rice (Malay: *nasi kunyit*) with chicken curry, accompanied by a sweet red-coloured dumpling made of soft rice and filled with mashed green or mung beans. A design on the sweet indicates the sex of the baby. A turtle and two marbles is the sign for a boy while a girl is represented by two peaches. Custom demands that the recipients reciprocate the gifts with fresh eggs, which symbolize fertility. These are usually accompanied by rock sugar and a box of dry vermicelli as wishes for a sweet long life.

There are no special ceremonies to mark children's reaching puberty, but in bygone days a stricter watch would begin to be kept over girls, who would no longer be allowed to play in the backyards of the houses.

The traditional Baba wedding

Matchmaking was the norm among the Babas until half a century ago. Many women believed that matchmaking gained 'merit' for the matchmaker towards going to Heaven. Her match had to be sanctioned by Heaven, which ordained all marriages. The compatibility of the match would be indicated in an almanac. Even so, the birthdates and 'animal years' of the couple were written in Chinese on two separate pieces of red paper by an astrologer and placed on the altar of each parental house for three days. That the couple, or even the matchmaker, could not read and write Chinese was no matter. Choosing the engagement and wedding days was also done through consultations with an almanac expert.

Besides earning a place in Heaven, matchmakers got earthly rewards in the form of cash (always discreetly slipped into a red envelope, hence called an *ang pow*, or red

packet), two bottles of wine and two legs of pork from both sets of parents. The matchmaker had to handle the sensitive issue of status.

Generally, while the bride's standing depended on the wealth of her family, the groom's bargaining power was his earning potential. If the groom was of high status, being from an affluent family, he would receive very special treatment and little effort was required of him.

The majority of Baba weddings for the wealthy were matrilocal, so that the husband lived with the wife's family after the marriage. Sometimes the groom even adopted the surname of the bride if she had no brothers to continue the family name.

Failure to observe social status was thought to show ignorance of repercussions because, as the first line of a Hokkien ditty in the form of a couplet moralizes, 'A phoenix mates with a phoenix'. The meaning is similar to 'Birds of a feather flock together'. There is further bird imagery in another Hokkien saying about ill-matched couples, 'A crow flying with the phoenix'.

In the past, the astrologer determined not only the day of marriage, but also the engagement day, which was only about two weeks before the wedding. A deputation of about six elderly ladies (blessed with longevity) brought gifts from the groom to the bride's family. Engagement gifts varied, but the symbolic ones included a bowl of *koey ee* (small round balls of rice dough in a light syrup), candles, part of a roast

A Penang bride and groom alighting from their motorcade procession during rounds of visits on the first day of the wedding. (Courtesy Penang Museum)

ABOVE LEFT: A groom wearing a skull cap of a formal Chinese style created by the Baba Straits Chinese, decorated with a star-shaped pendant-brooch. (Courtesy Low Hock Hoon)
ABOVE RIGHT: A Penang bride with her Mistress of Ceremonies.

piglet and two bottles of brandy; the last item replaced the traditional Chinese rice wine. These gifts were usually transported in tiered cane baskets. A well-to-do groom's family would add hairpins, a wedding dress, shoes and two diamond rings. Apparently the Malaccan practice of sending two red packets or *ang pow* did not apply in Penang. (One of the red packets was for the mother who had brought up the daughter.)

Among the gifts given in return from the bride's family were oranges, a silver belt, and men's slippers which should have been embroidered by the bride. The groom was sometimes given a fan to carry on the wedding day.

Before the advent of the invitation card, offering a quid of betel leaf signified the wedding invitation. A professional Indian ritual master acccompanied middle-aged and elderly ladies to distribute these invitations. The betel leaf was folded into a pyramid shape containing the ingredients for a chew. These little bundles were put in a silver bowl which in turn was wrapped in a large square handkerchief. The bridegroom personally invited close relatives by offering small bowls of *koey ee*. By the time invitation cards were in vogue, the Penang custom was for relatives to receive a special set of these cards. Family members who wished to hold a tea ceremony for the newlyweds kept the invitation and the couple would pay them a visit on the third day.

About two weeks before the wedding, a middle-aged or elderly lady ceremonially cut

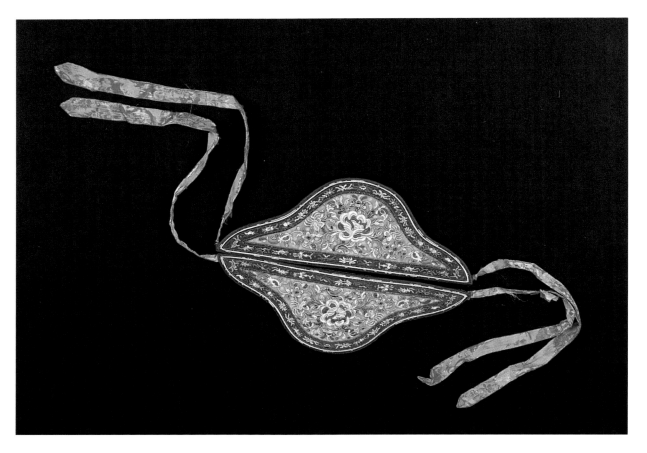

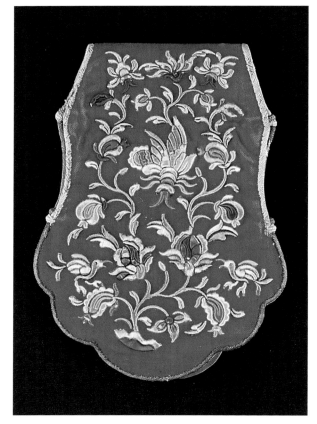

ABOVE LEFT: The Malacca bridal necklace called kalung papan in Malay. Filigree floral sprays are appliquéd on wire-mesh plates, whose upright edges are lined with a row of very fine rosettes. The plates, papan, are joined by nine strings of openwork florets. Gilt silver. (Courtesy Azah Aziz, photo H. Lin Ho)

LEFT: Star-shaped brooches, used singly or joined into a necklace, were preferred by Penang Nyonya brides, and also by some earlier generation Malacca brides. The grooms and men of both northern and southern Babas wore a single one on their hat or jacket (see page 75). (Collection Khoo Joo Ee, photo H. Lin Ho)

ABOVE: A pair of sunting mala worn by Malacca brides. The wavy shaft of the hairpin is inserted just over the ears so that the tiered rosette sticks out at the temple. Gilt silver and rose-cut diamonds. (Collection Khoo Joo Ee, photo H. Lin Ho)

RIGHT: A Malacca bridal couple
with their pages; the attire of the
bridesmaid was almost as elaborate as the bride's. (Courtesy
Dato' Dr. Lim Kee Jin)

BELOW: The Malacca style head-
dress of the bride on this photograph shows the *sunting mala*
(see page 77) jutting out perpendicularly from her temples.
(Courtesy Dato' Dr. Lim Kee Jin)

a length of white cloth (sometimes silk) into two. This ritual was conducted in the
groom's home and one piece of the material was sent to the bride. The couple would
each make their own pair of pyjamas from the cloth. The person chosen to cut the
cloth had to have a complete family still living: a husband, son, daughter and grand-
children.

Throughout the twelve-day wedding period, the bridal chamber was in the bride's
home whether the marriage was matrilocal or not. With the bedchamber already decorated, a special ceremony was held five days before the wedding day. A teenage boy
dressed in his best clothes rolled back and forth from one end of the bed to the other
three times; he was assisted by a mistress of ceremonies. Again, not just any boy
would do for this marriage rite; he should preferably have been born in the year of
the dragon, and come from a large family with both parents still living.

Four days before the wedding, friends and relatives would be milling around the
house especially to peel the mountain of onions required for the enormous amount of
food to be prepared. Usually a Hainanese chef would be hired to cook food that was
fine enough for such an occasion. Three days before the wedding a special sweet

appetizer was prepared from soya beans in spices. This, together with the ever-present sweet rice-flour balls in syrup, would be distributed to friends and neighbours.

With two days to go, the ritual of combing and trimming the bride's hair was performed, starting at midday. The fringe, after being trimmed, was tied into tiny tufts at both sides of the forehead. The ribbon was either white to signify the bride's purity, or red for the auspicious occasion; practices varied. The hairdresser was usually also the mistress of ceremonies for the wedding. Folklore has it that this experienced lady was able to determine whether the bride-to-be was a virgin or not. If the hairline along the forehead refused to respond to the comb but tended to curl, it was a sign of the girl's loss of honour. The tied tufts remained in place throughout the rest of the wedding ceremonies. Some brides retained this symbol of virginity until after the birth of their first child. Young girls also sported the fringe.

On the eve of the wedding there were more rituals to be followed. In Hokkien, the expression for the eve means 'to reserve the hall', which had to be thoroughly prepared and not used for any other activity besides the wedding. Ladies were invited for lunch and men for dinner. For both occasions, the meals were laid out on very long tables. Formerly, say before this century, ladies at this lunch ate with their fingers Malay style, while the Baba men, who were westernized far earlier than their women, dined with fork and spoon. Even though several sets of the same dishes were laid out at regular intervals on the table within reach of all seated, the Nyonya restricted herself to the dishes immediately in front of her; it was unbecoming for a lady to stretch for food. The more formal dinner for the men was served course by course.

The initiation ceremony symbolized the bridal couple's entry into adulthood and was conducted on the eve of the wedding. It can be considered the most sacred of all the many ceremonies and rituals. Tantamount to an exchange of vows, it was held in the homes of both the bride and the groom from late at night till the early hours of the next morning. The bride and the groom went through the same ceremony separately at the appointed time, which again had been chosen after consulting the almanac.

Facing the family altar, another altar to Heaven was set up, with a space left between

ABOVE: A pair of candle stands of lacquered, painted and gilded namwood. These flank the altar during festive occasions. (Courtesy Dato' Khoo Keat Siew, photo Cheang Yik On)

LEFT: Wooden rice measure (height 20.5 cm, diameter 29 cm), lacquered and gilded, and other paraphernalia used in the initiation rite on the eve of the wedding. (Courtesy Tan Joo Lan, photo The Pepin Press)

the two. The altar to Heaven was tall and narrow and below it was a square table which was wider and therefore protruded below the altar itself. This table was pulled out fully to accommodate offerings. Apart from the usual cooked foods, tea, wine, flowers and a pair of glass lamps, there was a special wooden stand (called *beet chien* in Penang and *chien arb* in Malacca) to hold decorative skewers spiked with slivers of crisp young papaya. During the ceremony, the whole stand had a cover to protect the sweetened fruit until it was time for it to be given as an offering.

The initiation ceremony was conducted in the space between the two altars. A large round tray of plaited bamboo with a red circle painted in the centre was placed in the middle of this space. There was a wooden rice measure on the tray with its mouth upwards and covered with a piece of red cloth. The bride, dressed in white pyjamas made from the cloth sent by the groom two weeks earlier, sat on the rice measure holding an almanac on her lap. The page boy who had taken part in the blessing of the bridal bed was present. He received symbolic objects from the mistress of ceremonies and passed them to the bride. These were a Chinese ruler, a razor and a pair of scissors. Then the boy himself held a Chinese weighing scale above the bride's head and slowly lowered it to her feet to remind her that now as an adult she should weigh all her actions.

Apart from the numerous pre-nuptial ceremonies and preparations, the wedding itself was a long drawn out twelve-day affair displaying a mixture of Chinese and Malay customs. The groom's family, after consulting the almanac, had chosen the date for the wedding. On the day itself, the house was decorated and the family lanterns hung up, which meant that the family was officially ready; this was called 'open hall', just as the eve of the day was named 'reserving the hall'.

The day started with a procession leaving the groom's house: his parents would lead him out to a waiting carriage. Before mounting it he was offered a cup of wine by his father as a parting gesture. This ritual is still called 'mounting the horse', harking back

OPPOSITE PAGE: A formal and ceremonial bridal handkerchief of silver. Auspicious Chinese and Hindu-Buddhist symbols are worked in repoussé and perforated throughout, suggesting that the piece, which is actually a flattened pouch, was also scent container. The apex is in the form of a bat while a pheasant hovers over a vase of plenty from which blooms a lotus and other vegetal elements. Length 40.5 cm, width 13.7 cm. (Courtesy and photo National Museum of Singapore, S0546)

BELOW: Ventilating vest of small bamboo tubes worn by both bride and groom underneath the heavy outer garments. (Courtesy and photo National Museum of Singapore, G0309)

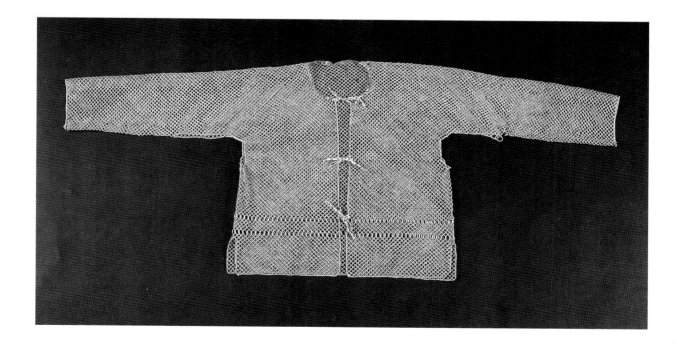

RIGHT: A sweetmeat rack (photographed from both sides, and with cover) called *beet-chien* in Penang and *chien-arb* in Malacca and Singapore. Skewers of glacé crystallized preserved fruits or other sweet meats are inserted into the protruding tubes at the top. The cover of the elongated hexagonal box is made of gilded lacquered wood, and decorated with legendary scenes. (Courtesy P. G. Lim, photo The Pepin Press)

OPPOSITE PAGE: A silver tray used to display jewellery and gifts during a wedding ceremony. While the rim of the tray is composed of ten lotus petals, decorations, executed in chasing, repoussé and applique techniques, are of vegetal, floral and zoomorphic motifs with the ubiquitous phoenix and peony in the centre medaillon. Diameter. 27 cm, 700 gm. (Courtesy Prof. Dr. Cheah Jin Seng, photo H. Lin Ho)

FAR RIGHT: Tiered red lacquered basket. (Courtesy P. G. Lim, photo The Pepin Press)

ABOVE: A bridal couple in Malacca in front of an altar.

RIGHT: The same dressed-up altar with the *chien-arb* carrying skewers of sweet meats. (Courtesy Amy Hamidon)

BELOW: A pair of gilt silver *kipas pengantin*, bridal fans. More practical fans are still used to fan the Malay bridal couple sitting in state. Length with tassels 29 cm, width 14 cm. (Courtesy Asian Art Museum, Kuala Lumpur, UM79.333, photo H. Lin Ho)

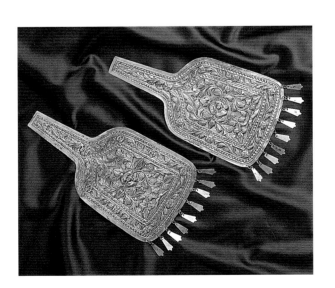

to old China where the groom went on horseback to fetch his bride from another district, i.e. exogamous marriage. These days, he goes to the bride's house in a motorcade, and even now we still sometimes see two sticks of sugarcane, symbol for a sweet long life, strapped on the back of the groom's car. However, we now rarely see that other ancient custom of placing a bamboo basket containing a young cockerel and a hen on the back of the vehicle. The groom was accompanied by a master of ceremonies, two best men, a cymbal player, a flutist and two gong beaters. The master of ceremonies was usually an energetic middle-aged man who helped the groom in the many rituals and was always by his side just as the bride had a mistress of ceremonies to attend to her.

The Baba gentry spent a fortune on the pageantry celebrating a traditional wedding, and the groom's procession was, of course, very lavish. Managing and heading this procession would be a professional Indian ritual master, who carried the groom's lantern and banner. He was followed by Chinese musicians playing Chinese intruments to accompany the marchers. Next came a display of items, purportedly gifts for the bride, arranged on large brass trays (in Penang it used to be twelve trays) which were borne shoulder-high by Indian labourers in colourful uniforms. They would be escorted by a deputation of the groom's close friends. The contents of the trays might have included jewellery from the bridegroom's parents for the bridal couple. Only a very small proportion of the gifts was actually accepted by the bride. They were meant only as symbols of a good life. In addition to the trays there were large lacquered wooden boxes hung on horizontal poles and carried on the shoulders of strong men — two per box. Inside the boxes were gifts for the bride's parents, including a roast piglet, ducks, chickens, fruit, wine and candles. To add the finishing touch to the spectacle, embroidered slippers were displayed on trellised wooden frames.

In rural China, a wedding box of polished wood decorated with colourful designs and storing the girl's trousseau, together with other pieces of the bride's dowry, was carried in a procession through the streets from the bride's to the groom's house, so that all could view the wealth and domestic skills of the bride.

Upon arrival at the bride's house, the groom was greeted by the sound of firecrakers. A page boy received him and invited him in. No Baba wedding was complete without the Malay *ronggeng*, dancing accompanied by music. The band and the dancers performed from morning till night, pausing every so often to rest or eat. Meantime, in the bridal chamber the mistress of ceremonies fussed over the bride. The girl's parents covered her face with a net veil which was black, symbolizing her sadness at leaving behind the carefree life of childhood, and her apprehension at entering adulthood. Sometimes the mistress of ceremonies had an elderly assistant, but it had to be someone who would not prove a threat to her business. Besides chiding the nervous bride to keep her in order, the usually formidable matron pinched her for all her mistakes and unbecoming behaviour.

After some time the groom invited the bride, who was by now arrayed in her finery, and veiled, to come out of her chamber. She was led out by the mistress of ceremonies. The bridal couple, having bowed to each other, were then led to the bridal chamber. It was the moment of truth. To the strains of Chinese music, the groom stood facing his bride ready to unveil her. Lifting the veil above her tall head-dress, he threw it up on to the canopy of the bridal bed. The bride had been instructed to keep her head low and her eyes modestly downcast. If she dared so much as raise her head to glance at her new husband, she would certainly receive a wicked pinch from the mistress of ceremonies. Folk belief has it that the speed with which the groom lifted and threw the veil up was indicative of how soon the first child would be born.

The couple then mimed the motions of feeding each other in a ceremonial first meal. Twelve dishes of food, tea and wine had been laid out for the purpose. Two pairs of silver or silverplated chopsticks were part of the table setting (although the Straits Chinese bride and groom normally ate with their fingers, or he with fork and spoon). The bridal pair shared a long red lacquered stool. Guests watched with curiosity and amusement for signs of matrimonial dominance indicated by one of the pair apparently stepping on the other's toes. If she stepped on his foot first, he would be under wifely control, but if the groom managed to place his foot over the bride's first it meant that he would be master of his household. On the table was a pair of tall candles, one for each of them. It was believed that if his candle went out before hers, she would be a widow and vice versa.

The final ritual, held in the bridal chamber, was concerned with the rooster and hen which had been brought to the house in the groom's car. They were released under the bridal bed and rice grains were scattered on the floor to entice the frightened birds out. This almost playful activity provided a break from the hitherto solemn for-

Rectangular bridal box. It can be carried by two men who shoulder a pole which goes through the handle of the box. (Photo Khoo Joo Ee)

OPPOSITE PAGE: Dressed up bridal
bed.
RIGHT: Detail.
(Courtesy The Baba Nyonya
Heritage Museum, Malacca,
photos H. Lin Ho)

BELOW: A pair of curtain hooks
used to hold up the front drapes
of the bed. Each stem plate,
worked in repoussé, is composed of two convex pieces
decorated with floral and
zoomorphic motifs, surmounted
by butterflies. Silver gilt, length
26.5 cm, 180 gm. (Courtesy Dr.
Chan Chin Cheung, photo H. Lin
Ho)

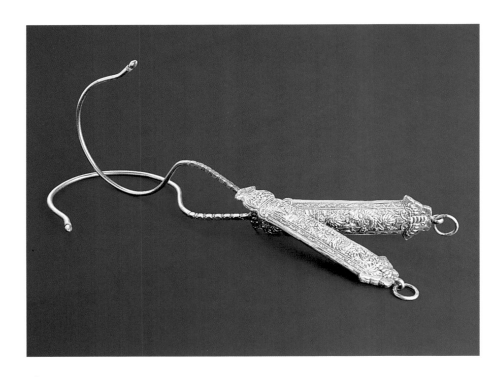

RIGHT: A pair of rectangular silver pillow ends. (Photo The Pepin Press)

BELOW: A pair of bed tassles, each strung by means of chained gold thread with three padded foliated shapes which in turn have tassles of strung metallic beads. Each pad is embroidered in gold-coloured sequins, metallic springy coils *(paku-paku),* Chinese-type flat silvery gold threads in relief in the Malay embroidery style called *tekat* and round silvery-gold threads couched down with coloured threads. (Courtesy Azah Aziz, photo H. Lin Ho)

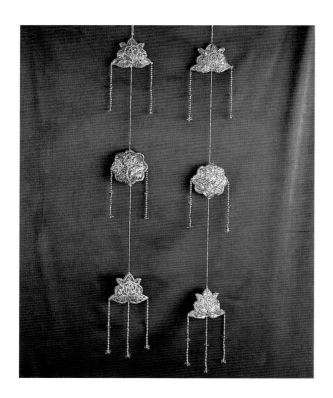

malities. If the rooster emerged before the hen, then it was believed that the first child would be a son. No doubt there would be some good-humoured betting on this prediction of the sex of the first-born. It is to be expected that extra encouragement was given to the rooster. At the same time, symbols of fertility such as the prolific yam plant, bananas and lemon grass were placed under the bed.

After paying their respects to the bride's parents by kneeling before them, the bridal couple departed for the groom's house to pay homage to his parents in a similar fashion before going on their rounds of temples and the homes of relatives. In Penang the bridal couple were accompanied by two page boys and two bridesmaids, while in Malacca they were attended by one page boy and one bridesmaid.

Later that night, the groom would be ceremonially invited back to the bride's house by the Indian ritual master and a page boy. They were supposed to make three calls before the groom accepted. The groom's friends were already there when he arrived at the bride's house and the newlyweds were subjected to a great deal of teasing. The merrymaking included the bride offering tea to the friends. The good humour and teasing, which inevitably revolved around the subject of offspring, drew out folksy ditties on the advantages and disadvantages of a son or a daughter. All the while, a mild contest, with betting, underlay the teasing: whoever managed to draw a smile from the bride won a dinner. The mistress of ceremonies had already commanded the bride to bite a piece of betel nut between her teeth; it would have been unbecoming for her to smile on such a serious and solemn occasion.

From the second day to the twelfth or last day, the groom was expected to rise at cockcrow and leave the bride's house early in the morning for his own home, returning to the bride by invitation each evening. The items for the groom's morning toilet were prepared by his bride and in recognition of this service he was expected to place the customary red packet of money on the washstand. This taxing ritual of daily departure and return was a sign of the privileged guest status of the son-in-law; the mistress of ceremonies had impressed upon the bride that the groom was her guest.

At the same time the ritual reinforced his continuing ties with his own house.

On the third day, the bride visited her in-laws; a retinue of older Nyonya accompanied her. The families exchanged gifts of food such as rice dumplings and sweet glutinous rice cakes which would also be distributed among relatives. The tea ceremony was held on this day; it was initially performed in the groom's home where his parents were offered tea first; the bride, having paid homage, was rewarded with cash in a sealed red packet. Other relatives, according to their seniority, were introduced by way of being served tea. The ceremony was repeated at the bride's home with the groom serving.

When the marriage was not matrilocal, the bride departed on the twelfth day for the groom's residence where a bedroom was appropriately furnished and decorated to receive her.

Whether it was a matrilocal marriage or not, the Babas always set up the bridal chamber in the bride's home and the furnishings were provided by her family. The preparation of the bridal bed meant the hanging up of embroidered drapes and bed curtains; the pillows and bolsters were encased in special covers and sewn with silver endpieces. The decorative hangings for the bed included talismans and perforated containers for potpourri. Incense and fumigants against insects and mosquitoes were present, even though netting enclosed the canopied bedstead.

During the wedding period there were some taboos. Entry to the bridal chamber was forbidden for 'unclean' (menstruating) women and anyone in mourning. Although it seems paradoxical that pregnant women were also not allowed to enter the chamber, considering all the decorations symbolic of fertility already there, perhaps the explanation was the belief that the fertility imbued in the chamber would be appropriated by the pregnant woman. Lest the empty bridal bed be inhabited by malicious spirits it was covered with auspicious items chosen for their sweetness, such as posies of fragrant flowers, flower petals mixed with shredded *pandanus* leaves (Malay: *bunga rampai*), sweet dishes made from rice and the ubiquitous betel leaf set.

ABOVE LEFT: Pillow ends come in various geometric shapes, and usually have holes along the edges for stitching. These hexagonal decorative silver plates feature very intricate floral motifs enclosing a crane in the centre. Width 9 cm (Photo The Pepin Press)

ABOVE: This round model is in its central medallion decorated with a *qilin* surrounded by a register of Buddhist symbols. Diameter 9.7 cm (Photo The Pepin Press).

ABOVE LEFT: A silver bridal water basin (top view). The centre of the well features two phoenixes while peonies and phoenixes, decorate the cavetto (the inner curved side of the basin). On the everted rim are the Eight Buddhist emblems among butterflies, birds and flowers. Diameter 38 cm, 2.3 kg, Ta Hing shopmark. (Courtesy Prof. Dr. Cheah Jin Seng, photo H. Lin Ho)

ABOVE RIGHT: A jardiniere decorated with peonies in *famille rose* colours against a brown background between an upper border of Buddhist emblems and a register of *fu* (Chinese character for happiness) symbols at the base. The mouth rim is painted with sprigs of prunus flowers. Height 23 cm, diameter 5.3. cm. (Courtesy Prof. Dr. Cheah Jin Seng, photo H. Lin Ho)

OPPOSITE PAGE: Bridal wash-stand of lacquered and gilded nam-wood. Height 182 cm (Courtesy and photo National Museum of Singapore, F0048)

BELOW RIGHT: A ceramic wash-basin of coloured enamels on a white ground. A peacock perches on rocks in the centre medallion and on the cavetto is the Hundred Antiquities motif. (Courtesy Penang Museum, photo Cheang Yik On)

RIGHT: A pair of gilt silver tea-cups, each with a cover and stand, used during the tea ceremony, where the bridal couple offered tea as a gesture of respectful homage to their elders. Total height 8.5 cm. (Courtesy Asia House, Hong Kong, photo Cheang Yik On)

OPPOSITE PAGE: A Penang bridal couple on the twelfth day of the wedding. It is unusual is that they both stand, instead of her sitting. The page-girl is also wearing a *baju panjang* and sarong. (Courtesy SCPA)

BELOW: The reformed style of wedding, with the bride's skirt maxi length. (Courtesy Penang Museum)

Such pageantry ended half a century ago. The reformed style of wedding was already in vogue in the 1930s. The elaborate and heavy Chinese costumes gave way to the white satin bridal gown with a bouquet for the bride and a western suit for the groom.

Registration of Chinese marriages has been a controversial issue, as can be seen, for example, from a report that in 1918 a group of Nyonya in Penang held a meeting to discuss monogamy and registration of non-Christian marriages (*Penang Gazette* 15.3.1918). They drew up a resolution and sent a petition to the Governor on the matter. The majority of Chinese men, except for a few 'enlightened' ones, opposed this women's group's advocacy of compulsory registration; all *Sinkhek* were against it. The Governor had to consult his advisors and a committee was formed to investigate which rites and ceremonies constituted a valid Chinese marriage. The feeling was that Chinese marriage rites were good enough for the Chinese and the Government should not interfere with long-standing customs. Marriage laws in China, however, allowed for voluntary separation though not divorce, so the Chinese in the Straits Settlements could arrange privately with an officer of the Chinese Protectorate for such a separation. Finally, a compromise was reached; registration was recommended by the committee but it had to be on a voluntary basis.

ABOVE LEFT: The twelfth and last day of the wedding. The groom wears a western suit, the bride a Malay costume; an elaborate *baju panjang* over a *sarung songket* (a silk sarong woven with supplementary gold threads). On her head she wears a tiara composed of hairpins and garlands of jasmin buds. (Courtesy Penang Museum)

ABOVE RIGHT: A Penang bridal couple on their third day. The bride wears a *baju Shanghai*, a creation by Shanghai tailors residing in the Straits Settlements. The dress is a long sleeve blouse over an A-line long skirt. Her hairstyle is the so-called telephone type with a fringe. (Courtesy Penang Museum)

BELOW LEFT: The elaborate hairdo of this bride is purposefully reflected in the mirror. (Courtesy Lily Khoo)

BELOW RIGHT: The reformed style of wedding.

94

Childbirth and confinement

When it was the norm for women to give birth at home, those who could afford to hire a midwife did so. She attended to the new mother from delivery through the period of post-natal confinement. The Nyonyas in Malacca usually chose a Malay helper, while in Penang a Siamese midwife was often preferred. The midwife usually stayed at the house only during the day.

Many taboos were observed during pregnancy, childbirth and confinement. As early as four months into pregnancy, the midwife was called in to give the mother-to-be a ritual cleansing. She recited incantations while sponging her ward with ordinary bathing water enhanced by limes and different coloured flowers. When labour began, the Nyonya mother was advised to insert a nail into her hair so as to stop any evil spirit from entering her body. It was believed that delivery would be easier if during labour all drawers and cupboards in the room were left open. In case there were difficulties, the pregnant woman would be given a glass of water which had a key submerged in it. In addition the skilful midwife might recite incantations.

It was believed that a woman who had just given birth, having had her body stretched open, was susceptible both to loss of body warmth and possession by malicious spirits. To give her back her body heat, she was put on a diet of 'heaty' foods. At the same time she was given foods considered able to build up her strength; seafood, however, was considered toxic.

A special daily treatment was administered by the midwife. She rubbed the mother with menthol-based oil, then a hot metal rod wrapped in cloth was applied against her womb with the intention of pushing it back into position. In addition to these treatments the mother was tightly wrapped up around the belly region with a six-metre long cummerbund to hold in the loosened muscles to help her to remain slim. Finally, she would be simultaneously 'fumigated' and given body warmth to get rid of flatulence by sitting on a chair below which was a charcoal stove with old ginger roots burning in it. The mother would be given two more ritual baths, on the ninth day and the thirtieth day.

Birthdays

The yearly celebration of children's birthdays is very much a modern western activity. Even adults celebrating their birthdays before they are sixty years old is a modern occurrence. The sixtieth birthday, however, is traditionally considered the first major achievement in one's lifespan. The number sixty may have been chosen because of the sixty year cycle which was important in the traditional Chinese calendar (i.e. before the adoption of the Gregorian calendar). The serving of a special birthday dish of noodles is a custom among the Hokkiens and even more so among the Babas. Noodles signify longevity, so close relatives would, as a symbolic gesture of goodwill, bring boxes of dry vermicelli and rock sugar. Patriarchs and matriarchs, from the age of sixty onwards, are honoured yearly with birthday celebrations, and on these occasions it is customary for them to give their offspring and other family members a red packet each, upon receiving birthday wishes. The standard birthday greeting wishes the person longevity.

Funerals

Many funeral customs of old are still strictly adhered to. When a death occurs, all reflective surfaces in the house are covered. Often, a Taoist priest or priestess is invited to help clean and dress the deceased before placing the body in the coffin. Previously, preparation of the corpse might include the traditional offering of a pearl placed in the mouth, sometimes wrapped in a betel leaf. If the deceased used leather shoes in his lifetime, they would be replaced by rubber or paper ones into each of which a pearl might be placed. The fear of corpses talking and rising from the dead prompted such rituals. In bygone days deceased Babas or Nyonyas would be dressed in the white pyjamas worn on their wedding eve. Together with the body, some of the dead person's favourite clothes were placed in the coffin. Finally, the whole body would be covered with silver paper replicas of bank notes. Although white candles were normally used for the dead, if the deceased was an octogenarian or of a ripe old age, red candles were burned instead.

Both a decent burial and a proper tomb are supposed to be provided for during one's lifetime. In ancient times coffins used to be purchased and kept in temples until needed. The choice of a tomb site according to geomancy (see Architecture), could involve quite a search. While awaiting its outcome, old Chinese practice allowed for Buddhist or ancestral temples to store the coffin temporarily. For use during the funeral itself, paper replicas of material goods were often made for the grave. (In ancient times this papercraft, or *kong teik*, included images of real people as a substitute for human sacrifice.) The goods which are represented are all necessary items for the living. Some of the objects made did not represent actual possessions of the deceased but items he might have wished for, including money. Nowadays, this papercraft, made in miniatures, may include modern consumer items such as television sets or motor cars. The underlying theory is that death is a continuation of living: therefore, the deceased

BELOW: A funeral procession.
BELOW RIGHT: The *keo*, sedan chair fashioned as *kong teik* (papercraft for the dead), carried as part of the funeral procession.

needed in the nether world everything he had possessed in this world. There are still undertakers who also run shops selling paper goods for the dead.

For the procession to the grave, ten or more strong men would traditionally be needed to carry the coffin. Some of the elaborate old-fashioned wooden coffins were extremely heavy and the men carrying such a coffin wore yokes on which it was placed. The eldest living son of the deceased carried a bamboo stave from which hung a paper lantern meant to guide the soul of his late parent. A son-in-law carried a red banner on which were written the name and age of the deceased. At the grave, following prayers conducted by the Taoist priest, all papercraft effigies and miniatures were burnt, together with plenty of gold and silver painted replicas of paper money to be used in the spirit world. It was, and is, common practice not to place the headstone on the grave until the third week after the funeral. Posthumous ceremonies are organized according to the number of weeks since the person's death; the first three

Funeral of a matriarch in Singapore. The paper replicas of worldly possessions carried in the procession to the grave site were burnt for the deceased. (Courtesy Ong Siong Ngo)

weeks, known as the 'first seven days', 'second seven days' and 'third seven days', are important, just as the seventh week or 'seventh seven days' is. Non-Baba Chinese usually have a papercraft burning ceremony on the hundredth day after death and perhaps also on the anniversary. Some posthumous ceremonies are held at temples. The traditional period of mourning for parents is three years although in practice it may be reduced to, say, twelve months of wearing black, three months wearing black and white or blue, and three months wearing green. Members of the household still in mourning may not visit others during the Chinese New Year and in turn others cannot visit a house still in mourning.

A funeral procession along
Heeren Street, Malacca.
(Courtesy Low Hock Hoon)

A set of *kerongsang* of silver and pearls worn during a period of mourning. (Photo H. Lin Ho)

BELOW LEFT: Bamboo strips are used for the *kong teik* armatures of the artefacts. (Photo Cheang Yik On)

BELOW: *Kong teik* being made in a funeral parlour in Singapore. (Photo Khoo Joo Ee)

Festivals

Chinese New Year

Chinese New Year is not celebrated on the same day of the Gregorian calendar every year; the date is calculated according to the lunar calendar. New Year is the first day of the first lunar month of the year: the full moon is on the fifteenth of the month. On Chinese New Year, all Chinese are considered to be one year older as though it is a national birthday. Since China is in the northern hemisphere, New Year is a Spring Festival in its traditional calendar, which was formulated according to the cycle of agricultural production. The beginning of spring is seen as marking the turning point not only in this cycle, but also in business and personal economic affairs. Straits Chinese, whose agricultural activities, if any, depend on the tropical monsoon rather than the four seasons, still calculate their festival in the same way as the Chinese of the northern hemisphere. It is always between January the twenty-first and February the twentieth of the Gregorian calendar. Only even-numbered days are chosen to start the new year. In China in bygone days, shops and businesses closed for as long as sixteen days, that is until the day after the full moon, but this is not usually so in Southeast Asia, where work and commerce sometimes recommence from the second day; only some tradesmen (e.g. carpenters and shoemakers) take a two week holiday.

In anticipation of spring, the Winter Solstice is already a very important day. The twenty-second of December is mid-winter and the turning point of the year in the northern hemisphere, with the sun directly over the Tropic of Capricorn. In the Peninsula, the weather may be sunny, but especially on the east coast which is affected by the north-east monsoon, this sunny spell is short-lived. Even so, the Chinese make offerings to God and their ancestors as those in China do, in celebration of the fact that days will soon begin to lengthen.

Chinese New Year gift of oranges decorated with strips of red paper. (Photo Khoo Joo Ee)

All debts have to be settled before New Year and the house gets a thorough spring cleaning. The superstition is that cleaning does away with ill luck and makes way for good fortune, but more often now it is simply thought of as a healthy habit. Some prosperous families give presents of dress materials or jewellery to their relatives and employees in a gesture of sharing their surplus or abundance. It was the custom in China for people to give each other good quality tea and rare fruit; for the Chinese here tangerines have always been the most common fruit given. Presents of food also have symbolic value and the word for orange or tangerine has the same sound as the word for gold in some Chinese dialects.

Much food is prepared on the eve of Chinese New Year or a day or two before. No knives or sharp instruments can be handled on New Year's Day, to guard against good luck being cut off. It is even more important not to slaughter animals for food because this signifies severing life's continuity. A red cloth is hung framing the entrance to a house, while commercial premises and homes are also decorated with strings of firecrackers which are often tied to bamboo poles. The characteristic loud popping sound of these bamboo pole firecrackers can be heard any time between the eve and the end of the fifteen-day celebration.

All Chinese communities, including Straits Chinese, and especially those involved in business, invite lion dance troupes to their homes to perform at New Year. This must be done no later than the fifteenth day, but preferably during the first few days of the festival. A small troupe has only one effigy of the lion, whereas a large troupe has

ABOVE: Baskets for steaming sweet rice pudding are lined with banana leaves, which flavour the pudding while it is being steamed. (Photo Khoo Joo Ee)

FAR LEFT: 'Year pudding', *tnee koay*, is made of rice flour. It is used as an offering to spirits or given as homage to the living. (Photo Khoo Joo Ee)

LEFT: The 'double happiness' character is cut out in red paper and pasted on a comb of bananas as a ceremonial offering. (Photo Khoo Joo Ee)

Rice flour cakes dotted with red food colouring. They are called by their Malay name *kuih bangkit*, 'risen cakes'. (Photo Khoo Joo Ee)

two — one black and the other white. The lion effigy is animated by two men, one taking the head and one the rear. As another dancer teases the lion with some kind of decorative ball representing a pearl (see Architecture, temples). A dance ensues to the rhythm of percussion music from drummers, and gong and cymbal players. The troupe is rewarded with a substantial *ang pow* which is hung from a pole and taken by the lion dancer who is held up by acrobats from the troupe.

Such a dance, manipulating an effigy, is similar to a masked dance which was meant (and still is) as a ritual of exorcism. Troupes of masked dancers would parade through the streets of village after village, performing the demon-expelling ritual to cleanse each village. The feared animal is represented by an effigy which is controlled by Man, thus by sympathetic magic the animal is controlled (see also Dragon Boat Race). The lion is not native to China. Latsch (1984:43) has suggested that its image in China was derived from itinerant Indian jugglers and animal trainers during the Tang Dynasty (AD 618-906). The pre-Buddhist demon-expelling ritual or exorcism was appropriated by Buddhism; in this the lion symbolizing a *Bodhisattva* became a Buddhist guardian.

The most important and even intimate family deity is the Kitchen God, who is reputed to be the inventor of fire. He presides over and protects the hearth. He also makes an annual visit to Heaven, which is presided over by the Jade Emperor, to report on the household. Representations of this god range from a simple piece of plain red paper in humble homes to fanciful paintings in more prosperous residences. The pictures seem to reflect the devotee's conception of this deity, who is depicted in various ways: as an old man accompanied by his wife, a younger man holding an ancestor's tablet or a man on horseback. The horse is thought to be his vehicle for the journey to Heaven. Offerings to the Kitchen God a few days before the New Year are almost always sweet dishes, the intention being to 'sweeten' him up so that he will give a good report. The Straits Chinese offer him a cylindrical pudding of sweet steamed glutinous rice, simply called 'year pudding'. This sticky dessert will either seal the Kitchen God's lips or sweeten him up for his important report to the Jade Emperor.

Chinese New Year is an occasion to renew family ties and it is mandatory for every member of the immediate family to be present for the reunion dinner on the eve and to remain together to welcome the new year (see p.38). Members of the extended family are also encouraged to be present. In the days when an extended family stayed under one roof it was relatively easy to hold such a gathering. Since extended families have become more dispersed, it is now much more difficult to keep this tradition intact but immediate family members still try to be present. Apart from the dinner, ancestors are remembered when homage is paid to the inscribed tablets enshrined on the family altar. In cases where family members have settled in different places and there is no such altar, they pay homage, when possible, to the eldest living member of the family and to the ancestral tablets, usually kept at a temple.

Ang pows, those well-known red packets containing cash, are expected by children as gifts from married couples. Family members who are still single, whatever their age, are also given *ang pows* by their elders, the implication is that these unmarried people have not been initiated into adulthood. A daughter-in-law pays respects to her in-laws first thing in the morning on Chinese New Year's Day. She serves them some kind of sweet infusion, usually of bird's nests or longan, and in return she receives an *ang pow*. A family often has group portraits taken at a photo studio. Various other tradi-

tional practices of the different language groups are still carried out during New Year. The Cantonese in particular celebrate the birthday of Man on the seventh day by eating salad with raw freshwater fish, carp being preferred. The food is symbolic, the salad being a sign of something living and fresh, as opposed to dead, cooked and processed vegetables. Eating this salad means that Man will stay alive and alert for the whole year until he is rejuvenated by the cycle of rituals the following year.

Thanksgiving

To the Hokkiens, the ninth day of the Chinese New Year is more important than the New Year itself because it is the birthday of the God of Heaven, the Jade Emperor. Thanksgiving to Heaven is expressed in lavish offerings laid out on an altar table in front of the house. The altar, besides being dressed with an embroidered apron, has at each end a full grown stick of sugarcane tied to it, the prolific growth of the sugarcane being symbolic of a former agrarian prayer for a bountiful crop. (It will be recalled that sugarcane symbolizes a long sweet life in wedding rituals.) In addition to the offerings given to usher in a season of regeneration, a brief pilgrimage is undertaken. This involves climbing steps to a hilltop temple dedicated to the God of Heaven. The procession of climbers begins around midnight on the eighth day and goes on through the ninth day.

Chingay ('floats')

Chingay is a procession of floats held in Penang which is somewhat like the Latin *mardi gras*. It attracts a large crowd; people even come from the mainland to watch the parade. Its popularity dwindled after the Second World War but interest is currently being revived. The spectacular procession is made up of various divisions repre-

senting groups living in different parts of the island. Each division carries, besides a
float, a huge triangular silk flag which reaches a height of eight to twelve metres.
Each of these colourful flags has Chinese characters or some kind of graphic design
on it as a sort of logo of the group which sponsored it. A long strip of silk flutters
from the top of each flag down to the ground, making a striking sight as the flags bil-
low in the wind. A giant bamboo pole is used to hold the flag up. About a dozen
bearers take turns to balance the pole, punctuating the feat with acrobatic stunts.
The Chingay street procession used to be held on the day of the full moon of the first

A Chingay in Penang in 1928 in honour of *kuan im* (the *Mahayana* Buddhist *bodhisattva* or Buddha-to-be). The float was donated by Lim Cheng Law. (Courtesy Prof. Dr.Cheah Jin Seng)

month in the lunar calendar, in honour of the immigrants' god of fortune, *Tua Pek Kong.* This deity, who bestows on us all the good things of life, finds a place in every home. He is depicted as a smiling old man with a long white beard. During the procession an exchange of lighted joss-sticks occurs when devotees hand over lighted sticks from their houses and receive in return some from the urn of the deity in the procession. It is a symbolic reinforcement of the deity's presence in the devotee's home. In former days, the Chingay procession and the flame divination mentioned earlier in this chapter took place on the same date.

Chap goh meh ('night of the fifteenth day')

One of the most important days for all Chinese during the New Year celebrations is *Chap goh meh*, the fifteenth and last day of the Chinese New Year period when the moon is full. It used to be celebrated very lavishly by the Baba.

In the past, the special attraction was that young Nyonya, after a year of cloistered imprisonment, made their appearance in public, on parade. In town, shopkeepers provided chairs, which were arranged closely packed along the pavement. From about seven in the evening to midnight, regular traffic was diverted to make way for the show. Wealthy Nyonya bedecked in jewellery sat in open horse-drawn carriages with their chaperons; at one time they used to travel in bullock carts. Poorer girls went in rickshaws while others were on foot escorted by their brothers. The girls tried to cross seven bridges, the symbolism of which may be interpreted to mean passing successfully through the different stages of life. It was the custom for the Nyonya to throw oranges as they crossed the bridges, making a wish for a good husband. In Hokkien the word for orange rhymes with the word for husband. Bachelors were on the lookout for prospective wives, and the bolder men would serenade the bevy of maidens *dondang sayang* style (see the Arts).

This public display of marriageable girls who, for the whole year through were virtually kept under lock and key, was a striking contrast to the usually genteel style of the Babas. A paradoxical, unsubtle and direct ritual courting, it was an urban representation of an agrarian harvest-time mating.

The Lantern or Moon Festival

Although originally separate and distinct, the Lantern Festival and the Moon Festival merged into one celebration in the Straits Settlements. In China, the Lantern Festival falls on the fifteenth day of the first lunar month, the same day as the Baba *Chap goh meh*. It is also called the feast of the first full moon. It brings the Spring Festival of Chinese New Year to a climax. The Moon Festival as practised in China is in mid-autumn, falling on the fifteenth day of the eighth lunar month. On this cool autumn day, the moon is furthest away from earth and is at its most luminous. In bygone days people gathered to view the perfectly round moon. Its unusual brilliance inspired Tang Dynasty poets to extol its beauty and moon myths have been created. The Moon Festival in the Straits is also on the fifteenth day of the eighth lunar month but it incorporates a Lantern Festival.

The purpose of the original Lantern Festival in China was to welcome the warmth and increasing sunlight after the winter and to pray for the right amount of rain — neither drought nor floods — for planting in spring. The variegated lanterns were made in a variety of animal and human shapes. Originally they were of white gauze or silk, transparent horn, or glass painted with legendary scenes. In the old days of the Chinese Dynasties, respectable married women, normally confined to the house, were at liberty to go out and view the lantern display. This is a contrast with the custom of the Babas, who did not allow their Nyonya maidens to see lanterns, but did allow them to be seen at *Chap goh meh*. Latsch (1984:42) records that, in Fujian Province in particular, a household would have as many lanterns as the number of people in it, adding that an intention to expand the family was shown by having extra lanterns.

The festival also featured various performances including masquerades, and dragon or lion dances.

Many ancient peoples worshipped the moon: farmers in particular, programmed their sowing, harvesting and animal breeding according to the phases of the moon, whose regular waxing and waning has long held Man in fascination. The moon cakes prepared for the Moon Festival are not always round like the moon, but may be square or oval, and they have decorated sides. Ttheir fillings vary and they may be either savoury or sweet. An offering ceremony to the moon is conducted in the evening, generally by women, because the moon is classified as *Ying*, the feminine force. On an altar table in the open, fruit with fertility symbols is offered along with thirteen mooncakes, there being thirteen months in a full lunar year.

Moon cakes were purportedly instrumental in the overthrow of a dynasty in China. The Mongols, with Kublai Khan, grandson of Genghis Khan, as their first emperor, ruled the country as the Yuan Dynasty (1278-1368). Rebellions against the Mongols began in 1351 and continued intermittently. It is believed that in 1353 a secret message was hidden in the moon cakes which were exchanged. The court was taken by surprise by a moon festival which turned out to be a mass uprising, with people armed with kitchen knives and wooden sticks. This moon cake story, however, has been refuted as unhistorical by Eberhard (1952:122), who proposed that it is probably a folktale invented during the Manchu period (Qing Dynasty, 1644-1911).

Everyday Life 3

Not so long ago, no matter whether a Chinese family was rich or poor, the norm was to live in an extended family group. Cousins of both sexes slept in the same room until puberty. Daughters-in-law did all the housework. Less fortunate girls who lived with their in-laws were often bullied, and they had an especially hard life when an unkind mother-in-law encouraged her sons to have more wives so that she would have even more daughters-in-law to dominate. Hence, wealthy Babas contracted matrilocal marriages to prevent their daughters being ill-treated by their mothers-in-law. Polygamy and concubinage were accepted practices.

Language

Most of the Babas are now English-speaking. Those of earlier generations were fluent in Malay, and although it may seem strange now, in the last century few of the Babas spoke either Cantonese or Mandarin. However, during the era of re-sinization, around the time of the 1911 revolution in China, many Baba families learned Mandarin. All they could manage in Cantonese would be a few phrases picked up during childhood from their *amah che* or nursemaid. (See servants and slaves).

Malacca, being the oldest foreign settlement in Malaysia, is the most appropriate place to trace the origin of the language which modern-day Babas speak. It seems likely that the first immigrants were from the province of Fujian, because nearly all the words of Chinese origin in the Malay language resemble more closely the sounds of the Hokkien language than those of any other Chinese language; also, the Babas of all the old families trace their origin to Fujian province. The children of the early immigrants spoke various different patois of Chinese depending on the locality, and these would have included a mixture of Malay words peculiar to each region. The second generation Babas could neither speak nor read much Chinese, and conversed mostly in Malay, which the early Straits Chinese traders had been forced to learn to communicate with the indigenous Malays. In the course of time, there was no need to know Chinese, as contact with the immigrants' former homeland became less important.

Baba Malay

As the name suggests, Baba Malay is a corrupt form of the Malay language: it borrows liberally from Hokkien. This patois spoken by Straits Chinese Babas is one of the most

OPPOSITE PAGE: Jazz band formed by the smart set of the day, Penang c. 1935. (Courtesy Prof. Dr. Cheah Jin Seng)

striking pieces of evidence of cultural integration between the Malays and the Chinese. It has also been called the Baba language because although the vocabulary is mostly of Malay origin, it differs from Malay in many important respects and is practically a separate language.

In this Baba patois, sometimes both Malay and Hokkien words are incorporated within a single phrase. In some situations this is really necessary: for instance, the Chinese have a wide vocabulary to describe specific family relationships while that of the Malays is more limited. Almost all forms of address expressing relationships are in Chinese, not Malay. Exceptions to this rule are the words for mother, younger brother or sister, and elder brother, where the Malay terms were adopted, although the Malay word for elder brother is not used in Penang.

The main difference between Baba Malay and the standard language was the introduction of words of Chinese origin, most of which were entirely unknown to the Malays. A large class of such words relates to household affairs. Although most kitchen utensils are called by their Malay names, anything peculiar to the Chinese inevitably got a Chinese name. Almost all methods of cooking have Malay terms except for steaming, and many cooked dishes are given their Chinese names. Chinese is also used to name the different areas of a traditional Chinese home, and a number of items of clothing have Chinese names. In expressing abstract ideas, and in religious matters, the Babas use Chinese. There are, in addition, a number of Chinese words which relate to business affairs, gambling games and medicine. Some of the introduced Chinese words have in turn been absorbed into the mainstream of the Malay language.

Apart from vocabulary, there are other aspects of the language of the Babas which make it more like Chinese. The most obvious similarity is in the sentence structure, which often uses Chinese syntax. In addition, the possessive particle is used in exactly the same way as it is in Hokkien. Even the pronunciation and speech pattern sound similar to Chinese and the idioms are Chinese rather than Malay.

The language differs from Malay in other ways; the basic verb 'to be' has a different use in Malay. Even now, the Babas are entirely unacquainted with a large number of Malay words which are in common use among the Malays themselves. It is well known that those who cannot read their own language use a very small number of words in ordinary conversation. One can only acquire a large vocabulary in one's own language by constant reading. With a few exceptions, the Babas read very little in the Malay language and consquently their knowledge of Malay words is very limited. Where a number of words have similar meanings, the Babas use only one or two to express them all. Most of the phraseology in use for topics such as religion, or even simple polite greetings, is unkown in Baba Malay. Malay grammar is mutilated. The rules for the formation of derived words from roots by means of prefixes and suffixes are disregarded; derived words are used without knowledge of their connection with the root. The Babas have even coined their own style of derivatives! The passive verb form, which is common in both spoken and written Malay, is hardly used. While speakers of both the Malay and the southern Chinese dialects use the glottal stop, the Babas apply it to some Malay words where it is not correct. Besides all these differences, the Babas mispronounce many Malay words, and in some cases have altered the pronunciation so much that the word is almost unrecognizable, although indigenous Malay words are less corrupted than those of Arabic origin.

The Hokkien language has very clearly defined tones, and the meaning of a word depends entirely on the tone of voice in which it is pronounced. Many Malacca and Singapore Babas do not pronounce Chinese words correctly as far as the tone is concerned. Thus, some Chinese words have been changed beyond recognition. The Hokkien words in Baba Malay are spoken with something like a Malay accent. The most frequently used words from the Hokkien language are the pronouns for I and you; the equivalent Malay words are not used.

The Babas learned Malay either from their local mothers, or from constant association with Malay children. As time went by and the Babas became more numerous, they began to form communities of their own, and would, therefore, not have come into contact so much with the Malays; this was certainly the case in the town of Malacca as compared with the villages. As the Babas in the town associated less with the Malays their peculiarities of idiom tended to become fixed and their speech was influenced less and less by Malay pronunciation and grammar.

Until after the Second World War, many of the Babas had no formal education in written or spoken Malay, hence their knowledge of the language was generally purely colloquial, and therefore more liable to be corrupted. Baba Malay became the language of the Straits-born Chinese, the most influential section of the Chinese community under British rule. This patois was also largely the language of the traders; it was more easily acquired than pure Malay and sufficiently expressive for all ordinary purposes. Besides, it had a remarkable capacity for borrowing and assimilating such words as it needed from other languages. The Baba Malay spoken by the descendants of the early Straits-born Chinese is distinct from the 'bazaar Malay' spoken by the *Sinkhek*, who do not use Malay pronunciation or accent. While those who speak Baba Malay may also mispronounce certain words, their overall accent and intonation are definitely much more Malay than the Chinese accent of the *Sinkhek*.

In the British settlements (Malacca, Penang and Singapore), the Chinese had a commanding influence in all business affairs and they left their impression upon the language in which the business of the Settlements was transacted. From the study of the Baba language one can obtain a good impression of the interaction that went on between the Malays and the Chinese.

Baba Malay originated in Malacca, and the Penang variety differs from it in many ways. While Babas in Penang and Singapore share some common characteristics with their counterparts in Malacca, in addition to speaking varieties of Baba Malay, Penang and Singapore Babas also converse in Hokkien; this is not true of those in Malacca.

In spite of its peculiarities, the Baba language is still a kind of Malay and is intelligible on the whole to most Malays.

Penang Hokkien

The Chinese in Penang are predominantly Hokkien. While this language group originated from the province of Fujian, as we have seen, the language itself has at least seven variants or dialects. The Hokkiens of Penang originate from three districts in Fujian which are near each other. The reason people from nearby districts in China settled close to one another on the same faraway island may have been that correspondence between friends or family in China and those who had emigrated to the Straits Settlements eventually led to business connections in their new homeland.

China's spoken languages such as Mandarin, Cantonese (originating in Guangdong Province) and Amoy or Hokkien of Fujian Province, and Hakka, to name but a few,

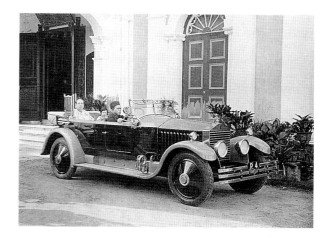

A Rolls Royce with a Nyonya and child on the back seat in front of a typical mansion in Penang, c. 1920. (Courtesy Prof. Dr. Cheah Jin Seng)

are not dialects of one language. They are cognate languages which have a relationship to each other analogous to that between English, German and Dutch. Within each of these languages there are dialects. Mandarin itself has three variants, originating from the north, south and west of the country. The Amoy vernaculars, the so-called Hokkien dialects, while of course having affinities with other Chinese languages, did not grow out of modern Mandarin but from an earlier, ancient form of the Chinese language. As already recounted, Hokkien was brought to Southeast Asia by immigrants from Fujian Province. The Zhangzhou dialect of Hokkien is the most common one in Java and the Straits Settlements while in the Philippines, the Hokkien was influenced by immigrants from Quanzhou.

In the region around the treaty port of Swatow, which is in Guangdong Province near the Fujian border, the 'Swatow dialect' is spoken. The forefathers of the people speaking it were from Fujian and the people of Guangdong referred to them as 'Hok-lo' or Hokkien people. They are known as Teochew in Southeast Asia.

The name *Yue* was applied to all the countries along the south and southeastern seaboard of China, and even to northern Vietnam, although the people in this large area were not all of the same race, and did not share a common language. This so-called 'empire of Min' of the Yue peoples included the whole of Fujian Province and extended into Guangdong, where the dialects of Swatow and Chaozhou were spoken. The term *Min*, which now simply means 'people' in general, was used for the peoples of the south, particularly around the province of Fujian. There are two groups of Min dialects: a northern and a southern. The southern group includes the dialects of Amoy, Swatow and Chaozhou.

As explained by Forrest (1948:232-340), some varieties of Amoy vernacular speech or Hokkien with certain special features were termed *Tang Min* because of the influence on them of northern Chinese speakers during the Tang Dynasty (618-906). Tang Min is essentially Hokkien modified by ancient Chinese of the Tang period. It can be seen from the phonetic table of Forrest, that the Baba Hokkien in Penang is closer to this Tang Min than is the type of Hokkien spoken by the *Sinkhek*, who use the standard Amoy variety. Penang Hokkien is even less closely related to standard Amoy because of the Malay words it has assimilated. It is different from other variations of Hokkien spoken on the mainland, or in Malacca and Singapore.

Education

Chinese schools

Protestant Christian missionaries of the London Missionary Society founded the first schools in Malacca around 1815. These were Malay and Chinese vernacular schools. Chinese education has always been given high priority in the Chinese community, and even the Babas supported the concept. In the early days the British authorities generally accepted that the organization of Chinese education would be done by the Chinese themselves and left them to handle their own programmes.

Guilds and clan associations set up schools with Chinese as the medium of instruction and Chinese temples also functioned as schools, besides being venues for meetings. The first clan association in Penang to start a school was the Khoo *Kongsi*. Its primary school, first housed in the clan temple, was founded in 1906, providing free education for clan members' children. Staff, who taught in the Hokkien language, were recruited from China. Towards the end of the nineteenth century, educational reforms in China stimulated the development of Chinese education in the Straits Settlements and elsewhere in the Peninsula. China's social and political reforms, which led to the founding of the Republic of China in 1911, had a profound effect, not only in the Peninsula, but throughout the *Nanyang*.

The earlier style of studying only the ancient classics and of rote learning was replaced by a modern curriculum which encompassed various aspects of the arts and sciences. Following this, there was a sort of political awakening in the Chinese schools.

The 1919 'Thought Revolution' in China proclaimed a standard national Chinese language, called *guo yu*. The teaching of this language was undertaken through night classes, organized by voluntary associations. One of these, in Penang, was the *Hu Yew Seah*, the League of Helping Friends, which was even officially requested in 1931 to run a government-sponsored kindergarten. Ironically, the anglophile Babas supported the teaching of *guo yu*. They were at that time in a dilemma about their loyalty to the British since the effects of the nationalist movement in China were spilling over into the *Nanyang*. Some Babas who attended English-medium schools received Chinese tuition at home.

With the Registration of Schools Ordinance in 1920, all schools, including Chinese ones, came under the control of the British authorities, who by then felt the need to control and curtail the influence of the new Republic of China. The political content of materials used in Chinese schools continued to be a cause for concern to the Government authorities throughout the 1920s and 30s, and text books were carefully inspected. Chinese schools were forced to close during the Japanese Occupation (1941-45) immediately after which, in 1946, guilds and associations were responsible for their re-registration.

After Independence in 1957 vernacular education in Chinese and Tamil lost ground to a national type of education using only English and Malay. However, there are still Chinese and Tamil medium schools, although they have been brought into the national system and now come under the jurisdiction of the Ministry of Education; the Khoo *Kongsi* school mentioned earlier underwent this change and opened to the public in 1959. A development in the opposite direction, as it were, was the establishment of the Nanyang University, using Mandarin as the medium of instruction, in Singapore in 1953.

English schools

At the suggestion of Captain Francis Light, a Catholic bishop invited the Eurasian Catholic community from Kedah to come to Penang, where they started the first schools in 1787. Since Penang was the earliest British settlement in Southeast Asia, its schools were also the Anglican Church's first English schools in the area. In 1816, the colonial chaplain of the Anglican Church started the Penang Free School which was modelled on the English public school system. Soon Penang became the centre for education in the region, and before the Second World War students came from as far as Thailand and Indonesia to study there.

The colonial government was not, in fact, enthusiastic about English education for local people. However, many Chinese pressed for it, in view of the better employment prospects and the increase in social standing offered by an education in English. The

St. Xavier Institution, Penang.

(Photo The Penang Museum)

Straits Settlements developed fast after the Depression years of the 1930s, and again in the late 1940s after the Second World War, so there was a growing demand for clerks both in the public and private sectors. Missionary schools accommodated this demand and they also recruited many non-Europeans as teachers. English was highly regarded by the local population, who associated it with progress and development: English was the language of the modern world and the British Empire. Even for local employment, a knowledge of the English language was useful because it was the language of administration. There was also a political factor: socially and emotionally it provided a sense of security and reassurance to have the privilege of British nationality; persons born in the Straits Settlements could claim this privilege, and were usually anxious to know English well.

Before long, affluent families sent their offspring to study in England rather than China. It is evident that this western education had a cultural influence; in nineteenth century photographs the Baba men are almost always in western attire, although the women are still in their Malay or Chinese costumes. Even among the English-speaking Chinese, however, the women (much more than the men) continued to observe traditional superstitions and customs. This was partly due to the fact that education was not considered necessary for girls: they were not sent to English schools, and their horizons were extremely limited. Until after the Second World War, it was unthinkable that a woman should pursue a career outside the home. The gradual emancipation of women began early in the twentieth century.

The idea of emancipation was in fact broached in modern schools in the 1920s by women's youth organizations, at meetings and in publications. Wealthy and middle-class families allowed their daughters to be educated in English, but usually only up to the end of the secondary school course. There was no popular demand for higher education for women. Although, generally, English-educated fathers were more lax about traditional values, there was still a reluctance to allow girls to continue training beyond the minimum standard that was required to earn a moderate salary.

In spite of this, education was regarded with reverence in the same way that scholarships and examinations were characteristically respected as a measure of academic distinction. The most prestigious award was the Queen's Scholarship, first started in 1885 in honour of Queen Victoria.

Because of the influence of the West in the eighteenth and nineteenth centuries, English became the second language of the Babas and even of the Nyonyas, who were tutored at home, usually by the wives of British officers or professionals living in the Straits Settlements.

Men's social lives

Many of the prosperous Baba families attempted to copy the English lifestyle in every respect. It was appropriate, therefore, that the anglicized élite kept pedigreed pets and were chauffeur-driven in Rolls-Royces. An eccentric might have preferred to be driven in a carriage drawn by two pairs of horses.

Other aspects of the day-to-day life of the wealthy Baba businessman were also very 'British', although the conservative patriarch insisted on being seated before the daily family meal started. His mansion was the envy of all the moneyed gentry and his passion for polo was the talk of the town. In those times, this well-to-do Chinese mer-

A formal dinner of an affluent Baba family in about 1930. Note the western attire of the men and the table decorations with an epergne and other European glassware. (Courtesy Prof. Dr. Cheah Jin Seng)

chant might have been the only non-European member of the Polo Club. The English-speaking Baba often entertained European guests. It was advantageous for his business to throw parties; it was also prestigious. After a while, it became the accepted lifestyle. Typically, printed invitations would be sent before a party. After dinner, guests were entertained with chamber music, or perhaps the daughter of the house might play the piano. There were recreation parties where guests had a choice of billiards, bowls, tennis or croquet. Sometimes the company gathered at a country estate, where they could take part in a hunt, complete with beautifully groomed horses and hunting dogs. The times when the Baba businessman entertained guests would often be among the few occasions when he was at home. Whether he was a white-collar office employee or someone of a higher station, he spent his time away from home mostly at work or in his social club.

Associations and clubs

'Members-only' clubs became the focal points of the Babas' social life. Some of these organizations resembled the traditional Chinese clan associations with objectives which included mutual help and brotherly love. One such club in Penang was the League of Helping Friends, already mentioned. It tried to bring together Chinese-educated and English-educated Chinese. Some English-speaking Chinese, however, regarded the League as exposing the Babas (especially) as denationalized Chinese. Ironically, it was the English-educated Babas who took over the leadership of this League. Of its many pro-China customs, one was standing in front of a portrait of Sun Yat-Sen observing three minutes' silence and, on China's national day, bowing three times before this portrait.

Besides these 'members-only' clubs, there were also associations, usually equipped with reading rooms and recreational facilities. One of the most popular activities was billiards. The Anglo-Chinese School Union appears to have been the only alumni group which conducted a more unusual programme for its members: they had Chinese story-telling classes. An inevitable drawback of these adult Chinese clubs, however, was the opportunity for gambling. Often after an initial declaration of noble objectives and a short span of keeping to them, a club would end up also functioning as a gambling den with its noble aims almost forgotten.

The reading material in the clubs' libraries was popular classical western literature. On the shelves were the standard works of Shakespeare, Dickens and Wordsworth; however, most of the time that was exactly where they stayed!

The Young Men's Christian Association, started by missionaries, aimed to develop the moral and intellectual well-being of all young men. Young Christian men from Baba families were particularly active. The association soon developed social and recreational activities, including billiards.

At the turn of the century, an exclusively Baba club was founded in Singapore. It was a weekly entertainment club which, besides its premises in town, also had a rambling

A glove puppet theatre.

(Courtesy and photo National Museum of Singapore, PB0028)

bungalow by the sea. The members were the smart set of the day. Sports clubs before the Second World War almost always had British-style indoor and outdoor games. The range of 'English sports' included football, cricket, tennis and rugby, which appealed to the English-educated who found themselves banned from the white clubs. The Chinese clubs in turn excluded non-Chinese. Even though such recreational clubs were open to all Chinese, the Babas dominated both in the sports field and on the committees. All meetings and minutes of such Victorian clubs in the Straits Settlements were in English. Occasionally, there may have been members who were Chinese speakers but English speakers dominated. Committee members were either professionals or men of leisure who were living on their inheritance. The clubs were rather 'upper-class', what with expensive sports equipment and rounds of drinks after a game. After the Second World War, sports which were more popular with the Mandarin-speaking sector of the community such as table-tennis, basketball, netball and volleyball were added to the range of activities. The Turf Club was much more exclusive: it was the only venue where finely bred horses owned by the élite Straits Chinese could compete with those owned by Europeans.

Other pastimes

Puppet shows have always been a popular activity in Southeast Asia. Of the three main types of puppets in the Chinese tradition — the glove, the iron-rod and the string — the first has the advantage that its theatre is easily portable. Glove puppet theatres are usually set up in the courtyard of a temple. The façade of the theatre is decorated with paintings of auspicious creatures like lions, tigers, dragons and phoenixes. In between are panels depicting well-known legends. The puppets appear on a small stage in the centre, and the painted canvas backdrop hides the puppeteers. For the plays, there is a limited repertoire of about ten to fifteen scenes. The stage faces the gods on the altar of the temple, because the performance is to entertain

BELOW LEFT AND RIGHT: Glove puppets. (Courtesy and photo National Museum of Singapore, PB0028)

them; the members of the audience, therefore, have their backs to the gods. Seating is not provided; people simply stand or mill around; some bring their own stools and chairs. There is no charge to watch the show, so the crowd does not feel obliged to be attentive. They chatter away amidst the din of the percussion instruments which often drown out the shrill singing. When a child loses interest in the play, he turns his attention to his own games. At the periphery of the courtyard, both adults and children have a wide choice of food sold by hawkers. Among the crowd are pious temple devotees bringing offerings for the gods. The air is filled with smoke from the burning of incense and joss sticks. The puppet-show in fact becomes a backdrop to a carnival that is a feast for the gods.

The festive mood also extends to the puppeteers backstage. They too engage in conversation, paying little attention to their own routine performance, but supplementing it with impromptu dialogue when they forget the script. Formal literary dialogue is not employed anyway; it would go over the heads of the audience. In any case the puppeteers themselves are usually not literate, having learned their lines by rote, although a troupe manager may have printed copies of some popular epics. A puppet troupe has about fifty to a hundred puppets, which are of two main types, with unpainted or with painted faces. Colours symbolize two groups: gold for gods and green for demons.

A *mah-jong* set. The four drawers each contains a suite. The sticks in the lowest drawer are used as chips. (Courtesy Penang Museum, photo Cheang Yik On)

A *mah-jong* table. The raised edges on the sides help to prevent the *mah-jong* blocks from falling off during shuffling. (Courtesy Lim Kean Siew, photo Cheang Yik On)

The Russian puppeteer Obraztsov, who studied different types of Chinese puppets, commented that they were animated so cleverly that even the features of the faces were alive. Before the days of the cinema in the 1930s, such theatres were an important form of entertainment. A theatre season was usually three days, with two sessions daily, in the afternoon and at night. Formerly, puppet performances were also staged on ceremonial occasions in people's lives, namely weddings, sixtieth birthdays and the subsequent birthdays of old people.

The white-collar, English-educated Chinese enjoyed picnics and weekends at beach bungalows or hill resorts. Bicycle rides along tree-lined boulevards and Sunday drives were standard pastimes. The usual recreational activities of the wage-earner were playing football and *mah-jong*, and going to the dance hall or the cinema. In addition to western dancing, fancy dress competitions were popular in the 1900s. The pastimes of the wealthy included motoring, racing, and gambling for very high stakes. The size of the playboys' bets would be the talk of the town. It was not unheard of for a wayward son to lose rows of houses at one sitting. To restore the family name, the doting mother would pawn her jewellery to bail him out.

Other more esoteric indulgences were flying, photography, game hunting or taxidermy. In the 1920s, the rich young gentleman of leisure dabbled in photography with his Brownie box camera. There was even a Wireless Society which was the forerunner of Penang's radio station. It was also fashionable for the young people of the smart set to form orchestras and jazz bands. These second or third generation offspring of wealthy Baba families fitted the image of the Roaring Twenties with their jazz bands and fancy cars.

Cinemas were introduced in the 1930s. They were often set up where there was already a large wooden stage for Chinese opera. The earliest silent movies, however, were first screened by mobile cinemas in open public spaces, and viewers sat wherever they pleased. War pictures with a romantic storyline were common. The young musicians of leisure played the background music. For scenes of soldiers at war, the lads played a lively march; a slow waltz was thought appropriate for the sentimental parts. After the silent movies came the amusement parks and theatres. Rudimentary air-conditioning was supplied using large fans blowing over blocks of ice.

The cabaret as a form of entertainment attracted the Babas especially. In the 1920s most of the Babas still had some of their inherited wealth, although it was beginning to dwindle. The popularity of western ballroom dancing in cabarets was echoed in Baba homes; in the corner of the living room stood a gramophone for playing records of English dance music.

At the cabarets there was 'taxi dancing' where patrons bought books of coupons to dance with their favourite hostesses. The dance hostesses and cabaret girls were numerous enough to form their own association. Besides the many musical groups and dance orchestras that sprang up, foreign bands, especially from the Philippines, were brought in. Even floor shows from the United States were featured; they included tap-dancers. While ballroom dancing remained the most popular style, it also became fashionable to learn to tap dance. Some cabarets introduced tea-dances. When they later started organizing stag parties, where wives and girlfriends were not included so that patrons could taxi-dance with their chosen hostesses, family quarrels ensued. While the younger Babas spent their wages and wealth in the cabarets, older ones and those disinclined to dance frequented parlours with sing-song girls called *Pipa chai*. During the drinking and merry-making these girls strummed their *pipa* and flirted with their clients.

Only about three generations enjoyed this high living, which crumbled with the Rubber Crash and the 1930s world-wide Depression. The Japanese Occupation put an end to this lifestyle, although some of its features revived after the War. For example, the cabarets reappeared, and the staff of the British Military Administration (BMA) and local people crowded into them.

Women's social lives

Since the Nyonyas spent most of their lives indoors they needed some form of recreation to fill their time. One such pastime was *chee kee*, a Baba card game. One image of a contented old lady has her playing *chee kee* and chewing betel. The mature Nyonya, who was ready to act as a hostess, had already taken to betel chewing. It has

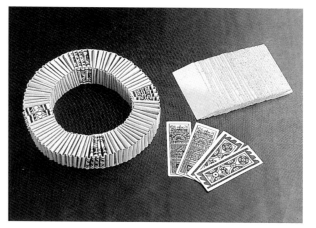

been pointed out earlier that offering betel was a gesture of hospitality and an invitation. The older Nyonya, known as a *Bibi* in Malacca and Singapore, had the social licence to attend or hold such sessions, which involved gambling. While playing, the women felt free to crack bawdy jokes among themselves. Another form of relaxation which the matriarchs loved was massage; a Malay masseuse was preferred.

Young unmarried women did not, however, lead such carefree lives. Whether well-to-do or not, a girl spent all her time indoors occupied with housekeeping activities. Cooking and sewing were mandatory accomplishments, inculcated to prepare a girl for the only profession open to her, that of wife and home-maker. Her first sewing exercise was to hem a sarong, her own customary attire. She graduated to making her own *baju panjang* (see the Arts, Costumes and Accessoires) and other items of clothing, and doing embroidery. If she was from a wealthy home with many servants she 'helped out' in the kitchen so that she would know how to supervise one later in life when she would be entrusted with running a household. Poor girls of course did their full share of household chores.

The young Nyonyas were taught at home by English tutors, many of whom were the wives of British officers, as we have seen. The very wealthy had English governesses for their daughters. Among the rich, education at home also included piano lessons for the daughters of the house. Living such a secluded life that they were almost cloistered, the Nyonyas could only peep through the slits of almost closed shutters at the outside world; a bench was placed permanently by the window for this purpose. On

ABOVE LEFT: The way the Nyonya holds the *chee kee* cards.
TOP: *Chee kee* cards.
ABOVE: The southern *chee kee* type is coloured. Nyonya handiwork from used *chee kee* cards.
(Photos H. Lin Ho)

The older Nyonya feels most comfortable wearing her sarong *kemban*-style when conducting kitchen chores. (Photo Khoo Joo Ee)

the whole, girls grew up ignorant of the outside world; they were not encouraged to be inquisitive. If a Nyonya so much as stood outside the house, she would be reprimanded with the Hokkien saying: 'bad tangerines are displayed at the shop-front, good ones are kept inside'. If a wilful girl challenged her elders' authority and remained outside the door, she might be told more brutally that only prostitutes display themselves outside houses.

This conservatism was not total; a girl was allowed to play in the house compound until just after puberty. Within the grounds of a mansion she might even learn to ride a bicycle. But, as we saw earlier, she originally travelled chaperoned, in a covered hammock-like contraption slung over a pole borne on the shoulders of two coolies. The privileged were transported in horse-drawn carriages, and later in motor cars. When girls finally went to school, a wealthy Nyonya did so in a covered buggy. From school she would be taken straight home. The only time of the year that the Nyonya maidens were seen in public was at *Chap goh meh,* that long awaited night of the full moon when they took to the streets in trishaws, horse-drawn buggies or motor cars for the sole purpose of being seen by prospective wooers.

The immigration of a significant number of respectable women from China occurred only around the beginning of the twentieth century. Until then, the number of eligible men far exceeded the number of marriageable Nyonyas. Since the Nyonyas thus had rarity value, a bride's family had great bargaining power, to the extent that they were able to arrange to keep their daughter at home after marriage, as we have also seen. This ran strongly contrary to traditional custom in China, where upon marriage the bride was permanently separated from her own family and bound to her husband's.

The over-protected Nyonya had greater freedom after marriage. If she was lucky, she might even accompany her affluent English-speaking husband for a drive in his car, although when her husband's men friends were around, she would not be allowed to be present. After she was married she went shopping more often; before then she perhaps did so no more than two or three times a year. There were servants to do the marketing while itinerant vendors hawked their wares from door to door, and the Nyonya hardly needed to run errands. Older matriarchs did go on social calls.

Around the house the Nyonya wore either the short inner blouse that went with the long dress and sarong, (see the Arts, Costumes and Accessories) or only the sarong as a *kemban,* i.e. tied above the breasts. The sarong was only worn in this way for temporary cooling off on a very hot day or for household chores where long sleeves would have been cumbersome. In the 1920s, it was fashionable for a Nyonya, with her husband's permission, to bob her hair or have a perm. Her elders were appalled. A few of the wealthy Nyonya even participated in the modish activities of the day, namely western dancing, croquet and tennis.

That highly domesticated creature the Nyonya was responsible for a good deal of the gentility of the Baba lifestyle. She led a protected, housebound existence, and so surrounded herself with extravagant creature comforts. The contents of the home, whether a handsome European villa or a Chinese residential terrace house, were chosen by the Nyonya. She, more than her male counterpart, produced the lavish Baba Nyonya material culture of the late nineteenth and early twentieth century.

While the public domain was dominated by the Baba, the home was more often than not run and ruled by a strong-willed Nyonya who had been trained to cope with a great variety of household and social tasks. She was managing director *par excellence*

and the supreme boss of the palatial Baba Nyonya residence. Upon marriage, the demure young Nyonya, still a child, found herself thrust into a responsible position which increased in difficulty as she embraced motherhood. Added to family duties were social obligations befitting her status in society. By the time she became a mother-in-law and grandmother, she would have acquired some confidence in social matters. When she rose to the position of matriarch in charge of running an extended family under one roof, the Nyonya would have emerged as an assertive, sometimes even bossy, woman. The mature Nyonya ladies who gaze confidently from old portraits have a commanding air, and also convey an impression of sound common sense. The matriarchs assumed precedence over their sons upon the death of their own husbands. While wielding their authority, Nyonya mothers doted upon their sons, and the result was that many a mature Baba, though he had status and was respected in the outside world, often continued to submit to an uncompromising mother at home.

It was only after the Great Depression of the 1930s that the idea of a woman having a career outside the home was accepted.

At home the Nyonya wore only an inner blouse and sarong. This blouse is called *tay snah* which is Penang Hokkien for short dress. Southern Nyonyas use a Malay term, *baju dalam* ('inner dress'), which sometimes is mistaken for the camisole worn with a diaphanous *kebaya*. (Courtesy Mrs. Ong Chong Keng)

ABOVE LEFT: Older Nyonyas have
the 'licence' to be seen in the
streets. These matriarchs wear
baju panjang with sarong.
(Courtesy Penang Museum)
ABOVE RIGHT: Unmarried Nyonyas
were under lock and key in the
house. (Courtesy Mrs. Ong
Chong Keng)

Servants and slaves

The Hailam cook-boy

The Hailam speakers from the Island of Hainan are reputed to be the best cooks and they used to be employed as such in the homes of Europeans and wealthy Chinese. Sometimes they doubled as houseboys and they were then called cook-boys. In practice, the cook-boy's family normally helped with the household chores: his sons helped with serving meals and his daughters with other housework. Most households had only one or two servants. In very wealthy homes there would be a male servant solely to attend to visitors, and he was often of Hailam origin. Although the services of a Hailam cook-boy were considered invaluable, the system lacked some of the amenities of the traditional forms of female domestic servitude, particularly as regards the services required by the women of the house.

Mui chai

Before the Emancipation Act of 1834, slavery in the form of domestic servitude was rampant. Even long after the act was passed, the wealthy still acquired and kept slaves because the law was lax. There were female slaves from Sumatra, India and

China. Many were from poor homes, and some were victims of confidence tricksters. There were few Chinese women in early colonial Malaya because, unlike the men, most of them emigrated only in the early decades of the twentieth century. In times of economic hardship in China young girls were sold or given away as *mui chai* — unpaid domestic servants — in return for food and shelter. From early in the twentieth century, the traffic in women and girls between South China and Malaya increased. *Mui chai* from China were acquired from traffickers or from the girls' parents by members of Straits households visiting China, or coming to join husbands and relatives in Malaya. They were bought when young and married off before they were twenty to artisans or petty traders. Some households collected bride-money when disposing of the girls after they grew up. Of course there was also the possibility of a *mui chai* becoming the wife or concubine of a male member of the household.

Local-born *mui chai* were acquired from impoverished families and single mothers, including prostitutes. In Malaya, the *mui chai* system was partly a result of the shortage of adult women for producing heirs.

Some households hired male domestic servants, who were not necessarily Hailam cook-boys or even Chinese, on a regular wage. This situation still exists but when it was relatively new and unfamiliar, such male domestic labour was more expensive; the fixed wages and conditions of work had to be negotiated. The male servants were organized in secret societies or groups, and so were in a position to bargain with the employers. There was even an organized male domestic workers' strike in 1888 led by the Hailam cook-boys (Song 1923:238-39).

Amah che

The term *amah* is derived from the Portuguese *ama*, meaning nurse. In the 1930s, there was an influx of paid domestic servants as a result of the abolition of the *mui chai* system. These professionals were known as 'black-and-white' *amah che* because they wore black silk trousers and white blouses. These unmarried Cantonese women, who formed a sorority or sisterhood (*che* is Cantonese for sister), tended to displace the Hailam 'cook-boys'. The *amah che* were most common in the 1950s. They were analogous to the Victorian 'maid-of-all-work' who carried out a strenuous and difficult job. With large families of perhaps more than twenty people under one roof, just doing the laundry was extremely hard work.

Before the advent of the electric iron, the old-fashioned charcoal iron was very tiring to use. It was made of cast iron and shaped like a bowl with a wooden handle. Red hot charcoal embers were placed inside it to heat it up. Such Chinese irons were widely used until the 1950s.

The *amah che,* who also functioned as a cook for a Chinese family worked even harder than her western counterpart. The Chinese custom of hospitality meant inviting even surprise visitors to stay for meals, and the resourceful *amah che* — 'superior servants' according to Gaw (1991) — seemed to be able to cook something out of nothing. The mistress, being excessively anxious about not providing enough food for guests in case she was called penny-pinching and niggardly, expected a spread on the dinner table. Chinese families had a tendency to entertain more often than their western counterparts: dinner parties were frequent. Apart from the cooking and the laundry, Chinese employers tended to expect their *amah che* to perform endless chores regardless of the time involved or their other responsibilities.

The home-made rice powder is acclaimed to cool the skin and absorb excess oil. It was not considered 'unsightly' to be seen wearing such a face in public. (Courtesy Lily Khoo)

ABOVE: The kitchen of the Chan house in Malacca. (Photo H. Lin Ho)

BELOW: Enamel trays, one featuring the English rose, are now used for a variety of purposes. Possibly they were formally used for communal eating in rural areas. Diameter 50 cm. (Courtesy Tan Kim Lan)

BELOW RIGHT: Two food covers made of gilded *pandanus*. The centre of the oval dome is embellished with beadwork. Such covers, called *tudung saji* in Malay, were brought over from Sumatra to Penang and Malacca. 57 x 49 cm. (Courtesy Asia House, Hong Kong, photo Cheang Yik On)

Although the *amah che* were noted for their honesty, there was a widely accepted practice of 'keeping the change'. An *amah* would be given a certain amount of money to do the marketing twice a day, and if she bought cheaply and well, she kept the money left over; it was not much. This practice was understood and was rarely mentioned. When these faithful and devoted servants were older, and if the employer had a chauffeur, they would be taken to and from the market by car.

In a wealthy family, an *amah che* would be appointed as a personal nurse for each child. The baby *amahs* and their charges used to congregate in parks and other suitable areas in the better parts of town. The *amahs* looked forward to these daily gatherings for some much needed rest and relaxation from the back-breaking and monotonous task of endless household chores from daybreak to late at night. Their favourite recreation, however, was popular Chinese opera. Dignified and immaculately clean professional servants, the *amah che* were excellent nannies, and there were even instances when they were employed as children's playmates.

All the *amah che* practised folk medicine and most of them were vegetarians. Often, in a household, they had their own sets of crockery and cooking utensils which they used for special vegetarian meals on the first and fifteenth of each month.

The *amahs* sent part of their earnings back to their families in China. Some of them were the only breadwinners of their families so there was always a need to supplement their incomes. Tips came from additional work done at special functions in the house, such as parties. Also, guests or winning players in *mah-jong* sessions tipped the servants, including the *amahs*. Some *amahs* added to their income by helping out at temples. Many invested in tontines, a type of life insurance scheme. This informal financial arrangement among voluntary subscribers was always open to abuse, partly because it was based on trust. The practice was finally banned.

Employers usually gave the *amah* some 22-carat gold item as a Chinese New Year gift which was meant as an investment for the future. Alternatively, *amah che* received clothing or material, together with the customary *ang pow*, which increased in value

each year. They put aside funds for a proper funeral, burial and posthumous ceremonies. These were taken care of by their *Kongsi*, the premises of which would also accommodate them in times of need, for instance when they were between jobs. When a servant had been asked by her employer to recommend another, and the former left or retired, the latter also left. It was an unwritten rule of their sworn sisterhood. After the Second World War, these 'black-and-white' *amahs* began to assert their rights as traditional employees. As their numbers are not being replenished, the *amah che* are fast becoming superior servants of the past. Blythe (1947:90-91) recorded that under the indenture system, domestic service made up a very small percentage of the labour force and the 'black-and-white' domestic servants, who were in demand, were relatively few in number.

Nyonya cuisine

From morning till night, the men were out at work or in a recreational club, while the womenfolk spent most of their time in the spacious kitchen. Family members and friends were, in fact, entertained there.

Before refrigeration, live fowls were kept in cages in the backyard. Food had to be stored away from ants and cockroaches, so a long hook used to hang from the ceiling and on this hook a food storage box was suspended. The box itself was encased in wire mesh to keep flies out, and just below the hook was a bowl or box filled with oil to keep rats away. Tall cupboards with fly-screen doors were later used for food storage. The four high legs of such *almari* stood in bowl-like ceramic moats filled with liquid disinfectant to discourage ants.

To the older generation of Straits Chinese ladies, cooking was an accomplishment, an

Nyonya deserts, including soya bean curd, *bubor chacha*, *tau suan*, red bean soup with lotus seed and *chendol*. (Courtesy King's Hotel, Singapore)

art to be proud of. The style of their cooking is one 'cultural marker' which distinguishes the Baba Chinese from the *Sinkhek*. Nyonya cuisine shows strong Malay, Indonesian and Indian influence, so curries and condiments are standard items on a Baba family table. In Penang, there is the additional Thai influence, with lavish use of spices, varieties of tamarind and coconut cream. Thus, Nyonya food, like other features of the Nyonya lifestyle, is a synthesis of many tastes. It is a blend of spicy, herbal, tangy and sweet dishes.

In the backyard of Nyonya homes an assortment of herbs was almost always grown, and many well-known herbs feature in Nyonya fare. The distinctively shaped leaf (like a figure of eight) of a variety of citrus called leper lime *(limau purut)* is added to many dishes whole or shredded. Fresh basil and coriander shoots are used lavishly. The delicate, frilly leaves of coriander, used for garnishing, have a pronounced and distinctive flavour which is less fragrant in younger leaves. The screwpine or *pandanus* is a standard flavouring for both savoury and sweet dishes. Leaves are often pounded to extract the juices, or they are used whole to wrap up meat or other food. The banana leaf is a good example of this. After the filling is wrapped up in leaves the neat little packets are deep fried or steamed. During the process the scent of the leaves is extracted.

Salads are of two types, dry and moist. A spicy yet sweetish dressing which has no obvious oil in it is given a heavy tang with lime. The basis of the dressing, which actually does contain oil in the form of coconut, comes in two forms: the southern variety, which tends to be drier, is made with roasted grated coconut, indicating Sumatran influence, while the Penang Nyonyas follow the Thai style of using coconut cream. The Penang variety of a savoury salad which is served with a peanut sauce and blanched vegetables (known by the Malay name *gado-gado*) is also mixed with seafood fritters and is then called *pasembur*. A spicy, pungent, shrimp-based sauce is also very popular as an accompaniment with raw vegetables; this is known as *ulam*. *Rojak* is a sweetish, mainly fruit-based salad with more of a bean paste dressing.

Unlike the Cantonese, the Hokkiens generally do not serve soup at daily family meals. For both language groups, however, soups are mandatory as part of the spread of ritual food offerings to gods and ancestors and also at meals on special occasions. Casserole-like dishes of rice and noodles are common. While soups are boiled and simmered in aluminium or enamel pots, traditional curry preparation demands the Indian clay pot. A good curry depends on the technique of sautéing. It should be done slowly on a low fire until the pounded ingredients dry up and release their aromas and the oil breaks through. In the past, coconut oil was always used for cooking but there is now a greater variety, including peanut and palm oils. Candlenut, a heart-shaped, creamy-coloured nut, is used as a thickening agent.

Curry Kapitan, a special Baba curry which is always cooked at festivals, is of Indonesian origin. The belief is that a Dutch captain asked what was on the evening's menu. His cook, having prepared curry, replied 'Curry, Kapitan'. In time this became the accepted name of the dish.

Cincaluk is a shrimp-based pickle, served as an appetizer or side dish, which has a decidedly strong flavour that makes it an acquired taste. It originated as the speciality of the Portuguese Eurasian fishermen in Malacca. This community itself became known by the name, *geragau*, for the very small shrimps used to make the pickle. (The Penang Baba call these tiny shrimps 'squirrel prawns'.) The northern variety of this sour, salty and spicy pickle is coloured dark pink with vegetable dye while the Malacca variety retains the original pale pink hue. The *Sinkhek* find this pickle revolting. They, however, eat a different variety of shellfish sauce which is similar to the fish sauces found on mainland Southeast Asia; it is used in the same way as soya sauce is in the island portion of the region. (Soya sauce is hardly used in countries such as Burma, Thailand, Laos, Cambodia or Vietnam.)

Traditionally, an assortment of other pickles were served in small porcelain jars during festive occasions or at a Baba wedding. Another standard dish of Malay origin is *serunding;* it is served cold and is a pungent, spicy shredded meat condiment.

A true Baba family is addicted to *sambal belacan*, a pounded condiment of chilly peppers and prawn paste mixed with lime juice, which is served with almost every meal. This ubiquitous paste is also eaten along with Chinese lettuce like a salad dressing. A particular style of shredded cuttlefish is said to go very well with this lettuce and *sambal*. Every Nyonya is supposed to master this almost ceremonial dish: ceremonial because it is obligatory in a spread of food offerings to gods and ancestors. Each Nyonya household would evolve its own style of fried cuttlefish.

Many traditional dishes are served only on specific occasions. *Nasi kunyit,* or yellow glutinous rice, which is steamed and coloured with turmeric, is just such a ceremonial food. Yellow, the royal colour, is added to enhance the life-giving qualities of the rice, which is supposed to have a soul (see Religion, ancestor worship). Its traditional accompaniment is chicken curry. This meal of yellow rice and curry is even more colourful when served with a sweet red rice dumpling filled with mashed green beans. These foods are auspicious in their colouring (see Religion, rites of passage). The dumplings come in different shapes and designs, especially during religious festivals. Their symbolic forms, which include a turtle, a mussel and a marble, have evoked some Hokkien proverbs. One of these verses attributes a windfall to a red marble. To obtain a good husband, one should choose a red mussel, while a red turtle will make one a landowner.

Koey ee, the dessert of glutinous rice balls mentioned as being a traditional food for marriage ceremonies, is also ceremonial fare to welcome the Chinese New Year. The rice is symbolically coloured bright pink or red for good fortune. Other staples for sweets are bananas, yams, tapioca, whole or powdered green beans and various types of seaweed. Desserts contain a lot of coconut cream and brown palm sugar. Sometimes, if a clear sauce is preferred, rock sugar is used instead of palm sugar, which colours the coconut cream brown.

The domesticated and cloistered Nyonya had time to practise and perfect dishes and even to evolve her own version of especially festive dishes — gilding the lily, as it were. Plain boiling or even steaming would be too bland for her. A pungent dip would accompany boiled seafood, which was soaked in gravy. Alternatively, the fish was stuffed or marinated in herbs. Food had to be in bite-sized pieces when served. All cutting and chopping was done in the kitchen, not at the table. Cakes and vegetables were always cut at a slant. To cut foods into dainty decorative shapes was considered refined.

Even rich men's wives were proud of their cooking and did not regard it as beneath their dignity to sell their home-made foods. While the Malacca Nyonya sold her shrimp pickle from the kitchen, Penang Nyonya wives hired vendors to sell their specialities.

RIGHT: Nonya cuisine. Among the spread are five teacups in a ceramic tray contain *koay ee*, the coloured rice flour balls in weak syrup — a ceremonial dish (see weddings).

OPPOSITE PAGE: A variety of Nyonya food. In the centre is a bowl of *laksa*. (Courtesy King's Hotel, Singapore)

RIGHT: Soya bean curd in brown and in white syrup. (Courtesy King's Hotel, Singapore)

Architecture 4

The architecture of the Straits Chinese is often referred to by the term 'Straits Eclectic'. This hybrid building style has also been given several other names — some of them facetious — such as 'Sino-Malay-Colonial', 'Sino-Malay-Palladian', 'Tropical Renaissance', '*Towkay* Italianate', 'Chinese Palladian' and 'Chinese Baroque'. Because of the combination of influences, a building of the nineteenth century may have a Chinese roof crowning a Palladian elevation supported on Malay-style stilts. The late nineteenth and early twentieth-century style, which has been termed 'Chinese Baroque', is more like classical Chinese architecture than the earlier Straits Eclectic styles. The layout of the classical Chinese house was usually copied for temples, *Kongsi* houses and large mansions with courtyards. Traditional Chinese houses were more formal and austere than Malay houses.

The evolution of Straits Eclectic architecture may have begun in the fifteenth century when Chinese traders brought their Southern Chinese styles to Malacca. Until the late eighteenth century, Malacca was the only place in Malaya where Chinese buildings were seen. With the coming of the British, the pace of construction by the Chinese increased and it continued until the Depression of the 1930s, after reaching a peak early in the nineteenth century.

The history of Chinese building in Malaya can be roughly divided into three phases: the first from 1511 to 1641, the period of Portuguese rule in Malacca; the second from 1641 to 1797 and from 1818 to 1824 — the two periods of rule by the Dutch, when they constructed forts and dwellings along the river and by the seafront; and the third from 1786 to 1957 when the British were in Malaya, building forts, government offices and bungalows for civil servants, businessmen, planters and others. The architectural style of the bungalows was derived from India. During the seventeenth to the mid-twentieth century period, which roughly corresponds with the British colonial era in Asia, a lot of building was undertaken by engineers and architects in the service of the East India Company or the British Government. Some of those who had served in India brought with them to Malaya what is termed the Anglo-Indian style.

The houses created by early architects were adapted to the tropical climate, with European, especially Portuguese, Dutch and later British influence incorporated. Several features of the houses were especially designed to keep their interiors cool, such as large verandahs, wide overhanging Chinese roofs, Anglo-Indian white stucco walls and high ceilings with *punkahs* (large swinging cloth fans operated by pulling a

OPPOSITE PAGE: A terraced house with forecourt in Singapore. (Photo H. Lin Ho)

Corner lot of nineteenth-century terraced shophouses with a 'five-foot way' arcade. (Photo Cheang Yik On)

cord). Good ventilation was achieved by incorporating jack-roofs (see page 137), elevated floors and airwells. Throughout Malaysia wherever there is a substantial Chinese population there are variations of this Straits architecture. The Portuguese introduced the arch; the Dutch erected imposing public buildings and cosy private dwellings; the British introduced Anglo-Indian buildings with Palladian features and local touches like elevated structures and shaded porches. These were the main identifying features of the Straits Eclectic style, a form of urban architecture unique to Southeast Asia.

Secular structures

The shophouse

The early traders lived and conducted their businesses in the same building, as the very term shophouse indicates. The earliest shophouses were single-storeyed wooden structures with *atap* roofs which were usually half-hipped and half-gabled. Such single-storeyed shophouses are still seen in rural areas today.

Along the open front of the shophouse, goods were displayed on a counter which stretched the width of the building. The shopfront had no wall — it was boarded up at night — so that there was really no façade. The private living area was at the back of the house, or sometimes in an attic. Because the building itself did not provide much protection against theft or bad weather, the shrewd trader built a brick vault inside it to store valuables (Newbold 71:72). The early shophouses were usually on the waterfront so that boats could load and unload at the back of the house from a platform which projected over the water on stilts. The front of the house was at ground level, not on stilts.

Shophouses began to look a little more like their modern counterparts when they acquired an upper residential storey. At first, both floors had open fronts and a bal-

RIGHT: A row of terraced houses with arcade in Penang. (Photo Cheang Yik On)

OPPOSITE PAGE: A 'five-foot way' arcade in Singapore. (Photo H. Lin Ho)

Shophouses in Penang. (Photo
Cheang Yik On)

cony ran the full width of the upper floor. The next logical development was to close up the front of this floor with shutters. The residential floor was reached by stairs which led from the street at the side of the house, although occasionally the staircase was at the rear. The front of the shop on the ground floor was still open. The next step came when the lower part of the shuttered verandah was walled in, leaving a large window above the wall. Later still, a masonry wall with two or three windows in it was built up to the roof of the upper floor. The early permanent shophouses were quite low and had squat pillars and steeply pitched tiled roofs; it was the decorative motifs on the stucco-finished walls of the upper floor which gave them their unique character. Through the nineteenth century, the initially simple upper floor gradually became more elaborate. By the time the shophouse became the characteristic form of housing in the urban areas, decorative tiles were also being used on the outer stucco walls.

The shophouses were built in rows with a shared wall between each of them. These 'row houses' may date from the mid-eighteenth century in Dutch Malacca. Already established in Malacca, Penang and Singapore in the early nineteenth century, the architectural style of the shophouses spread to other towns in the Peninsula in the second half of the century. The basic design has remained the same from then till the present day. The building is long with a narrow frontage. Rows of such long narrow houses were built to form streets and squares; only the façades differed significantly. Shophouses were normally thirteen to twenty feet wide but their depth was two or three times their width. The early Malacca shophouses, which were very much deeper than others elsewhere, were up to a hundred and fifty feet long. Blocks of such shop-houses with party walls faced on to streets in a grid pattern.

The early Chinese often named a street according to the number of shophouses that stood in it, for example 'ten-house street', 'street of twenty small houses' and 'back of the fifteen-house street'.

A conspicuous feature in shophouse design was the continuous covered arcade in front of the shops, providing protection from the sun and rain. This passageway, besides making a transition from the house proper to the street, linked the houses, thereby giving the block some unity. In addition, the arcade gave the shopkeeper extra space to display his wares. He could also easily visit his next-door neighbour and still keep an eye on his own shop. In 1822, while he was working on Singapore's town plan, Raffles laid down a specified width for the arcade. It was to be at least five feet wide; the Hokkien Chinese therefore called it 'the five-foot way'.

The façades of shophouses have an unlimited variety of styles. The range of these from different periods is sometimes confusing, but at least there was an attempt at coherence within each group of houses. In the early 1900s there was a mixture of Chinese, Malay and European styles. Between about 1910 and 1930, the simple wood-en shutters of the 1880s and 1890s gave way to ornate window frames with Roman and Greek columns, complete with pediments. This type of ornamentation was derived from the European neoclassical style. An almost fully Europeanized façade emerged by the early decades of this century; ornate columns, stucco decorations and glazed ornamental tiles vied for attention with Palladian windows and Venetian bal-conies. There was a brief Art Deco period in the 1930s.

The adoption of all these styles gave an impression of a frontage which was quite incongruous with a simple building. However, even in its final phase of a wonderful eclectic mix, the shophouse remained a narrow building no wider than twenty feet, and only the upper floors were elaborately ornamented. Although the design of the shophouse façade sometimes followed European styles, because of a time lag certain styles occurred after they were no longer in vogue in Europe. It would appear that wealthy merchants, having visited Europe, sometimes included designs from its classical monuments in their shophouses. There are rows of shophouses which are quite cluttered with a profusion of eclectic creations in plasterwork. The attention given to the façade is more a western practice than a Chinese one; Chinese architecture emphasizes the roof, and despite the European style of the upper façade of these shophouses, the roof remained Chinese. It was often steeply-pitched, which helped to keep the interior cool.

Ventilation for these compact row houses was provided by airwells which admitted sunlight (but not the sun's full heat), natural breezes and rain. While each house had an airwell, some very deep houses had a second, or even a third. The airwell was designed to channel and collect rainwater and to drain it away. Quite often the rainwater flowed from the roof down charming ceramic fish-shaped gutters.

Further air circulation was afforded by ceilings twelve feet or more in height, and the jack-roofs already mentioned, which helped protect the main roof below from direct heat. It is often asserted that the design of the jack-roof (which is a smaller roof above and overlapping the main roof, leaving a space between the two) was brought to Malaysia from India by the British. However, Kohl (1984:158) has shown that an illustrated record of rural China features the jack-roof. The space between the jack-roof and the main roof admits natural draught. The Southern Chinese design of the jack-roof can still be seen in areas inhabited by hill tribes in the so-called 'Golden Triangle', a region bordered by Burma, Thailand and Laos. These tribes are pre-sinized South Chinese ethnic groups.

Vents in the ceiling and in the wall below the eaves of the roof allowed air flow. These vents came in an infinitude of decorative designs. The top portions of partitions between rooms had lattice-work, which facilitated ventilation. Finally, balconies on the top floors of houses contributed further to ventilation of these narrow elongated buildings. Pot plants formed a little garden behind the balustrades.

Shaped gable walls rose between the gabled roofs of groups of shophouses and functioned as 'fire walls' because they prevent fire from spreading.

While more than one household might have lived in one shophouse, especially during hard times when the residential area would have been subdivided, originally only the merchant's family and those involved in his business lived in the building. The upper storeys of modern buildings could lodge many households, but nowadays two-storeyed or three-storeyed buildings normally accommodate various commercial enterprises, including light industry: shophouses originally had businesses only on the ground floor and residential space above, but the upper floors were later built for or converted into office space. Shophouses built by the Chinese were not only for their own use but were also let to other merchants.

Shophouses were, and still are, very common in coastal south China, where they have similar floorplans to those in Malaysia. The shops are of about the same size, share party walls, and are built tightly packed together. Occasionally awnings span the narrow streets joining the overhanging eaves of the houses. The shops have shelves and counters at the front where goods are displayed. Signboards are a feature of the

The Poe Choo Seah, a nineteenth-century association of Straits-born Chinese, was housed in this three-storey shophouse in one of the earliest main streets in Penang. (Photo Cheang Yik On)

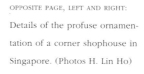

OPPOSITE PAGE, LEFT AND RIGHT:
Details of the profuse ornamentation of a corner shophouse in Singapore. (Photos H. Lin Ho)

streets, either hanging (with the Chinese characters reading horizontally) or standing vertically on bases. In the former Straits Settlements, elsewhere in Malaysia, and all over Southeast Asia the doorways of shophouses are adorned with signboards hung on brackets. Very often shop signs and streamers blend in with strips of red paper which are part of a miniature shrine, a perennial prayer for good fortune.

The shophouse, an importation from South China, is one of the most common house forms in Malaysia, especially in urban areas. Because of its dual function it enables high population coupled with intensive trading. It was originally purely utilitarian, created to suit the purpose and the environment — trading in a tropical climate.

Terraced houses

Terraced houses are the residential counterpart of shophouses. There are a number of different types, but the earliest examples are similar to shophouses in having porches and arcades. Some of the earliest terraced houses were built in Malacca in the latter half of the seventeenth century.

By the 1700s the Dutch had built sturdy dwellings with thick walls. These houses had the characteristic long narrow design because taxes were calculated on the width of street frontage. In keeping with the narrow houses, even the streets were narrow. Malaccan terraced houses, though narrow, are spacious, and bigger than those in Penang and Singapore.

In the western part of Malacca there was a wealthy residential area which the Dutch named Heeren Street, literally Street of the Gentlemen. It had rows of elongated nar-

Terraced house façade in
Malacca (Photo H. Lin Ho.).

row terrace houses. These Malaccan homes, built in long rows, belonged to wealthy Baba merchants and are usually considered as the prototype for other terraced houses. Carved wooden plaques displaying the family name in gold calligraphy still hang above the doorways of some such houses. This practice is reminiscent of the office buildings of Mandarins in China, where the entry porch had ideographs engraved on the lintel or flanking the door.

Nowadays many of the houses in Heeren Street no longer belong to Baba; those that do are maintained as ancestral homes for use on special occasions. Many of these ornate houses were bought from the Dutch or converted by wealthy Baba into either warehouses, or dual purpose residences and storehouses. The design of the houses has Chinese influence combined with the characteristic Dutch style of houses built in rows.

Heeren Street was the main street in Malacca town and was strategically situated by the sea near the Dutch Stadhuis building, which was the equivalent of today's City Hall. When these houses were first constructed during the Dutch occupation of Malacca, the back portions jutted out over the waters of the Straits. At high tide, boats could reach the doorsteps to load and unload. Cargo boats could do the same at buildings similarly constructed by rivers (Bird 67:132). Now the houses are on higher ground some distance from the water's edge, and reclamation is pushing the shoreline even further away.

While several building periods can be distinguished within the era of terraced house construction, there are two main house designs. Up to the mid-eighteenth century, between the upper and lower floors of houses in Malacca, there were secondary roofs, the eaves of which were tiled. The exteriors of houses of this age used more wood and were less ornate than those of later times. While the houses were of different heights, they all had only two storeys. The party wall continued to the end of the porch so there was no continuous covered walkway. This was the main difference between the shophouses and terraced houses of those times.

After the mid-eighteenth century, buildings could be either two or three storeys high and they began to acquire decorative plasterwork. The upper floors of these later houses overhung and shaded the porch without a secondary roof between the two floors.

When the Dutch reoccupied Malacca between 1818 and 1824 they decreed that no new houses were to be built, so the Chinese altered and adapted existing buildings.

Even though the earliest terraced houses were built in Malacca, the Chinese terraced house became the standard form of housing in the other two colonial settlements of Penang and Singapore. These port cities became prosperous trade centres with large Chinese merchant communities. In Penang especially, during the 1870s when various styles were gradually mixing, many terraced houses were built. In Singapore, terraced houses built after the passing of the 1822 Town Plan 'showed good manners' in that they were of similar depth and floor height, resulting in unity and harmony of design. The individuality of these row houses was expressed in the diversity of decorative details.

Embellishing the façades of terraced houses with extravagant decoration was particularly in vogue from the beginning of this century till around 1920. Therefore, both in Singapore and Penang, shops and terraced houses displaying a great variety of decorative styles can still be seen. Palladian columns on the ground floor may have green ceramic Chinese balustrades above them on the balcony. The front porch may have imported European tiles in pastel colours depicting flowers or birds. Porch pillars which rest on carved granite bases may be pseudo Doric or Corinthian and may incorporate jossstick holders. Windows and doors are arranged symmetrically in the Chinese style: two windows flank the door. These windows, however, may have Art Nouveau stained glass panes with wooden or even lead tracery frames. Above large windows are ventilators which are very often of the Chinese-style bat-wing or fan shape. French windows with fanlights above them are also popular. The fanlights often have wooden bars radiating in a fan shape. Later fanlights have glass against carved timber panels, showing Malay influence. Windows may have wooden louvred shutters in the European style. Occasionally, the jalousie is seen: a type of shuttered window with slats which slope upwards from the outside, and which may have been introduced by the Portuguese. Such a shutter keeps out sun and rain but provides ventilation and privacy.

In this riot of mixed designs, the Palladian styles of the British period predominate. Favourite features are Corinthian capitals, broken pediments and French windows with fanlights. The façades are painted in the pastel shades of Victorian rococo, while painted scrolls in the Chinese manner may be found above windows. The plasterwork ornamenting the upper storeys of terrace houses displays the most diverse designs, ranging from Chinese symbolic motifs, mythological animals and whimsical creatures to European festoons, bouquets, posies, English roses and Grecian vases. A mid-nineteenth century house with a rococo façade in Singapore, with unique, frivolous plasterwork mouldings, shows a pair of Sikh guards toting rifles and bayonets beside the main entrance (illustrated on pages 138-139).

The heavy main door of the house was usually left open during the day, and a swinging half door allowed privacy and ventilation. Some of these half doors were very ornately carved and gilded. The main doors, which were usually stained black or lacquered red, had decorative panels that had scenes carved on them, or were composed of openwork. Very often mirrored *yin* and *yang* discs were hung on doors as protective charms. Decorative green ceramic Chinese tiles, shaped like bamboo, covered the overhang of the arcade. The steeply pitched red-tiled roof had rounded gable ends. Timber fretwork on fascia boards, eaves and balustrades was influenced by Malay woodcarving. Decorations on the house often disregarded aesthetics in favour of symbolism and the all-pervading belief in geomancy.

Immigrants who had come from South China were used to elongated plots of land and houses with a narrow street frontage because these were common in the port cities of China; such homes also had the arcaded porch. While both northern and southern Chinese homes were formally planned with symmetry around a central axis, the northern buildings were austere, while the southern homes were extravagantly ornamented. The interiors of most terrace houses were similar in layout and there were also some standard features in their furnishing. The three most important areas of the house were always the ancestral hall, the sitting room and the airwell. Doors, window frames and teak panels enriched the interior, complementing traditional Chinese furniture. In the front hall an altar, ornately carved, stood against the dividing screen wall, which faced the front door. Red and black ancestral tablets with gilded calligraphy were placed beside portraits of the more recently deceased ancestors. Other decorative objects such as vases for flowers, accompanied the portraits. Chinese side tables,

ABOVE: Detail of a terraced house façade in Malacca. Between the first floor windows a pseudo-Corinthian pilaster, with a ceramic figure on top, and moulded in plasterwork a relief showing a 'Greek' vase, set against Chinese clouds and the *lingzhi*, the sacred fungus of immortality. (Photo H. Lin Ho)

BELOW: Bamboo-shaped, green glazed roof tiling in Malacca. (Photo H. Lin Ho)

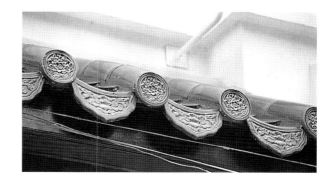

Terraced houses in Singapore.

(Photos H. Lin Ho)

ABOVE: Row of terraced houses with a forecourt.

RIGHT: The half swing-doors have been removed. Gilded plaques are placed above the windows, and above and flanking the door. The one above the door is called *ji hoo*, and indicates the family name. (Photos Cheang Yik On)

tea tables, and straight-backed chairs were arranged along both the side walls of the front room of older homes. The tables were of the same depth as the chairs. A guest could use half of the table on each side of his chair as a tea table or as an armrest. The floor was laid with large, rust-coloured square clay tiles arranged in a diagonal design. Later houses had imported European tiles, usually French or Italian.

The front hall led into a second hall, the living room, usually through two doorways, one on either side of the central screen partition, although some houses had only one doorway. The partitioning screen was a 'spirit wall' to keep out evil spirits by obstructing their straight paths. The living room faced an airwell beside which was a staircase leading to bedrooms on the first floor. These bedrooms opened on to the airwell, thus benefiting from the ventilation and natural light. The airwell and staircase arrangement could be repeated in a very long house with additional airwells.

The airwell was important because it was a reduced version of the traditional courtyard. It was bordered with granite and had a stone floor which was about one foot lower than the level of the surrounding floor so that rainwater could drain off. In China, the open courtyard with trees was very important in a building. The smaller, paved airwell, the equivalent in Malaysia, was never roofed because air and water are regarded as bringing tranquillity and peace, besides good luck and prosperity.

Because of the narrowness of the terrace house it was not possible to have rooms on the ground floor flanking the airwell. The result was a series of rooms arranged longitudinally. They had high ceilings from which hung Dutch kerosene lamps or chandeliers.

A passageway connected the front hall first to the living room and then to the kitchen. Along this passageway were cupboards built into the wall facing the airwell providing

ABOVE: Terraced houses in
Malacca. (Photo H. Lin Ho)
LEFT: Shophouse façade in
Penang. (Photo Cheang Yik On)

145

light and air for the living room. In the kitchen there was another airwell, with a platform for cooking placed near it. In some houses the entrances to bathrooms, which
were usually on the far side of the kitchen airwell, were through elaborate doorways.
Water was stored in a tank about three feet deep, built of solid brick and tiled. In
older houses the water would have come from a well. Fresh air and sunlight entered
through jack-roofs built over the bathrooms.

The Straits Chinese furnished their houses in a variety of styles, among which a few
main types predominated. Firstly, some furniture from China was of blackwood or
rosewood with mother-of-pearl inlay, while a style favoured by the Straits Chinese

ABOVE LEFT AND ABOVE: Terraced house arcades in Malacca. (Photos H. Lin Ho)

LEFT: Shophouses and shophouse temples in Penang. Clearly visible are the 'fire walls' on the roofs between the houses. (Photo Cheang Yik On)

OVERLEAF LEFT AND RIGHT: Terraced house façades in Malacca. (Photos H. Lin Ho)

was of lacquered and gilded namwood. A lot of lacquered furniture was imported. In 1833 a cabinet cost two hundred and fifty Spanish dollars (Begbie 67:367). In the latter part of the nineteenth century Cantonese screens of carved openwork, which were often gilded, were popular. Anglo-Indian teak furniture was comparatively more streamlined. The 'colonial furniture' was more varied, in that besides perforated carving and marquetry, the designs themselves could range from Art Deco to the less common Dutch cupboards, French-style consoles and chairs, and the occasional Dutch ladder-back chair.

The namwood of Straits Chinese furniture (as distinct from the rosewood in furniture from northern China) is found both in China and Southeast Asia, the latter type being darker in colour. South Chinese lacquered woodwork was often gilded. This type of furniture could be either imported or locally manufactured, with the former tending to be more intricate. All Chinese furniture was dovetailed and easily dismantled, making it less cumbersome to transport and store. Generally, the silhouette was streamlined, without unwieldy projections which could easily be broken off.

The bedrooms of the terraced house, upstairs and opening on to the air-well, usually contained a four-poster bed which was adorned with openwork and gilt cornices. Other bedsteads were massive, with ornamental hangings, some of which were crafted by women during their leisure time. Pillows, for daybeds especially, were of wood, bamboo or ceramic materials.

The most elaborate furnishings were in bridal chambers, which were graced by teak wardrobes, toilet tables and carved gilded chests of drawers. Round portable boxes were always at the ready for both clothes and ceremonial foods. Before modern plumbing, a portable wash-basin and its stand were placed in the bridal chamber. The stand, unlike its prototype in China, had a mirror and, as with much other Straits Chinese furniture, it was lacquered red and gilded. The sumptuous bridal bed whose inner side and two ends were embellished with gilded carvings had a high canopy. The bed was enclosed on three sides with drapes and only the front was left open. Fancy hanging lanterns were placed around the bed.

There were also lanterns in the front porch of the house, but these had a more solemn purpose. Two permanently installed family lanterns flanked a special one to heaven. The family surname on the lanterns on either side of the central heavenly one augmented the calligraphy plaque above the door.

Some terraced houses were set in from the others with large forecourts, while others had low masonry walls between the house and the street. Traditional terraced houses were usually two storeyed, but a third storey was sometimes added as the family expanded, especially when some married children continued to live with their parents.

OPPOSITE PAGE: House in Malacca with typical eclectic ornamentation. (Photo H. Lin Ho)

LEFT: The interior of Jonkers, a terraced house converted into a restaurant, in Malacca. The air-well and the wrought iron circular straircase are typical.

RIGHT: Stairs and airwell in the Chan House in Malacca (see following pages).

(Photos H. Lin Ho)

The Chan House — currently
the Baba Nyonya Heritage
Museum — is one of the best-
preserved Straits Chinese 'mansions' in Malacca. It consists of
two adjoining terraced houses.
LEFT: Decorartive details of the
exterior of the Chan House, and
the front façade.
ABOVE: The stairs to the first
floor.
(Courtesy the Baba Nyonya
Heritage Museum, photos H. Lin
Ho)

LEFT: Decorative tilework on a
'five-foot way' in Malacca.
TOP: Fan-shaped moulding above
a 'five-foot way' arcade in
Malacca.
ABOVE LEFT AND RIGHT: Glazed
mouldings in the shape of
scrolls in Singapore.
(Photos H. Lin Ho)

LEFT AND BELOW: Chipped glazed ceramic decoration on terraced houses in Malacca (left) and Singapore (below). (Photos H. Lin Ho)

160

Semi-detached houses

The semi-detached house, a cross between the terraced house and the detached house, was at one time mainly the abode of the small middle-class businessman or shopkeeper. Not many of the original semi-detached houses remain, but by far the best examples are in Penang. By the end of the 1930s such houses were no longer built. Semi-detached houses in Penang were double-storeyed with plasterwork-embellished columns and elaborate window frames. In those still standing, the first floor verandah has often been covered up, but the arcade on the ground floor remains.

The bungalow

The Hindi word *bangla* means belonging to Bengal. The Anglicized form 'bungalow' evolved into a term for any single-storeyed dwelling in the cottage style. Although a bungalow is strictly a single-storeyed structure in India and England, in Malaysia the term is applied to any detached house.

Bungalows in this sense were initially the homes of British civil servants and colonial entrepreneurs, especially planters. Originally the roof was thatched and the main building material was timber. These homes had extensive gardens. While bungalows faintly resembled English cottages, modifications were made to suit the tropical climate: floors were raised on pillared supports, ceilings were high and there was a spacious verandah running the length of the house which was shaded by roller blinds known locally as 'chicks'. These symmetrically planned, well-proportioned houses of the colonial period were built both in towns and in the plantations (known, still, as 'estates'). By the first quarter of this century, similar buildings of more permanent materials had been built in place of the original bungalows, but the characteristic style was preserved.

Colonial bungalow in Penang.

Bungalows located in mountainous areas were built for a special purpose — to afford a refuge from the sweltering heat of the plains. Penang Hill (which rises to 2720 feet) was the first hill station. Initially, ponies imported from Aceh in Sumatra were used to scale the difficult track to the top and ladies were carried up in sedan chairs by coolies. However, that was before the funicular railway, with its sturdy arches and tunnels, was built by Indian labour.

In the style of the English gentry, it was fashionable to have a country residence by the sea or on Penang Hill. Wealthy Baba merchants in Penang had mansions on both locations. There was a spate of building on Penang Hill in the 1920s. The earliest bungalows on the summit were built for the Europeans, but later holiday homes for wealthy Chinese *towkays* were built on the lower levels. These weekend retreats were set in manicured lawns dotted with flowering trees. The English landscaped garden was simulated as plants from temperate zones could be grown. Some time after the bungalows on Penang Hill were established, a convalescent home was built there by the English East India Company.

The setting on Penang Hill was meant to remind people of landscapes in faraway lands and the houses were given romantic names. Many even had fireplaces and chimneys installed! Others, more usefully, had terraces. Generally, hill bungalows were built on a smaller scale than those in the city, but they were still furnished in the same style, with teak panelling, stained-glass windows, brass and gilded fittings and trimmings, baroque lamps, rosewood furniture and fancy flowerpots with matching stands. Teak colonial or Anglo-Indian furniture had the simpler lines of the Art Deco style, which was also used for garden furniture. The Baba gentry liked strolls and walks, and on Penang Hill trails spread out in all directions for miles into the jungle. Some of these are now overgrown, although at sea level the promenades of colonial days still survive.

Villas

At the beginning of the nineteenth century, there was a burst of house construction in both Penang and Singapore, and in the course of the century, European bungalows changed hands to non-Europeans. By the late nineteenth century, the upper class of wealthy merchants that had emerged had built their own bungalows or *ang moh lau*, ('European houses' in Hokkien), in the suburbs. Such Sino-European villas were mostly put up in Penang and Singapore, especially at the beginning of the twentieth century when European influence was greatest in those two towns.

The preferred model was the Palladian villa as it had evolved in England from the work of Andrea Palladio in Renaissance Italy. The Sino-Palladian mansions were thus influenced by both the villas of Italy and the country homes of England, and included other neoclassical European elements and Chinese ornamentation. There were also copies of the French chateau style, which sometimes incorporated an asymmetrically placed dome. The adaptation of English Palladian might well be called Tropical Renaissance style, while the Italianate mansions here are reminiscent of fashionable villas around London's Regent's Park. The Malaysian adaptations had spacious verandahs and courtyards to create a cool airy interior.

On the whole, these stately homes showed a good deal of uniformity in their planning. The approach to the front entrance was usually a lush tree-lined avenue leading from a splendid gateway through a rambling landscaped garden with immaculate lawns. The extensive grounds had tennis courts, and further lawns for bowling and croquet. There would perhaps be an aviary or even a menagerie; arbours were very popular. Some gardens even boasted a fountain with a statuette of Cupid as its centrepiece, and sometimes there were statues of nymphs or sculptures of lions and eagles in real or simulated bronze scattered here and there.

Driveways were often circular, passing through the porch in front of the main entrance to the house. Passengers were protected from the sun and the rain as vehicles stopped for them to board or alight. Some of these porches had oyster glass panes. Fencing and balustrades of interlaced wrought iron were imported from England. The mews and the servants' quarters were tucked away out of sight.

The 'Duke of Edinburgh House' in Penang (so called after the Duke stayed there in 1869); a typical eclectic-style villa.

163

The front of the mansion was divided into three horizontal sections, namely a raised base, a very high mid portion emphasized by an impressive door and perhaps French windows, and an upper storey which was not as high as the one below. Another common item was the broken pediment adorned with decorative mouldings. In its centre, the Chinese symbols for luck and for prosperity, a bat and a coin respectively. The entrance portico might be bordered by a row of columns. A design which copied the front of a Roman temple, a very popular feature from Renaissance Italy, was used for both the front and back elevations. Very often the finished result of these Palladian-inspired villas was decidedly different from the buildings they had been modelled on, because the classical support columns were transformed into decorative pillars or appeared in clusters. The addition of the upper storey cut the columns short, spoiling the impression of great height.

The Palladian style of villa had a central hall around which other rooms were symmetrically arranged. Quite often, there would be two such halls, each in a separate wing of the mansion and both formally and grandly furnished. Fine mosaic floor tiles were laid in floral patterns and in panels. The panels were designed in Italy and exported from Naples to be assembled locally. Sometimes Italian-style mansions had Carrara marble floors.

One of the two halls was used to receive fellow Chinese business associates and was filled with Chinese blackwood or rosewood furniture with intricate carving and inlaid mother-of-pearl or marble-topped tables. These heavy pieces of furniture were arranged symmetrically along the walls and a set comprising of a round marble-topped table with accompanying stools stood in the centre of the room. A touch of brightness was added to the room the so-called Straits furniture — elaborately carved

OPPOSITE PAGE: Dutch-style villa in Malacca, situated in a row of terraced houses. (Photo H. Lin Ho)

BELOW: Grand villa built in 1924 on Gurney Drive in Penang. (Photo Cheang Yik On)

namwood finished with red lacquer and gilded. However, not much of this type of furniture would be in the reception halls; it was used mostly in bridal chambers. In this hall, with its distinctly Chinese character, hung calligraphic or pictorial scrolls. Some of the scrolls displayed poetic couplets but these were rarely read by either the host or the guests.

The wealthy Chinese merchant's business associations were such that he had one foot in the East and the other in the West. It was appropriate, therefore, for him to entertain Western guests in another hall appointed with European furnishings. Teak Anglo-Indian settees, tables and cabinets kept company with Victorian lamps whose shades were often adorned with tiers of crystal bead fringes. Venetian-glass mirrors, marble statues and chandeliers completed the setting. Besides the drawing room, whose furnishings included a piano and portraits in heavy frames of gilded brass, there was a library which had both English and Chinese books. The dining room inevitably had at least one epergne on the table. Carved and gilded wooden screens were of large proportions because the ceilings were high. Staircases leading up to bedrooms were wide and decorative. Finally, recreational facilities included a billiards room. One of these palatial villas even had a theatre big enough for staging Chinese operas.

Penang's Italian-style villas with exotic names were either in a northern residential suburb fronting the sea or on the Hill, and in the latter case they had terraced gardens. Along the street of seafront villas, dubbed Millionaires' Row, where many owners had their own beaches, newer houses were built in the compact Art Deco style of the 1930s, which was revived in the 1950s. These more recent villas stand side by side with others which are decorated with fanciful mouldings and curlicues. There are also later 'Art Moderne' streamlined houses influenced by the Bauhaus. Mansions on the mainland of the Peninsula developed from the Italian-style villas on Penang's north beach. A combination of diverse architectural elements was used in indiscriminate profusion as a result of the whimsical fancies of wealthy merchants. Needless to say, this produced some rather disastrous creations.

FROM LEFT TO RIGHT: Blackwood armchairs with ceramic backs and marble seats (courtesy Dato' Khoo Keat Siew); A traditional Chinese round table and stools, to be placed in the centre of a hall (courtesy Lim Kean Siew); Chinese-style table and stools made of teak wood (courtesy Dato' Khoo Keat Siew); A rosewood two-seater bench with marble backs (courtesy Lim Kean Siew). (Photos Cheang Yik On)

LEFT: A lacquered and gilded cupboard. This piece is most unusual because the front is curved. (Courtesy Dr. Chan Chin Cheung, photo H. Lin Ho)

LEFT: A European-style teak side-board, flanked by Chinese chairs. (Courtesy the Baba Nyonya Heritage Museum, Malacca, photo H. Lin Ho)

RIGHT: A bedroom dresser of red lacquered and gilded namwood with Ming-style legs. Height 89 cm, width 104 cm, diameter 54 cm. (Courtesy Lim Kean Siew, photo Cheang Yik On)

RIGHT BELOW: The main hall of the Hardwicke villa in Penang, with Chinese blackwood and European furniture. The side-boards are French-style. The cut-glass chandelier was a standard fitting in many villas. (Courtesy Lim Kean Siew, photo Cheang Yik On)

LEFT: Victorian cut-glass bases, to be used for lamps or as candle stands. Height 26 cm.
BELOW: Two Art Deco Italian marble statues, which were in vogue in the 1920s. Height 44.5 cm (left) and 59.5 cm (right). (All courtesy Lim Kean Siew, photos Cheang Yik On)

The courtyard mansion

In Penang and Singapore in the late nineteenth century, there was a vogue for building houses as authentically Chinese as possible, in the style of the traditional courtyard mansion, which is similar in many ways to the Chinese temple. In most cases, craftsmen from China accompanied the imported building materials. Generally, the mansion was still of mixed styles, combining Oriental and Western motifs, but the form of the finished house was essentially classical Chinese, with its Chinese roof, walled and landscaped garden, internal courtyards and Chinese cantilevers. The central courtyard of this type of mansion was paved with stone slabs and was bordered by halls, corridors and rooms which accommodated several generations of the same family. Usually, two main halls flanked the central courtyard along the east-west axis. This arrangement was sometimes repeated around additional adjoining courtyards, resulting in a large square or rectangular complex, which faced the rising sun. Because all the rooms opened on to the internal courtyards, these mansions were distinctly 'inward-looking'. The extended family and servants occupied outer wings of the complex. The courtyard functioned as a garden, with ornamental pot plants and miniature rockeries, but it was also a working area in the same style as the airwell of the terraced house, which was a reduced version of the courtyard.

The Cheong mansion in Penang is the only one of its kind in Southeast Asia. Because of the owner's high office as a Mandarin and Consul (see Chapter 1, The China Connection), it was appropriate for him to have at the front of his house four red pillars. In this mansion there was also the Fujian porcelain mosaic found on so many temple decorations. The well-known mixture of styles is still, however, very much in evidence. The interior has Chinese lattice screens side by side with Victorian grillwork, while wide Chinese capitals of carved and lacquered wood are set on top of thin Victorian cast-iron columns. There are seven iron spiral staircases. Other European elements are louvred windows in either Gothic or Roman style and Art Nouveau stained glass, floor tiles in geometric designs, and ornamental ceilings. Chinese furniture is accompanied by imported mirrors and chandeliers. Blackwood and rosewood furniture from China seems to have been preferred to that of Straits Chinese namwood. The imported furniture was still from the south of China, with marble or ceramics as table tops or back-rests for chairs, and inlays which included mother-of-pearl and silk embroidery. The street on which the Cheong mansion is located was, and still is, called Lotus River after the lotus garden of the mansion.

The Cheong Fatt Tze courtyard mansion in Penang (1896-1904), built in keeping with the owner's mandarin status conferred on him by the Empress Dowager. (Courtesy Cheong Fatt Tze Mansion Sdn. Bhd., photo Cheang Yik On)

Mosaics made of chipped glazed ceramic are called *jian nian*. The Cheong Fatt Tze mansion features several of these mosaics.

LEFT ABOVE: Fan-shaped mosaic depicting a tale from classical Chinese literature.

LEFT: Highly elaborate mosaic in the shape of a scroll.

RIGHT ABOVE: All gable ends of the building are embellished with *jian nian* mosaics.

RIGHT BELOW: Decorated support of the first-floor verandah. (All pictures courtesy Cheong Fatt Tze Mansion Sdn. Bhd., photos Cheang Yik On)

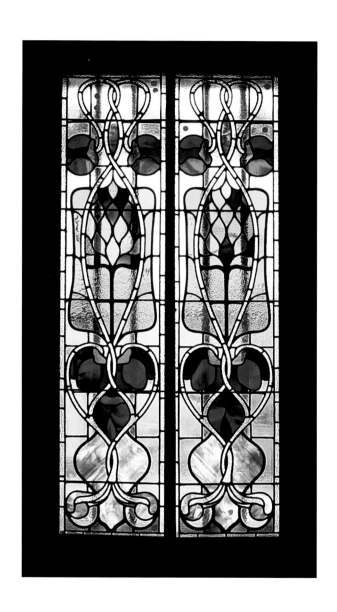

ABOVE: Art Nouveau in a Chinese
house; the Cheong Fatt Tze
mansion features several of
these stained-glass windows.
(Courtesy Cheong Fatt Tze
Mansion Sdn. Bhd., photo
Cheang Yik On)

The Chinese garden

The private garden of large Chinese villas was always one of the most important areas of the house. One such was the lotus garden of Penang's Cheong mansion, which may have included many of the following features. Walls ten to twelve feet high provided privacy and protection from fires. The walled garden, which was an extension of the house and a space for relaxation, contained small structures such as pavilions, bridges, arbours, shrines, libraries or theatres. Paths of paving stones laid in patterns wound in and around these architectural forms. Other elements of the garden included plants, rockeries and water. Certain plants and trees were preferred: of the so-called 'three friends', bamboo was the most common (the other two being pine and plum). The resilience of the bamboo is likened to a wise person who bends instead of breaking under pressure and rises up again when adversity has passed. The rockery is obviously a human imitation of nature, but it also represents an interest in minerals. Water is perhaps the most important element in the garden, and the natural ponds or artificial pools and lakes contain two powerful living symbols. The first of these is the carp, which is an extraordinary fish admired for the tremendous effort it expends in reproducing as it leaps upstream to spawn. The other is the white lotus, which represents hope and life because the immaculate flower rises from dark and murky stagnant water.

The white surface of the garden wall acted as a background for other garden elements, while there were openings in the wall which framed the scenery beyond. Texture was introduced by grillwork and latticework. The garden was not meant to be seen all at once as a whole, but as an ever-changing composition to be taken in in parts as one moved around it. Similarly, views of the sky were framed by the wavy border of the tiled eaves overhanging an airwell in a terraced house.

Temples

Although temples are generally separate buildings in their own right they are sometimes part of a complex which may include pagodas, memorial arches and gardens. Temples can even be attached to caves or graveyards. The style of the Chinese temple has remained unchanged for centuries and attention has always been focused on the exterior front elevation. During the 1870s and 1880s, many existing temples were rebuilt in permanent materials. The roof, which is the crowning glory of a temple, is never the hip-roof of domestic architecture. The most popular form in the Straits Settlements and elsewhere in Malaysia is a gabled roof in three sections, of which the middle one is usually raised, following the practice in southern China. Raised copings separate the three sections.

The central section of a temple roof is elaborately decorated; the ornamentation varies, but a common theme is a central bluish-green glass ball encircled by flames and flanked by a pair of dragons. This icon is variously called 'Dragon Pearl' or 'Dragon Bead', while the pearl or bead itself is often referred to as the blazing or the night-shining pearl. Some people think of this circular object as representing the sun, or the positive *Yang* principle or the head of the Buddha. Since it represents elevated ideas or concepts, it is placed on a pedestal on the top ridge of the roof. The dragons, which appear to be gambolling, climbing or crawling, are supposedly struggling towards the perfection represented by the central blazing pearl. Dragons are regarded

Temple roof decoration. The symbolic dragon and pearl motif forms the visual centre of the design. (Photo Cheang Yik On)

as malevolent in the West, but they symbolize justice, authority and strength in China, where they always guard temple roofs. The tendency for the elongated ends of the eaves to curve upwards reached an extreme during the Qing Dynasty. The upward sweep is named according to the variations in its form, e.g. 'curling wave', 'rolling wave', 'fish-tail' or 'swallow-tail'.

Perched on the ridge end is some aquatic creature whose symbolic function is to spout water in case of fire. The fire/water dualism is sometimes depicted by fire-spitting dragons gambolling on undulating roof tops, which represent ocean waves.

The concept of the eternal struggle between water and fire, light and darkness, *Yin* and *Yang*, or good and evil is not exclusive to the Chinese; it is practically universal. Sometimes this dualism is thought to be embodied in one entity with two facets. At other times, the dualism is manifested in two opposing but complementary entities. A dragon-related motif sometimes found on roof ridges or on friezes is the carp; it represents the average human being who, by tremendous endeavour, can become highly intellectual and hence powerful. This analogy comes about because of the carp's successful leap up the rapids of the Yellow River, which are collectively called the Dragon Gate. Carp which succeed in entering the Dragon Gate, i.e. in leaping through the rapids to spawn, are said to become dragons and are inconographically depicted as fish with dragon heads (see also The Arts, Jewellery).

The coping ends in between roof sections are profusely ornamented. The most common theme is a boat filled with smartly dressed figures, which is significant, because the maritime flavour is reminiscent of the origin of most of the Straits Chinese — coastal South China. Whether the reference is to actual journeys made by the earliest clan members or to some cultural ancestors far away in time is not clear. Roof-top figurines are always in odd numbers, in the belief that the strong *Yang* (associated with odd numbers) dominates over the weak *Yin* (even). There are two main methods for making these ceramic figures, namely those of Fujian and Guangdong.

The Fujian method of sculpture called *jian nian*, literally 'cut and paste', is a form of mosaic using ceramic shards embedded in cement to form the figures; even fine lines are made of these fragments. The ceramic pieces used are of thin translucent porcelain. Mirror chips add to the glitter. Such mosaic compositions are sometimes painted over when they are on gables or panels of shophouses. The Fujian *jian nian* style was fashionable in Canton in the 1870s.

The Guangdong method differs, with the figures being cast in moulds, as is pottery in the kilns of Shiwan in South China. Whichever method is used, the figures are prefabricated before being placed on the roof. Skeletal wire armatures may be used in both methods.

The gable walls of temples are often decorated with bands of multicoloured floral designs. These friezes are bas-reliefs in stucco. Gable walls do not usually extend above the roof, but look very striking when they do because their outlines can be seen against the skyline. Shaped in various ways, they have fanciful names such as 'crawling cat', 'five peaks adoring heaven' and 'ears of a Chinese cooking pan'.

Frescoes on walls depicting legends are worked in black ink, as in Chinese calligraphy. The adhesive used is animal glue and salt with a touch of vinegar. To accelerate drying, methylated spirit is added. Such ink frescoes are very durable. Oil paintings are also found in temples, usually on timber beams and panels; these paintings have a shorter life span.

Dragon-shaped decorations on the ends of the eaves. (Photo Cheang Yik On)

In front of temples are courtyards, which may be paved with brick, asphalt or stone. Friezes are painted under the eaves above the doors and windows. The entrances are guarded by pairs of lions, one of which carries a cub and the other a bale of coins. Such pairs of lions are symbolic of one's parents and are meant to instil a sense of filial piety. The main doors, made of wood, have paintings of door guardians, one on each panel. Inside the temple are gilded lacquered friezes depicting the life of the Buddha or Taoist legends. Gold leaf acquired by donations embellishes these paintings, which are usually placed above altars to deities. There is usually a pond somewhere in the temple where captive tortoises are reared to be released on festive days. Pagodas are sometimes freestanding structures but are more commonly part of a temple. Their designs vary between countries, and in Malaysia there is a mixture of styles. The eighty-foot-high, seven-tiered, octagonal Pagoda of the Thousand Buddhas in Penang, which was completed in 1927, has niches with pointed arches that suggest Indian influence. Inside the niches are small statues of Buddha. Werner Spieser

The Chung Keng Kwee temple.
(Courtesy Asia House, Hong Kong, photo Cheang Yik On)

(65:347) sees European baroque influence in this pagoda's circular galleries, which become smaller towards the top. While most Chinese pagodas have a circumambulation path inside the building, this one has it on the outside. Although the octagonal base is Chinese, the middle tiers are Thai and the upper ones Burmese in style.

The Penang Buddhist Association building, erected in the 1920s, is an unusual temple in that it is of Straits Eclectic style: Czechoslovak chandeliers and Buddhist images sculpted in Carrara marble accompany Chinese furniture. In its gardens is a three-metre-high, seven-tiered miniature pagoda.

Chinese temple architecture is, of course, full of symbolism and references to mythology. The conglomeration of colours is not chosen for aesthetic reasons, but purely for symbolic purposes. The five elements required in a temple to ensure harmony are represented by yellow for earth, black for water, green for wood, red for fire and white for metal. In other cultures these colours have different symbolic meanings. While it might be commonly agreed that red represents happiness and good fortune, white represents purity in many cultures, but for the Chinese generally connotes sorrow and tears. The Chinese also believe that blue is for peace, while yellow, being an imperial colour, is used liberally for religious but not for domestic buildings.

The shophouse temple

Temples are sometimes located in the middle of a row of shophouses. In construction, such a temple is not substantially different from the neighbouring shophouses. Even an ordinary shophouse can be adapted for use as a temple or clan house; usually only the ground floor is used for the purpose. The exterior is simple, featuring two windows with fanlights on the upper storey. There is usually a bas-relief frieze under the porch roof. In an inner hall, cubicles for ancestral tablets stretch from floor to ceiling, flanking an ancestral altar.

The Cantonese and Hakka temple to *Tua Pek Kong* in Penang. It conforms to a row shophouses. (Photo Cheang Yik On)

LEFT AND RIGHT: Inside the Chung Keng Kwee temple are highly elaborate three-dimensional friezes, decorating the walls below the roof. The tableaux illustrate Chinese legends, and are fashioned in both the *jian nian* and Shiwan techniques. (Courtesy Asia House, Hong Kong, photos Cheang Yik On)

The clan temples of Penang

Not only does a *Kongsi,* or clan temple, function in a similar way to a regular temple, providing for the worship of deities and ancestors, but it is also architecturally very similar. The Penang *Kongsis* are unique in having evolved from a mixture of South Chinese, Malay, Chinese classical and possibly Anglo-Indian designs. The roofs are mainly of the gabled type, but over porches they are sometimes half-hipped and half-gabled. The feature which is least typical of Chinese architecture is that in each case the temple itself is on an upper storey that is supported on heavy foundation pillars. The space between the pillars is closed up, making a lower storey which is used for various purposes — for instance as a meeting room, a school, a store, or even as a shrine to lesser deities. Building on stilts is generally considered to be a Malay practice. However, the exterior of such a clan temple resembles that of northern Chinese temples, which are built on solid plinths. Because they are built up on pillars, the Penang *Kongsis* have both the advantage of a lower storey for multipurpose use and the grandeur that comes from a building standing on a platform.

In many *Kongsis,* the upper floor projects over the forecourt below in the form of a portico. This feature may be seen as representing Anglo-Indian influence. The protruding porch has a railing which cuts across the front elevation, visually interrupting

The grand staircase leading to the entrance of the Khoo *Kongsi* building. (Photo Cheang Yik On)

the façade. This balustrade is often of intricately designed wrought iron.

The interior layout of a *Kongsi* retains the characteristically Chinese arrangement of two side halls flanking a main hall. All three halls open on to the front verandah. While most forecourts of temples do not open directly on to the street, but have an entrance through some kind of gateway, the Penang *Kongsi* temples have a forecourt which is enclosed on all sides by houses. A narrow passageway between these buildings is the only access to it and to the *Kongsi* itself.

The buildings surrounding a *Kongsi,* usually residential terrace houses or shophouses, are part of the *Kongsi* complex and are meant for clan members who rent them from the *Kongsi* authorities. The extensive main Khoo *Kongsi* complex in Penang, for example, centres on a large square courtyard which is approached by a narrow paved driveway in between rows of houses belonging to the *Kongsi*. Above the entrance to the temple complex are the ideograms for Sin Kang, the name of the village in China from which the clan progenitor originated.

At one time, the name Sin Kang was also above every doorway of the clan's adjacent terraced clan houses. In addition, on either side of each door was a pair of verses, one of which began with Sin and the other with Kang. The verses were engraved on long pieces of wood and hung vertically like scrolls. Today, not all of these clan houses are inhabited by Chinese named Khoo.

There are several clan temples in Penang for Chinese with the surname Khoo, but the main one represents the culmination of the trend for authentic Chinese buildings, and is the epitome of the Fujian style. It was rebuilt in 1906. It is both a temple and a repository for ancestral tablets. It has three halls, of which the central one houses the clan's patron saint. To the right of the main hall is the hall containing ancestral

ABOVE: The Penang *Kongsi* exemplified by the oldest: the Cheah *Kongsi*. The building has a bungalow-like design, with a wooden verandah on the upper floor. The verandah railing is cast iron, fashioned in a lacy Victorian design. (Photo Cheang Yik On)

BELOW: The *Kongsi* building of the Yeoh clan. (Photo Cheang Yik On)

The Ancestral Hall of the Leong San Tong Khoo *Kongsi*. At the back of the hall are ancestral tablets, and the side walls carry merit plaques of illustrious living sons. Both tablets and plaques are heavily gilded (Photo Cheang Yik On)

Roof decoration of the Khoo
Kongsi. (Photo Cheang Yik On)

The stage of the Khoo *Kongsi*
clan temple. (Photo Cheang Yik
On)

tablets. The god of prosperity is enshrined in the third hall. His altar spreads across the width of the room and above it hangs a Victorian lamp.

Emphasis on the roof in classical Chinese architecture is well exemplified by the roof of the Khoo *Kongsi*. This replaced the imperial double roof of the original building, which was burned down. Estimates of the weight of the newer roof, which supports a large collection of ceramic immortals, mythological creatures and flora and fauna, range from twenty-five to fifty tons. The roof decorations are made in the Hokkien *jian nian* style.

Supporting the front verandah of the temple are four granite columns with dragons carved in relief, and hence called dragon pillars. The *Kongsi* is of considerable proportions and its array of sculptured stones, wall frescoes and gilt woodcarvings are replete with ornamental detail.

Theatrical stages

Stages which are used for any form of entertainment performed at temples are separate structures facing the temple or *Kongsi*, usually within the grounds, and most often in the forecourt. The precursors of such permanent stages were the temporary makeshift platforms erected for specific ceremonies. These were sometimes even set up by the roadside. Small stages for puppet shows were on wheels, and therefore more mobile than those for Chinese opera.

The permanent stage is a platform about four feet high with trap doors in the floor. A back wall and flat ceiling help with sound projection. Traditionally, the emphasis on costumes compensates for the absence of scenery and stage curtains. The audience sit on simple benches directly in front of the stage.

Commemorative structures

The celebration of Queen Victoria's Diamond Jubilee in 1897 prompted the building of clocktowers in the Straits Settlements. The Penang clocktower is a good example; it is sixty feet high to mark the sixty years of the queen's reign. Edifices of this nature were gifts from philanthropic merchants who, for other occasions, financed the building of fountains or commemorative archways.

Freestanding monumental gateways, called *pai-lou* or *pai-fong* in China may date from the Buddhist period. Such a gateway could be the grand entrance at the approach to a palace or a tomb. It could also be a memorial built to honour a particular deceased person. Such gateways spanned streets in towns or roads between villages; sometimes they were built in isolated spots in the countryside. A *pai-lou* has three, five or seven arches while a *pai-fong* has only a single archway. A *pai-fong*, also called a 'widow's arch' or a 'chastity arch' was often erected by filial sons to honour their mothers who had led virtuous lives and were respected by the public. These gateways were of wood or stone. If they were of wood they were brightly painted and those of stone were carved to look like wood but left unpainted.

Triumphal gateways in the Straits do not seem to have exactly the same function as those in China. The single-arched *pai-fong* is more common in Southeast Asia. It may mark the entrance to a secluded building approached through a corridor and if this building is indeed a monument it has a function similar to the original *pai-fong*. However, *pai-lou* have a totally different purpose; for instance a three-arched *pai-lou* built in 1901 in Singapore commemorates the visit of the Duke of York. Archways

built in Malaya were also meant to be decorative structures.

Bukit Cina, literally Chinese Hill, a one-hundred-acre cemetery in Malacca, is the oldest Chinese cemetery in the Peninsula. Many of the twelve thousand graves there date from the seventeenth century. A *Kapitan Cina* bought this hill from the Dutch and donated it to a temple which was to oversee it as a burial ground for the Chinese. A special feature of Chinese graves in the Straits Settlements, or for that matter Malaysia generally, is the presence of a shrine to *Tua Pek Kong,* the god of good fortune and prosperity.

Cemeteries provide for the burning of token offerings by having altar ovens, some of which are of brick while others are metal furnaces. The wealth of the deceased and their families is indicated by the size and elaboration of the tombs, which have a shape reminiscent of an armchair, a horse-shoe or the Greek capital letter omega. An ideal location for a cemetery is on a hillside with a clear view of the sea; this has good *feng shui* (see Geomancy). The belief that all life emanates from mountains also makes a hillside an appropriate site; the dead return to the mountain.

Geomancy

Feng shui ('wind - water') is the art of divining an auspicious, and thus suitable, site for a building and it even extends to the interior of a house — furniture is arranged according to the principles of *feng shui.* Professional *feng shui* practitioners use a *feng shui* dial to determine placement. Good and evil are believed to be related to supernatural forces. A *feng shui* dial is shaped like a disc with a compass needle in the centre. Markings on the dial are in concentric circles with the eight trigrams *(ba gua)* nearest the needle. These are signs arranged in a circle and each made up of combinations of short straight lines; the continuous or broken lines are said to have been the basis of mathematics, and figuratively represent the cyclic changes of nature. In this art of divination, apart from the natural configuration of the land, the five elements, the seasons and the points of the compass are taken into consideration. Thus, the location of hills that are visible, the direction of the road in front of the house and the direction of the rising sun all have some bearing on the calculations for the siting and orientation of a building. Evil spirits are more likely to enter a house that faces a back lane or a road junction — that is, unless the individual's 'aura' is strong enough to repel them. Another thing to be avoided is a so-called 'chimney house' where the front entrance has a direct passage to or a view of the back door. This facilitates a clear run for evil spirits. Even though it is unlikely that a visitor on first entering a house could have an uninterrupted view of the whole interior, such a situation should also be avoided. One of the other principles of *feng shui* is that a house should not have a hill directly in front of it; it is also good *feng shui* to have an unobstructed view of the sea or any expanse of water. The maxim 'sit on a hill, view the ocean' is recommended for both the living and the dead.

Building materials

Both Malays and Chinese use mortise or rattan-bound joints when working with wood. The wooden houses of Chinese farmers, like those of the Malay farmers, are portable because the joints are slotted, so that the prefabricated house parts can be dismantled and stored if necessary; the same is true of furniture. It was not only because nails were scarce that they were hardly used, but because it was thought that they split the wood and encouraged rust and wood rot.

Wealthy Malacca Chinese merchants employed *Sinkhek* woodcarvers and carpenters. All the carpenters in Penang are from Guangdong province and they have their own guilds. There is even a temple to the gods of carpentry in Penang. Chinese carpenters dominated the building industry which went through a boom period in the 1820s.

In the early nineteenth century the use of bricks was limited. After the 1826 fire in Penang, permanent building materials, including bricks, were used. Chinese roof tiles replaced *atap*. An 1887 ordinance forbade *atap* being used in the town. As trained architects and designers were few then, it was the technicians, carpenters, masons and contractors who actually built the houses. This may be a factor in accounting for the eclectic nature of the buildings.

The house on stilts

Writers on Straits architecture repeatedly identify this house form as Malay, thereby sanctioning the term 'Sino-Malay-Palladian'. I have previously made a case that the house raised on stilts is characteristic of a maritime monsoon and riverine terrain, and not only a Malay but generally a Southeast Asian and also southern Chinese building tradition (Khoo, J. E. 1988).

In the large cultural group of maritime peoples which stretches from southern coastal India, Southeast Asia, and South China to parts of Japan, similarities in architecture and customs include granaries on stilts, the longhouse, dugout canoes and betel-chewing (for other shared characteristics, see Religion, Customs and Festivals, Common Origins).

Southeast Asia is as much a sea-girt riverine land mass as is China south of the Yangtze river. South China, like Southeast Asia, was also originally covered with impenetrable subtropical forest, a rugged terrain broken only by rivers. A lifestyle depending on proximity to navigable streams accounts for the building of houses on stilts erected close to water, though not necessarily in it.

The entrance to riverside houses is usually on dry ground above flood level. The backs of such houses project towards the water and are set on stilts. The height and the distance of the houses from the shoreline depends on the tide. Historically, South China has no pit or underground dwellings like those of North China, where the cold encourages this style. Even up to the present day, rural houses in North China are of dried mud, while those of the south are of split and plaited bamboo with thatched roofs.

Raising a house on stilts or on a platform keeps the inhabitants above the cold earth, the damp soil and the mud of the farmyard. With urbanization, the lower portion of the house on stilts was closed up, resulting in a two-storeyed house built directly on the ground. 'Pre-sinized' and pre-industrialized South Chinese ethnic groups which migrated to non-maritime areas often retained the house on stilts although some abandoned it in terrains where its special features were irrelevant. The homes of minority hill tribes in the so-called Golden Triangle bordered by Burma, Thailand and Laos are good examples.

Having identified the house on stilts as generally a rural form, as opposed to the house built directly on the ground, which is urban, categorizing Chinese houses as those built directly on the ground and Malay houses as those on stilts means that the Chinese are urban and the Malays rural. Yet there are rural Chinese farmers and fishermen living in houses on stilts both in Malaysia and in South China. Fishermen's houses in riverine areas and along coasts are usually clustered together, partly to afford more stability to individual houses. Houses are also often clustered in clan groups, Penang's clan jetties being a good example. When these houses are built out over water, the cooler marine environment means airwells are not a necessity. There are still, however, half swing-doors.

The original rural southern Chinese house was a longhouse exactly analogous to the Iban longhouse on stilts. It very often functioned like a matriarchal village commune. It was a long narrow bamboo structure raised on wooden stilts with ladders as a means of access. The house had a gabled roof, and each room, which accommodated one family, opened out on to a front verandah which stretched the length of the building. The area below the house was used for storage, for example for keeping animals and farming and fishing equipment, and also as a place for dumping rubbish.

Early tin miners in Malaya lived in such longhouses, indicating that these indentured labourers were recruited from rural South China. The traders and merchants who had come before them to the Straits were urban people already used to building their houses directly on the ground.

The Penang clan jetties. (Photos Cheang Yik On)

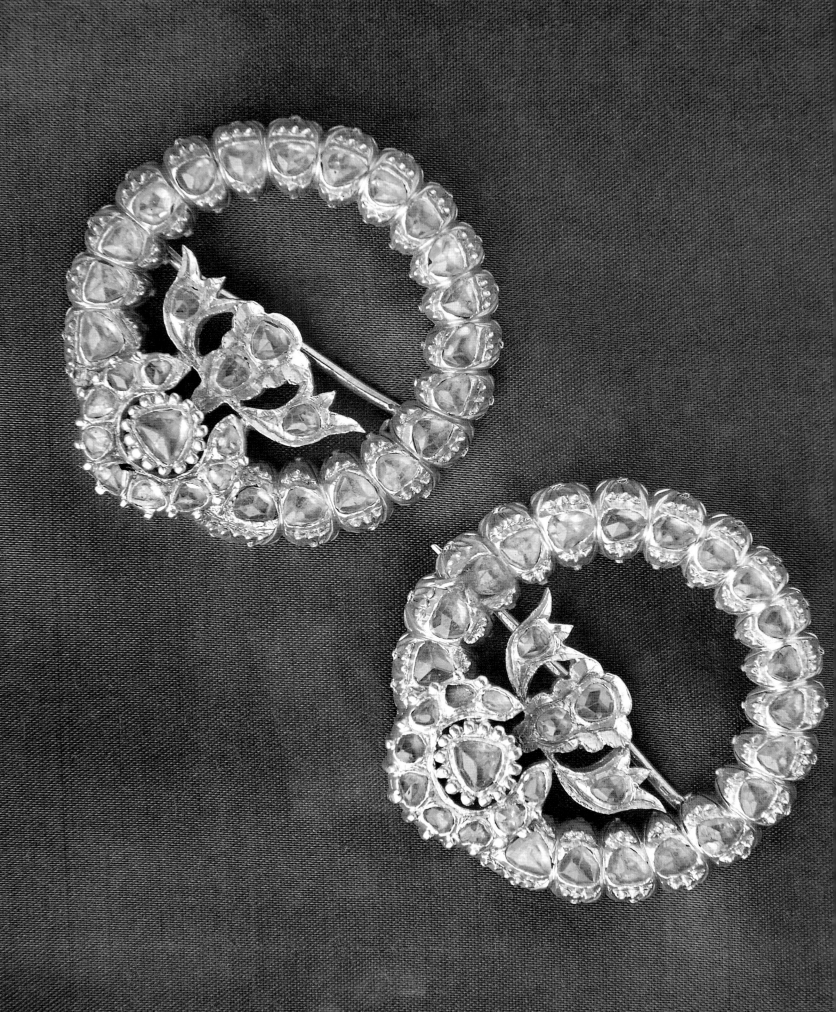

The Arts 5

Arts and crafts

During the times of the great dynasties of China people were very supercilious about arts and crafts. The literati, from about the Song Dynasty (907-1279) onwards, contemptuously referred to folk art as the 'small skills of carving insects' (Berliner 1986). The Mandarins asserted that folk art had neither moral benefit nor philosophical content and that it was only decoratively symbolic, not analytical. Sophisticated arts were popular in court circles and used technology considered more advanced than that of the villages. The products were supposedly the models for folk art done by the poor urban classes and the villagers. Some forms of courtly art, however, could actually have vanished or are only vaguely remembered. The urban poor and the villagers should really be seen as part of the court culture because they were familiar with sophisticated art forms. However, when they practised these arts themselves they did not employ either complicated techniques or expensive materials. This distinguishes folk art from primitive and popular art because the latter two are not derived from court art.

This is not to say that the élite group had no feeling for simple art; the intelligentsia may have admired the simple bamboo used to make a scholar's brush holder. Intellectuals could appreciate unpretentious natural objects such as pebbles or driftwood as points of interests on a desk or elsewhere in a study.

'Fine art', a Western categorization, is well known in stratified societies. While the general public are occupied with producing the necessities for survival, the upper classes, who have a more leisurely life, can devote their time and energy to creating things for aesthetic pleasure.

Although the masses, or 'folk' could only spend their spare time on the creation of works of art, the upper classes could devote all their time to perfecting such skills, or, if they were not artistically inclined themselves, they could hire artists to do the creating for them. These hired artists were professionals, whereas the generality of the upper class, who viewed art as a leisure pursuit, were amateurs. Since people of the working community were responsible for producing the necessities of life, they created utilitarian objects. The élite studied history, painting, sculpture, literature, music and the dance. The common people had similar art forms but they lacked polish and finesse. The distinction drawn between 'fine art' and utilitarian crafts resulted in a dis-

OPPOSITE PAGE: Two smaller brooches from a *kerongsang* (see pages 223 and 224). (Courtesy Azah Aziz, photo H. Lin Ho)

189

dainful attitude among the élite to certain media. For example, ceramics, weaving, printmaking (and later photography) were considered mere technical skills that could never reach the lofty heights of fine art.

In the late eighteenth century, and in various parts of the world, a Romantic Movement explored the possibility that people with 'simple' lives were closer to the source of romantic truth because they possessed primeval vitality. Those subscribing to this new philosophy believed that over-education dulled the senses, resulting in a loss of vitality. The admiration for naive folk arts culminated in Japan, where it is called *mingei* (Japanese for folk art). It is ironic that during a time of increasing industrialization and of the disappearance of some aspects of village life *mingei* became a stylized art form practised by sophisticated urban artists. This is an example of folk art becoming formalized, but in such a process much of the naivety is inevitably lost.

Among the Straits Chinese, appreciation of the arts was not affected by the Romantic Movement of the late eighteenth century because at that time *Peranakan* art was still evolving.

Much *Peranakan* art is 'folksy', emulating both Qing court and European styles. The results are not folk versions of these models but unique creations with a certain naivety of their own. Various arts and crafts were practised, but people worked on them for different purposes; for some they were mere pastimes, for others there was a utilitarian aim, and again there were crafts for specific purposes, e.g. to produce articles for religious ceremonies. In addition there were artisans who specialized in some particular field, producing unique work, most of which was ornamental.

Adaptation of the techniques used in and alteration of the design of any art or craft always takes place as it evolves. Some handicrafts, and their designs and techniques, have probably been independently re-invented over the years, although there is far less evidence of this than there is of copying.

Developing a sense of group identity by relating to certain aspects of one's heritage, and particularly of arts and crafts, is very important. This cultural pride grows with the interaction between people and their artefacts. Thus, arts and crafts as manifestations of one's material heritage are not merely badges of identity; they are actually a necessity. Material culture encompasses all forms of artefacts, from very sophisticated items used only by the upper classes to almost mundane pieces of clothing for primitive man. When we look at the history of arts and crafts we should be concerned not only with the finished article but also with its shape, size, material make-up, method of manufacture and purpose.

Embroidery and beadwork

Time hung heavy for the cloistered young Nyonya girl, so she was expected to engage in domestic accomplishments. One of these was needlework, in which most Nyonya excelled. Evidence of the amount of leisure time the young Nyonya had, and the nurturing she received, could be seen in the quantity and quality of her handiwork. As a result, a display of items embroidered in gold thread or beads became an indication of wealth and status. Embroidery and beadwork, besides being costly to produce, were accomplishments of the well-to-do who had plenty of leisure time.

All young Nyonya girls were taught the art of sewing and embroidery at an early age:

Embroidery with silk threads; the earliest form of Nyonya embroidery. (Courtesy Raymond Kam, photo Khoo Joo Ee)

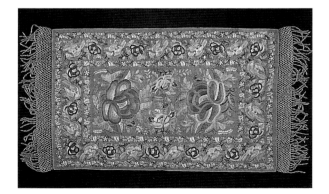

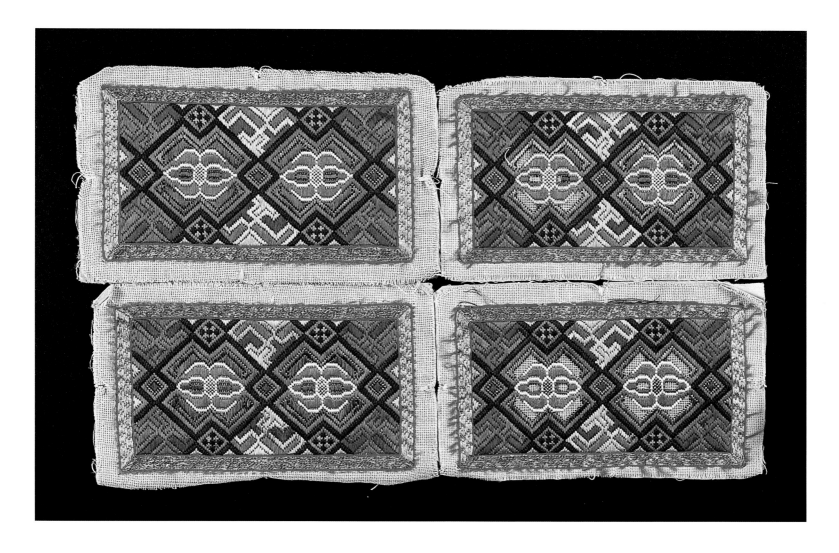

Embroidered pillow ends.
(Courtesy and photo Singapore
National Museum, G0837)

they started learning when they were eight to ten years old. Talent for this craft was a favourable qualification for marriage. While large embroidered bed-hangings and wedding costumes were ordered from China or made by professional tailors in the Straits Settlements, the Nyonya bride was expected to produce a variety of smaller items for her trousseau. These included costume accessories for herself and her groom as well as items to decorate the bridal chamber.

Because her marriage was the most important event in her life, all the skills of the young Chinese girl went into making her wedding costume and trousseau. The relatively pampered Straits Chinese Nyonya did not embroider her own bridal costume, apart from perhaps adding extra decoration on the sleeves of the purchased or rented dress. The short jacket worn by the groom was also bought or rented from an agency which was usually run by the mistress of the wedding ceremony.

Techniques and styles of embroidery

Some of the embroidery of the Malacca and Singapore Nyonya is strikingly similar to that of the Minangkabau Malays of West Sumatra. The proximity of Malacca to the state of Negeri Sembilan would account for this type of cultural exchange because a substantial number of Minangkabaus migrated to Negeri Sembilan in the late seven-

The Peking stitch gives texture to the smooth silk. (Courtesy Lee Siew Ee, photo Khoo Joo Ee)

teenth century. Minangkabau hangings on bridal beds include long panels shaped like neckties and sumptuously embroidered with couched gold threads. Similar decorative hangings featured in southern Nyonya bridal beds, but they were not seen in Penang. The northern Nyonya preferred a different type of embroidered hanging, more in keeping with the Chinese style, which had padded replicas of fish, birds or fruit alternately strung together with colourful tassels.

Generally, two types of stitches were used for embroidery work. The first was satin stitch, which is a smooth-finished filling stitch used to give solid blocks of colour. The other common stitch goes by various names. The Chinese term translates literally as 'making seeds'; foreigners living in China called it the Peking knot or Peking stitch, while in Europe it was known as a French knot (Cammann, 1957). Here it will be referred to as the Peking knot or stitch.

The Peking knot was first used during the Ming Dynasty (1368-1644) but was employed only sparingly in embroidery until the Qianlong period (1736-1795). During the nineteenth century, it gained further popularity. To produce the stitch a knot is made by winding twisted silk thread around the needle several times, piercing the needle through the cloth and pulling the thread tight. The result is a tight seed-like stitch looking much like a knot. Besides producing a rough texture, colour is intensified when these knots are placed close together. This is similar to the painting style called pointillism used by the French post impressionists, where light and shade are built up by dots of paint.

The association of Beijing and its Forbidden City with the Peking stitch in the name 'the forbidden stitch' is erroneous. Contrary to some speculation, there does not seem to have been any law against its use outside the court. The stitch was, and still is, widely used in China. The name could have meant that it originated in Beijing (Peking). A suggestion that it was forbidden because it ruined the embroiderers' eyesight is also unfounded. There are, in fact, other stitches and methods of sewing which cause far more eye strain, and certain types of darning are extremely taxing on the eye.

Although the Peking and satin stitches on silk are traditionally Chinese, couching is widely used in Malay embroidery, which also uses more gold and silver thread. This is also true of embroidery done by the Nyonya of Malacca, whereas their northern counterparts in Penang normally used more silk thread and beads.

Both European and Chinese gold and silver threads were used by the Nyonya. The European type is rounded and the alloy contains less gold, giving it a silvery tint. Chinese gold thread is characterized by the higher gold content in its fine flat wires. To make this yarn the metallic threads are wrapped round a core of silk or cotton thread. Earlier seventeenth and eighteenth-century Chinese court embroidery used a profusion of gold thread; even iridescent threads made from peacock plumes were employed. The Straits Chinese did not continue this style, possibly because they were not acquainted with it.

Sometimes metallic thread was braided with strands of coloured threads. Plaiting the thread thus, and using metallic thread generously, produces an effect called basket weave. This embroidery stands out on the base material because the technique used is that of looping the threads over large needles which are later removed. When the background cloth was to be almost completely covered with metallic threads, then gauze was used as the base material because it was cheaper than velvet.

Just before the advent of beadwork in embroidery, and before the demise of gold and silver thread, a cheaper substitute was found in tinsel which also came in stretchable spring form. This tinsel thread came from India. A somewhat cluttered design resulted when both gold and silver tinsel twinkled beside sequins on a dark velvet background.

For this method of cut-work embroidery, an embroidery hoop is used to indicate a shape in satin stitch. The cloth within the outline is then cut. (Photo Khoo Joo Ee)

Velvet, being firmer than silk, was also used as the base for silver appliques which were specially made with tiny holes for threads to pass through. All the metallic decorations used in embroidery were recycled: these expensive materials would be carefully removed from a worn-out item which was being discarded.

Most of the equipment used for embroidery, such as patterns and stencils for slipper uppers and other work, was imported from China. A lot of the later embroidery of the 1920s to 1940s, however, copied European designs and motifs. Some of the ideas for patterns came from sources which had nothing to do with embroidery, for example, designs on chocolate boxes or illustrated books of European fairy-tales. Other items like ceremonial costumes or house decorations were, and still are, brought in from China. The Straits Chinese worked additional embroidery on to already finished fabrics and garments, which is the *Qing* style of treating costumes. Apart from the standard valances, curtains and outer wedding garments, most of which were and are bought and sometimes given additional embroidery, smaller items which were embroidered included handkerchiefs, covers for mirrors, purses, decorations for the bridal bed, and table runners. These common items can be very Chinese in style or they may look very European even though they are distinctively Straits Chinese, especially in the choice of colours. Nowadays the subtlety and subdued hues of European or Chinese embroidery are no longer seen; instead there is a directness which sometimes approaches garishness because of the choice of harsh colours.

There is another distinct form of embroidery executed by the neighbouring *Peranakan* women of Indonesia. This is embroidery on pillow and bolster ends. While the Straits Chinese have abandoned the old traditions of rural China and now use metallic pillow ends, their Indonesian counterparts have preserved this craft, which is characterized by the use of silk thread on gauze, couching and geometric patterns. The gauze lends itself to a type of embroidery called counted thread or counted canvas stitch. Both Europeans and Chinese employ these stitches, but the former use a linen or canvas background, hence the name. The Chinese use gauze, which is more closely woven, and lends itself to geometrics. It is arguable that there is Islamic influence in the choice of geometric patterns. However, a great deal of both folk art and fine art uses geometric forms in the absence of Islamic influence; these forms are the basic shapes for designing and pattern-forming.

Counted canvas stitches are very regular and easily formed; they resemble tapestry stitches in the arrangement and direction of the thread. Among the various types of counted canvas stitches is the flame stitch, which is staggered and is used to give an impression of light and shade. Known in Europe as the Florentine stitch, it was the most popular stitch for Chinese mandarin squares. The Chinese called this kind of counted thread work 'gauze stabbing'. Towards the very end of the Qing Dynasty (1644-1911), petit point or tent stitch became popular: this is a tiny filling stitch worked diagonally, as in a tapestry. The most common type of counted canvas stitch, however, was the cross-stitch or gros point, which was in very wide use in China for peasant embroidery but not for the aristocratic mandarin squares.

Besides couching, all the counted canvas stitches mentioned above feature in the Sumatran cloth pillow ends, but the craft is also practised by villagers in south and southeast China, and minority groups in south China produce the same style. Indonesian cloth pillow ends may portray East European and Indonesian aboriginal images (Ho, 1987:122), but they definitely show Chinese folk art influence. Chinese courtly embroidery also features decorative cushion ends (Cammann, 1962:37) resembling the *Peranakan* pillow ends, although it has been suggested that these were unknown in China (Maxwell, 1990, Pl.373).

Another distinctive type of Nyonya embroidery is known as cut-work. The outlines of a pattern are sewn in satin stitch on the cloth. Next, the cloth enclosed by the outlines is cut out. Cut-work was, and still is, very common on the blouse called the *kebaya* (see costume). The cutouts seem to have developed from embroidery on gauze. The weave of the material forms a pattern of small square holes which become enlarged when two or more of the warp or weft threads are stitched together. Some of the pieces of embroidered gauze from Sumatra used to decorate the ends of pillow cases (and also tray cloths and suchlike), have cutouts at regular intervals following the weave of the material.

The cut-work technique can easily be used on other materials; for instance it was worked on voile which was then made into blouses. Elaborate cut-work embroidery was shown to advantage around collars, cuffs and hems as well as down the front lapels of Nyonya attire. Sumatran ladies excelled in this handiwork, and indeed Penang Nyonya recall the Medan connection with regard to such embroidery.

Embroidery on footwear

Special wedding shoes were worn by brides and these were the subject of much care and attention. They were made from the same material as the wedding dress and had ankle straps of satin ribbons. Such shoes were bought, but slippers were always embroidered by the bride-to-be, who was expected to do a pair of them to be presented to the groom at the engagement ceremony when there was an exchange of gifts. Nineteenth-century footwear was intricately embroidered with silver and gold thread. Beaded shoes and slippers came into fashion only in the first decades of the twentieth century.

Nyonya girls learned to embroider the slipper tops, which were then sent to the cobbler to be fitted with leather soles. Good quality gold and silver embroidered slipper uppers were carefully protected by layers of tissue or cloth remnants while awaiting these soles. Bridal slippers were made from two types of material. Velvet-based uppers were often bought ready-made with paste-on stencils for satin stitch embroidery. However if the alternative material, silk, was used, the Peking knot was normally worked on it. This was because the rough texture of the velvet complemented the smooth satin stitch, and in a similar fashion, Peking knots with their rough finish contrasted with and stood out on the smooth silk. The earliest type of slippers used the traditional materials of Chinese embroidery, silk threads on silk or satin cloth. The silk uppers, after being embroidered, were attached to layers of cotton or muslin, using home-made sago paste. Because there was no built-up heel, the design of the earliest slippers was a cross between a slip-on shoe and a slipper. The stub toe was reminiscent of a western ballet shoe, and it became known by the northern Nyonya as the 'frog slipper'; the southern Straits Chinese called it the 'bum-boat shoe'.

These quaint slippers remained popular till the very end of the nineteenth century and were part of the costume of the generation of genteel Nyonya who dressed in long, diaphanous over-dresses worn on top of blouses and ankle-length sarongs. The tunic-like over-dresses are called *baju panjang* ('long dress').

Velvet, a European import, was more popular than Chinese silk by the turn of the

Kasut kodok, or bum-boat shoes.
(Courtesy Khoo Boo Kang,
photo Khoo Joo Ee)

RIGHT TOP: Men's slippers embroidered with metallic thread. Such slippers were traditional wedding gifts, crafted by the bride.

RIGHT MIDDLE: Ladies' slippers. The gold threads used could be of either Chinese or European manufacture.

RIGHT BELOW: Bead slippers. Such slippers became popular in the 1920s, and superceded the ones embroidered with metallic thread. The earliest beads used were microscopic in size, and made of glass — those too small to be sewn with a needle, were threaded. (Collection Dr. Khoo Joo Ee, photos The Pepin Press)

OPPOSITE PAGE: A length of threaded beads made in Penang. It was probably used as a decorative bolster cover. 84 x 19 cm. (Courtesy Datin Patricia Lim Pui Huen, photo H. Lin Ho)

196

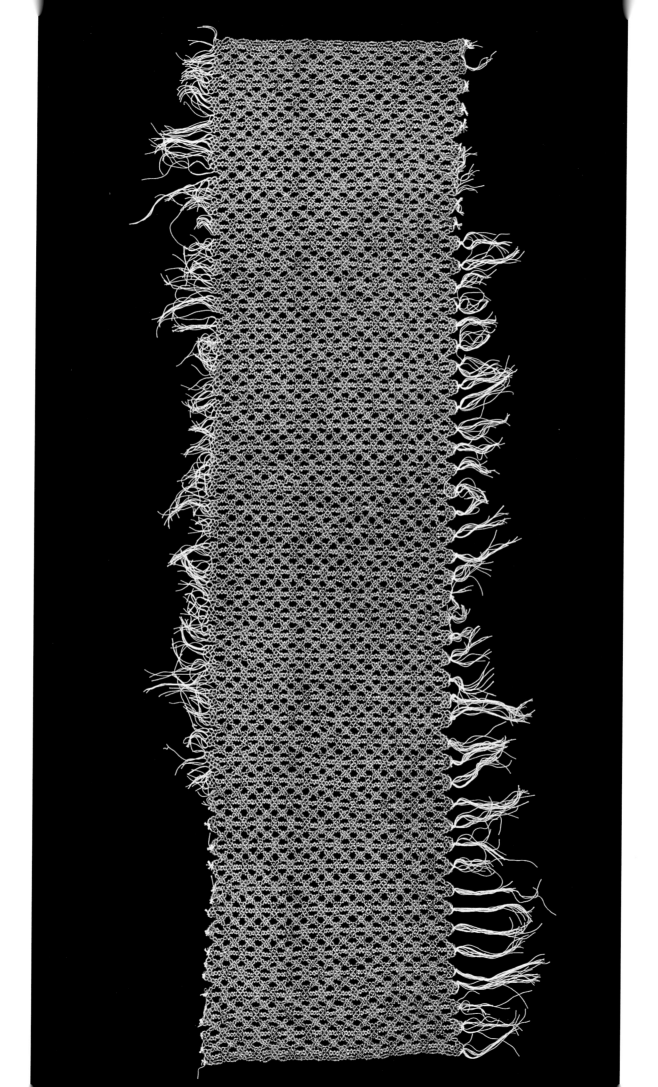

century, and by the 1910s it was used with gold or silver metallic threads. About this time, 'frog slippers' went out of fashion, giving way to flat leather-soled slippers with rounded toes. Gold and silver threads were arranged on the cloth of the uppers and a couching stitch was worked in silk thread to keep them in place.

Beadwork

Beads, those small, hard, perforated objects which have played such an important part in world trade, have been made from an enormous variety of materials, including glass, precious and semi-precious stones, amber, wood, metal, clay, ivory, pearls, shells, bone, feathers, straw, teeth, stalactites, marble, seeds and plastic. The earliest beads were of animal teeth and bones and date back to around 38000 BC: they were found in France (Dubin, 1987:21). Beads can be strung or threaded together, or sewn on to various fabrics to form decorative articles.

Throughout the history of Mankind, beadwork has been used for rituals, adornment and as a status symbol. Some tribes living in remote areas even attribute magical power to certain beads although the materials they are made from may not have any intrinsic value. For example, the Dayak men of Borneo design beadwork for their women to execute, and before imported beads were available, manufactured their own. These large 'home-made' beads are still held sacred and are believed to be imbued with spiritual power. We may perhaps liken this to the rosary of sophisticated urban dwellers, which is just as sacred to them.

The Nyonya did not adorn herself with beadwork jewellery in the way that women of many other cultures did, for instance the ancient Egyptians, North American Indians, Africans and some ethnic groups in Asia. Unlike the Dayaks, the Baba men had absolutely nothing to do with the process of beading, and for the Baba and Nyonya, beads had no ritualistic connotations.

Foreign beads made their appearance in Southeast Asia with West Asian, Indian, and Chinese travellers bringing beads to the region in the early historical period. Such beads, which have been found in archaeological sites, are generally large and pre-sixteenth century. They are sometimes referred to as 'trade-wind' beads because the sailing ships of traders followed these winds. Later, the bead trade became a European monopoly and this continued from the Renaissance till the present century, coinciding with the period of most rapid development and industrialization in Europe. Because of mechanization it became possible to produce 'seed beads' which ranged from 0.5 mm to 2 mm in diameter.

By the fifteenth century, when the port of Malacca had attracted a cosmopolitan trading community, Southeast Asians coveted stone and glass beads. These scarce luxury items were obtained from West Asian, Indian and Chinese traders. It was common for European explorers, traders and missionaries to carry glass beads as gifts or objects of barter, so they became well known and found a ready market. While a bead trade had existed in most parts of the world since prehistoric times, glass beads became an important commodity in international trade during the post-Renaissance European commercial expansion.

European centres of glass bead manufacture started in Venice, Holland, Bohemia and Moravia (the present-day Czech Republic). There were other glass factories in Italy, France, Belgium, England and Germany, but Venetian glassmakers dominated the world market for beads up till the twentieth century.

Glass beads can be made in several ways. The molten glass can be wound around a wire, giving the bead a smooth straight perforation with little danger of sharpness at the ends. Alternatively, the glass can be drawn into a tube and cut into small cylinders which are mechanically tumbled in a bowl of sand to polish off sharp edges. They can also be made in individual bead moulds or by the technique of glass blowing.

By the early nineteenth century, new techniques in the industry produced perfectly round beads. One development was the extremely small microbead, frequently less than one millimeter in diameter. As it was impossible to thread these miniscule beads with a needle, they apparently went out of production.

The Bohemians and Moravians had learned Venetian beadmaking techniques by the seventeenth century and in the eighteenth century their products were already vying with those of Venice. The Venetians, however, maintained their supremacy throughout the eighteenth century, although they suffered a temporary setback when the Venetian Republic fell to Napoleon in 1797. The North American Indians were producing bead-work with colourful seed beads by around the mid-nineteenth century. They used the standard sized beads two millimetres in diameter obtained from Venice or Bohemia. By that time the manufacturing process for bead-making had been mechanized.

It is very difficult to know whether particular beads were made in Venice, Holland, France, Bohemia or Moravia because Venetian beadmakers and Venetian techniques had spread to the other areas. The many middlemen who travelled all over the trading area often dealt in beads because they were easily portable. The trade was very complex: some beads went on long circuitous journeys, and trans-shipment in the days of sail made it even more difficult to trace their origins.

The beadwork produced in China was quite unlike that of the Western style. Although various forms of the bead necklace appeared in the Americas, Africa, India and tribal societies, they did not feature in China, where only jade beads were used as jewellery. The Straits Chinese, true to Chinese tradition, did not use beads for costume jewellery either. However, the Nyonya did develop their special type of beaded embroidery on which, apart from a limited number of motifs and symbols, China had little influence.

Seed beads were never widely used for embroidery in China; the preference was for thread embroidery. This is not to say that glass beads were unknown there: antique glass beads, not the tiny ones used by the Nyonya, were valued in China, but they did not develop into an export industry. Later nineteenth and twentieth century glass beads traded in India were not seed beads either.

Pieces of mica or glass were used for applique designs in some Indian embroidery. Similarly, Malay, or more specifically Sumatran (Minangkabau) embroidery employed mica chips — not beads — to complement thread and gold foil. Nyonya beadwork is quite distinct from these crafts and does not seem to have been inspired by them.

The Nyonya employed three methods of beading, namely stringing, threading and stitching, the last being the most popular. Strung beads were reserved for tassels and fringes. Threaded beadwork was relatively rare, at least in Malacca; the threading technique is found more often among other ancient Southeast Asian cultures. Yet this method was also often employed in Penang beadwork. Threading beads without a supporting material to form patterns requires considerable skill in manipulating the beads, which move along the threads unless knotted down. As multiple threads of beads are used simultaneously to create patterns, tangling inevitably results when this is not done with a practised hand.

A rectangular piece of beadwork with peony-like roses and European bluebirds, made by a Penang Nyonya. Such pieces were used during festive occasions, for instance to cover a side-table. (Courtesy Mrs. Lim Teik Ee, photo Khoo Joo Ee)

OPPOSITE PAGE: Ceremonial bridal handkerchief, decorated with faceted metallic beads and sequins on velvet.

BELOW: Ceremonial bridal handkerchief, embroidered with springy metal coils called *paku-paku* (Malay: ferns). The Nyonya would slip the ring over her third left finger, and swing it to echo her swaying gait. (Collection Muzium Negara, Kuala Lumpur, photos The Pepin Press)

In most of the beadwork done by the Nyonya the beads were stitched on to a backing of cloth: this backing fabric is stretched taut across a frame, just as it is in thread embroidery. The frames used for beaded embroidery ranged from the simple to the very elaborate. Some were rudimentary, consisting of strips of wood fixed together to form a rectangle, but others were made by skilled carpenters and lacquered. A stand with drawers was often made to accompany the frame.

The techniques employed in making beaded embroidery are still the same as they were many years ago. Although some experts can compose a design freehand, it is usually traced on to the backing material, which ranges from velvet to fine canvas, gauze and netting. Beads are attached to the backing either singly, or in a threaded group sewn down at each end. Alternatively, individual beads are sewn on to the backing material using a gros point stitch with all the beads facing in the same direction, resulting in a smooth even surface. The difficulty with this kind of embroidery is that the beads may 'bunch up' if not caught down properly with stitches of even tension.

While there is a predominance of Chinese motifs in metallic thread embroidery, beadwork, which became popular later (when the British and European presence in the Straits Settlements had increased) shows more Western influence. For instance, a pair of mandarin ducks, the Chinese expression of conjugal fidelity, was sometimes replaced by a pair of European bluebirds. The elegant crane gave way to the graceful swan. The soft kittens and cute puppies that appeared were more English than Chinese. Penang Nyonya tended to make their peonies resemble roses. The designs even included references to European fairy-tales: Snow White and the Seven Dwarfs were often seen on slipper tops.

The Nyonya used tiny seed beads which were produced in glass, metal and plastic. She bought her beads from her itinerant neighbourhood haberdashery vendor. The beads, available in a wide variety of colours, were sold in threaded bunches according to colour, or by the spoonful out of bottles. Very old glass beads are miniscule, less than 0.5 mm in diameter. These microbeads were threaded with waxed silk threads because no needle could pass through them. The long fringes of valances were threaded with such beads. Later glass beads were rather larger, but still less than 1.0 mm in diameter. Present-day beads would be considered huge and coarse.

There were both translucent and opaque glass beads. Just as granulation (see Jewellery) in antique jewellery is often faceted, so are some old beads. They sometimes have a film of some metallic oxide giving them a shiny surface which catches and reflects the light. Such variegated small beads were not common. They were accordingly more expensive and used sparingly, being reserved for precious wedding accessories.

Beading first became popular in Europe in the sixteenth century, when even pearls and jewels were embroidered on to personal and household items. Beading continued to be popular right into the early nineteenth century, when the medium was extensively employed for costume jewellery and household furnishings. Both costumes embroidered with beads and costume jewellery used tiny beads sometimes called birdseed beads. Some Victorian four-poster beds had complete surrounds of beading up to four kilograms in weight. Pastel blues and pinks were popular in mid-nineteenth century Victorian Britain. This fashion eventually reached Southeast Asia and was adapted by the Straits Chinese, but it was not until the early twentieth century

that beadwork became popular among the Nyonya. Together with Venetian and Bohemian beads and French velvet, Victoriana were shipped to the East. Furnishings in neo-Rococo and Art Deco styles, Venetian mirrors and French accessories were soon seen in the Baba villas.

In the early decades of this century it became fashionable to use some types of beads for certain items of personal adornment and decorative objects. Eventually beadwork superseded silk and gold thread embroidery. On their wedding both the Baba and Nyonya wore some form of beaded attire, the most common being beaded slippers. An unusual bridal accessory, a ceremonial handkerchief, was occasionally embroidered with beads. The bridesmaid wore a headdress fashioned partly of beads. Beaded belts were worn by both men and women. Ladies' beaded purses and handbags were also fashionable then. Almost all these personal accessories and other hand made items were reserved for festive occasions, like the New Year, weddings or birthdays.

The earliest beadwork was stitched with silk or metallic thread on to the same Chinese silk which had long been used for embroidery. These old beads were very fine faceted metallic ones. Later, velvet was used as the base material. Even before the appearance of beads it was common for slippers decorated with metallic threads to be crafted on long-piled furry velvet, which was used for both the upper and the sole. The long-piled velvets were succeeded by the usual short-piled velvets for beaded work; the colours available in the Straits appear to have been predominately oranges and greens. The styles of the beaded slippers generally evolved through many more stages than the earlier metallic thread ones.

The top of the beaded slipper, called the 'face' by both the Straits Chinese and the Malays, started with round toes. At a later date the toes became more pointed — just like those of some contemporary shoes. Scalloped edges appeared on older beaded slipper tops, just as they did on yet older metallic thread-embroidered ones. By the 1930s and 1940s European cross-stitch patterns were popular. The background material, velvet, was slowly replaced by other materials which were more suitable for this type of stitch. The new materials included a fine light canvas, but eventually firm netting was the most popular. Later work featured regular or chequered backgrounds besides the central motifs. Still later, the slipper tops had purely geometric designs.

Generally, the older metallic thread slippers were worn with the traditional *baju panjang*, and the beaded slippers, being more modern, went with the *sarung kebaya*. However, during the transition period at the turn of the century, flat metallic thread slippers were sometimes worn with the *sarung kebaya*. The Nyonya of the 1920s continued embroidering slippers with beads to complement her *sarung kebaya*. For formal wear, or for special occasions like Chinese New Year or grand birthday celebrations, new slippers were made for every member of the household. The Nyonya embroidered bead slippers not only for herself but also for her elders for festive occasions or for going out. (In the house the women wore wooden clogs.)

Neither the Nyonya bride nor her Baba groom wore the older gold thread or beaded slippers on their wedding day itself. They usually wore silk-embroidered shoes of cloth in keeping with their Chinese wedding costumes. However, the hand-made gold thread or beaded slippers were worn on every day but the first of the twelve-day long wedding ceremonies — more often by the new bride than by the groom, who frequently continued to wear Manchu boots. By the time beadwork became popular in the 1920s, the practice of the bride sewing her groom a pair of slippers (in gold thread) was dying out.

The bridal handkerchief was a unique accessory worn by the Malaccan and Singaporean bride on the third, fifth and twelfth day of the wedding ceremonies. It was like a large handkerchief shaped as a long triangle. It was usually made up of two pieces of decorated and stiffened velvet sewn together. Attached to this formal handkerchief was a ring which the bride wore on the fourth finger of her left hand. It has been suggested that this peculiar personal ornament is Malay in origin because the Straits Chinese adopted the Malay name for it (*saputangan*) (Ho Wing Meng, 1987:118). The southern Nyonya have always spoken Malay and would often use Malay words even for things Chinese. It is also possible that the original Malay article which influenced this Nyonya handkerchief was not a handkerchief but a fan. This is the *kipas pengantin*, or bridal fan, which is often one of a pair. These bridal fans were used to cool the Malay bridal couple as they sat in state during the *bersanding* ceremony. It appears that the stiff, formal and ceremonial handkerchief was an ingenious accessory replacing the hand-held fan which was originally unfoldable and unwieldy. It is also possible that this peculiarly southern Nyonya bridal handkerchief evolved from the Chinese handkerchief purse. The initial striking similarity is the triangular shape, even though the purse was used with the apex of the triangle at the bottom. The Chinese handkerchief purse was so named because it was intended for keeping a handkerchief.

The most interesting thing about the postulated transformation of the Chinese handkerchief purse into a formal bridal handkerchief is that a ring was attached to it. The ring was worn and the handkerchief dangled from the bride's hand. The ring itself may be related to the European practice of wearing a wedding ring on the third finger of the left hand, to symbolize love and marriage. The superstition that there was a nerve, vein or artery running from this finger straight to the heart appears to be based on the ancient Aegean practice of using the finger in magic medicine. The fact is that this finger is the least independent and weakest of them all; perhaps placing the wedding ring on it signifies the weaker, submissive and subordinate role of the wife (although, of course, the men of some European and American communities also wear wedding rings).

It is possible therefore, that the southern Nyonya invented the ceremonial bridal handkerchief under the combined influence of three objects from very different traditions, namely the Chinese handkerchief purse, the Malay bridal fan, and the European wedding ring. When traditions become established they sometimes seem to be 'frozen' in time; just as the Malay bridal fans became 'immortalized', as it were, in the more permanent materials of silver or gold, so the Nyonya handkerchief also had a double layered metal version.

Whether the two joined pieces were vestiges of a purse or a fan is debatable. The metallic Malay bridal fans, produced in pairs, were one-sided; they could be joined with their undersides facing inwards to form one fan — perhaps the ancestor of a stiff handkerchief.

In general, silver or gold belts were naturally for the more affluent. As an alternative, a silver buckle could be fitted to an embroidered or beaded strip belt of stiffened fabric. The latter often had an accompanying purse with a loop which slipped over the belt. Belts embroidered by the Nyonya of South Sumatra had built-in purses.

Beadwork pouch, possibly used as a spectacles case, decorated on both sides with fine glass beads. (Courtesy Lim Suan Har, photo Cheang Yik On)

OPPOSITE PAGE: Belt purse with floral patterns worked in tiny glass beads. The plain felt back extends above the beadwork to form a loop for the belt to pass through. Length 12.5 cm, width 9 cm. (Courtesy and photo National Museum of Singapore, G0296b)

RIGHT: A pair of beadwork vases, each with a bulbous hexagonally panelled body, tapering to a narrow neck and slightly wider mouth. Such carefully crafted Nyonya handiwork would be placed in the bridal chamber. Penang, early 20th century. Height 14.8 cm (without stands, which are not authentic). (Courtesy Prof. Dr. Cheah Jin Seng, photo H. Lin Ho)

BELOW: Beaded belt from Palembang, Sumatra. (Courtesy and photo National Museum of Singapore, G0866)

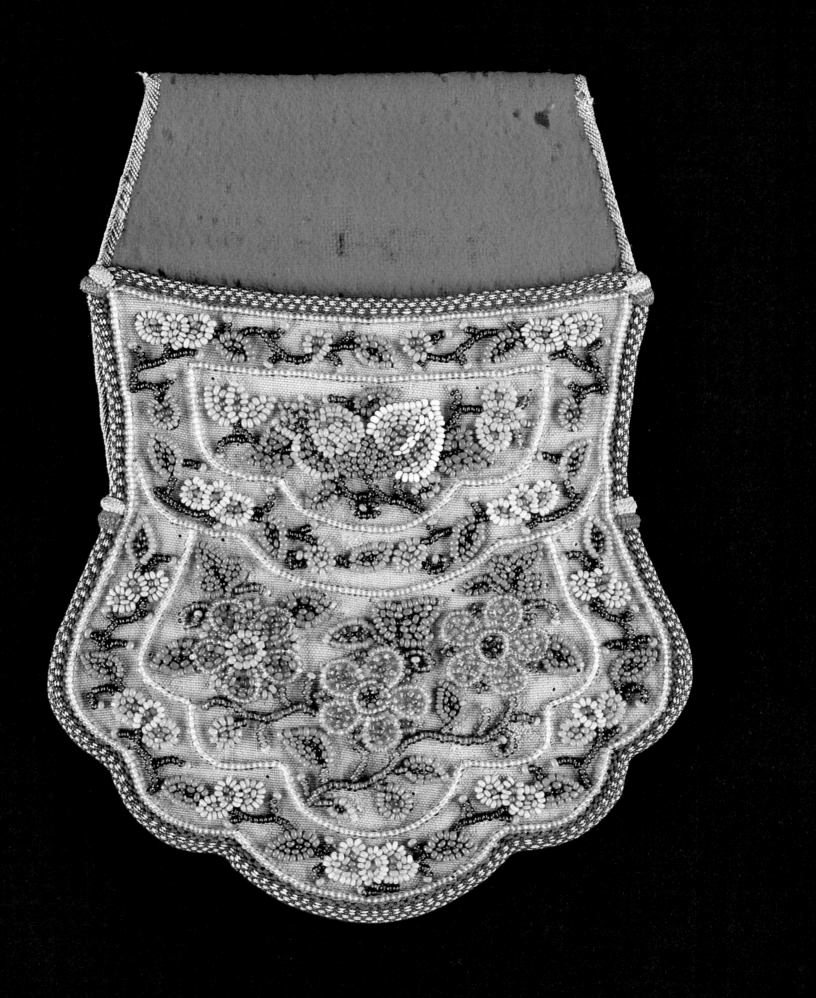

Sometimes though, only part of the belt was shaped to look like a purse. The Straits Settlements Nyonya did not practise this form of needlework. As with weaving on a loom, where it is possible to have a continuous warp by rolling or shifting the position of the warp after the weft threads have been woven in, the long fabric of the strip belt worked on an embroidery frame could be moved. Generally though, the strip belt was made in two sections of equal length, instead of as one continuous piece.

There were many types of purses because the Nyonya preferred the purse to the pouch. A typical Nyonya purse had a loop which slipped through a belt. The loop was a rectangular band forming an extension of the purse proper. The purse itself was actually pouch-shaped, but it had no gathers. It often had a scalloped edge and it was closed with a front flap. Such belt purses might even have a silver gilt panel at the front. The usual backing material for these embroidered or beaded purses was either velvet or felt. As part of her trousseau, the bride would have embroidered a matching pair of such purses, the one for the groom being larger.

Another type of purse was made from a rectangular panel formed into an envelope shape. This purse, which also had a front flap, was a later development showing Western influence. All of these purses had to contain at least a token amount of money; empty purses have always been considered unlucky.

Also related to the envelope purse was the document holder in which the important marriage certificate was kept. This was presented by the groom's family to the bride's parents. Sumatran Nyonya made these 'letter-holders'. The narrow strap used to tie up the holder was sewn at the tip of the flap of the envelope. The Straits Chinese wrapped their marriage contracts Chinese style in a large square of red or pink silk.

The Nyonya also made other items similar in construction to the flat document holder, which basically consisted of two panels sewn together. These included imaginative articles like spectacle cases which are not too different from modern ones. Decorative beaded items were produced in the form of rectangular panels or circular pieces, some of which were finished off with tassels. The rectangular mats were meant to be displayed on blackwood or rosewood Chinese side tables. They were only used on special celebration days. Circular covers were used on the lids of jars which contained sweets or other delicacies: they had a hole in the centre to slip the knob of the jar through.

A special type of beadwork was done for the traditional wedding mirror cover. It was a rectangular panel composed of three sections. The narrow rectangular piece at the top was sometimes beaded, the central portion was always beaded, and to finish it off there were long tassels strung with beads. The central panel of the cover inevitably featured auspicious symbols of fertility appropriate for a bridal chamber. Personal mirrors which are often small and hand-held have covers of beaded embroidery.

Very long bed-runners or mattress panels, and fringes for the other draperies were laboriously crafted in beads to decorate the wedding bed. Some of these strips, which were about two metres long, combined silk thread, metallic thread and beads, but the finest ones were done solely in minute beads. Penang Nyonya who excelled in beadwork created three-dimensional forms as well. The panels, stiffened with backing, were bent, curved, joined and composed into imaginative forms. Some of the items produced included vases to hold tinsel flowers, and multipurpose receptacles. In addition, all sorts of three-dimensional objects were encased in beaded covers.

Costumes and accessories

Cosmetics

Be it for vanity, modesty or just basic hygiene, people not only dress up the body but also the face. In the past the face powder applied by Nyonya, both young and old, was home-made rice powder. To make this cosmetic, rice was soaked till it was about to disintegrate, then it was strained and dried into a crumbly cake. It was ready for use after being scented with jasmine flowers and shredded *pandanus* leaves. The rationale for wearing this rice powder was that it had a cooling effect. Later, commercially manufactured, scented face powder came in compact blocks packaged in pictorial cardboard boxes. It was imported from Java.

Chinese styles of clothing

Many different types of clothing were worn by the Straits Chinese. The choice of style often depended not only on the job of the wearer, but also on his or her social status within the group. The *Sinkhek* labourer wore short baggy trousers secured round the waist with a piece of string. If he was not actually bare footed, he wore only straw sandals. His hair was tied in a queue. A *Sinkhek* in a less menial occupation often discarded his pigtail and wore a blue cotton jacket and trousers. The wealthier Chinese wore an outer robe, thick-soled shoes and a skullcap or conical hat. Beneath the robe were long baggy trousers and a loose-fitting shirt. The wearer also sported a queue.

Curiously enough, the anglicized Baba men retained the queue, although in China it was imposed on the ethnic Chinese by the ruling Manchu Qing Dynasty. Perhaps the Babas thought it was a Chinese tradition, a status symbol, or the fashion in China, not realizing its political significance. The *Sinkhek* seemed to be more aware of this, as some of them soon discarded the pigtail.

Female Chinese domestic help wore the *samfoo*, a blouse-and-trousers combination, and later immigrant Chinese women also wore Chinese costumes, the typical ensemble being a long blouse with full-length wide sleeves, worn with a long A-line skirt.

The Baba wedding costume copied both Ming and Manchu styles (see chapter 2, The Traditional Baba Wedding). The bride always clasped her hands to show the wide, heavily embroidered sleeves of the Ming Dynasty jacket to advantage. An elaborate caped collar with overlapping layers of material rested on her shoulders. To complete the outfit, she wore a pleated skirt. While the Penang bride wore a Chinese-style headdress with colourful pompoms, her Malaccan counterpart had a glittering crown of floral pins inserted into her large chignon.

The groom was clad in a Manchu-style three-quarter length embroidered tunic over an ankle-length gown. He wore either a skullcap or a conical hat and soft cloth shoes. The wealthy Baba groom wore a silver belt with an ornate silver gilt or even gold buckle under his gown. He also wore leggings around which contoured knee pads were tied with thin ribbons. The pads were made and ornamented for him by his bride. A special undergarment known as the ventilation vest was worn by both the groom and the bride. It was made of small bamboo tubes held together with cotton string, and was worn between the lavishly embroidered wedding gowns and the plain white cotton or silk pyjamas used in the initiation ceremony on the eve of the wedding. Small wedding purses designed for the belt to loop through were worn by both bride and groom.

The *sarung kebaya* ensemble.
Early *kebaya* had lace borders.
(Courtesy Lily Khoo)

The page boy was dressed in traditional mandarin style, with an embroidered outer jacket over a long silk gown. A black skullcap, leggings, white socks and cloth shoes completed his outfit.

Malay styles

Only the Babas, and not the *Sinkhek*, wore the *kain pelekat* as casual home attire. This cotton sarong in a checked pattern of muted tones is still worn by some Baba men. The *pelekat* is a type of Indian cloth (from Pulicat on the Coromandel coast) that is about two metres long and 1.2 metres wide. The ends are stitched to form the sarong commonly worn by Malay men, Baba men and even the early English planters. This type of cloth is, however, also worn by some women in Medan and Penang, mostly those of the older generation. Nowadays, we know *kain pelekat* as a woven material, but the patterns on early pieces produced in Pulicat were resist-dyed, as in the batik technique. *Kain pelekat* for the Southeast Asian markes are woven with a central panel in the pattern and a border, a characteristic of the Malay sarong. Cheaper varieties of the *kain pelekat* now include those made on power looms with partly synthetic yarn.

The Nyonya wore Malay costume, so their basic attire was the sarong worn with various styles of blouses as a two-piece ensemble. The combination was of two main types.

The *baju panjang*, (Malay for 'long dress') was the original traditional costume; it consists of a long tunic worn over a sarong. Cartwright (1907:731) observed that '*towkays*' wives, called Nyonya, wore a neat-fitting garment of some bright hue that envelops them from neck to foot'. The dress, traceable to the Javanese, was the Nyonya's attire in the late nineteenth and early twentieth centuries. It was worn by the older generation of Nyonya.

The long-sleeved tunic was usually starched and stood stiff like a tent. The ends of the sleeves were tapered, partly to facilitate eating with the fingers, but also to show off any bangles which were worn. The tunic, fastened with brooches called *kerongsang* in Malay, was worn with a colourful sarong imported from Pekalongan, a textile manufacturing town on the north coast of Java. A formal ensemble included 'frog slippers'.

Many types of material were used to make the *baju panjang*, changing with the fashion of the time. The early tunics were made of cotton gingham in a small check called *chooi mua see* (in Hokkien) which was in vogue from the 1900s. It came in sombre browns or reddish browns. The Malays called the material *Bugis* cloth. The fine checks in earth colours were characteristic of cotton produced in the Indonesian island of Sulawesi (Celebes) whose inhabitants, called *Bugis*, are great mariners. There was also *Bugis* silk in the same fine check.

Around the 1910s, organdie with white thread embroidery was fashionable. Floral sprays within a diamond shape made a popular pattern. There were also some with wavy vertical rows of flowers, leafy stems and tendrils with birds, butterflies and bees. The locals called it 'lace cloth' in Hokkien.

German organdie in colourful prints, called 'German cloth' or 'stiff fibre' by the Hokkiens, superseded the lace cloth in the 1920s. Sometimes its floral designs were superimposed on a background of white horizontal or vertical lines. Organdie is an almost transparent fabric so when it was used for the *baju panjang*, an inner vest was

The earliest type of *baju panjang*, made of Bugis cotton with a fine check design. (Collection Dr. Khoo Joo Ee, photo H. Lin Ho)

needed. This took the form of a long-sleeved white cotton blouse with stand-up mandarin collar. The stiff organdie long dress, or rather tunic, was donned when entertaining guests or venturing out of the house. At home, at leisure, the Nyonya wore only this inner blouse with the sarong. The blouse was only hip length and was simply called a 'short dress' in Hokkien. This short, jacket-like garment was fastened with removable stud-like buttons. Originally, two of these buttons were placed on the high mandarin collar; five further buttons down the front were linked with a fine chain.

The V-shaped neckline of the *baju panjang* revealed the inner blouse and its high collar. It appears from old photographs that when the Nyonya of around the turn of the century wore the *baju panjang*, there was no inner blouse; it would not have been needed as the *Bugis* cloth was not transparent like organdie.

A formal and ceremonial *baju panjang* is only complete with a large square batik handkerchief, called the *saputangan* or *setangan* in Malay. This is folded into a triangle and pinned across the right shoulder with a special type of brooch that is often shaped like a crab from which emanate tiny keys.

The Nyonya wore this *baju panjang* ensemble during the less formal days of the wedding celebrations. On the twelfth day she wore a much more lavish *baju panjang* of Chinese damask referred to as the 'hidden flower pattern' which may even have been trimmed with gold thread. The accompanying sarong was often of a special cloth with a woven pattern in gold threads, which is a Malay handicraft known as *songket*.

Perhaps the colourful transparent organdie material of the *baju panjang* was the first step in modernizing the dress of the staid Nyonya. Following this, the effects of the 'roaring twenties' were felt even in Southeast Asia, where the Nyonya women adopted a relatively new and more daring type of blouse known as the *kebaya*. This style became firmly established as the successor of the *baju panjang* and is still popular as present-day traditional dress.

By the end of the 1920s, the Nyonya started wearing a much shorter *kebaya* that ended around the hips, and was made of embroidered sheer fabric and worn over a cotton camisole, which was embroidered along the top edge. The body-hugging *kebaya* was secured in front by *kerongsang*, or brooches, which usually came in a set of three, joined by a chain. The skirt worn with the *kebaya* was still the sarong. This style of dress, also called *baju Nyonya*, or dress of the Nyonya, became the new style of daily wear. The modern fitted sarong, which often has sewn pleats or even a slit at the front, is its descendant.

The word *kebaya* is believed to be derived from the Arabic *habaya*, which means a long tunic with an opening down the front. The earliest Nyonya *kebaya* was not embroidered but edged with broad lace. Lacework suggests Portuguese or Dutch influence. The Portuguese *kobaya* was a lace blouse. That the Portuguese word *kobaya* is from the Arabic word *habaya* is highly probable, considering the historical background of the Muslim Moors who occupied the Iberian lands in former times. It is plausible that *habaya* and *kobaya* influences were absorbed independently by the Malays and *Peranakan* respectively. The *kebayas* of Malay ladies have always been longer and even the earlier ones did not have lace borders; they were thus more like the Arabic *habaya*. However both Malay and Nyonya *kebaya* are basically the same in design although they are made from different materials: the cut-work embroidery of the Nyonya version is distinctive. A Malay *kebaya* is usually made of cotton or silk while a Nyonya *kebaya* is of embroidered sheer fabric, as we have seen. Traditionally the Malay *kebaya* is knee-length, again making it more like the Arabic *habaya*. However, some Malay women also wear a short hip-length *kebaya* like the Nyonya one.

Not to be confused with the type of *kebaya* worn by the Nyonya of the Malay Peninsula, is the *baju Bandung* named after the town of Bandung on the island of Java. It has an inserted piece at the front, separating the lapels. This type of blouse is sometimes worn by the *Peranakan* ladies of Java but not by the Straits Nyonya. Normally the *baju Bandung* is not embroidered.

The characteristic hip-hugging skirt which the Nyonya wears with her *kebaya* is called *batik Cina* ('Chinese batik'). This was in the form of hand-drawn batik sarong lengths from the north coast of Java. As with Malay sarongs, there is a vertical panel called the *kepala* ('head') which is usually more elaborate in pattern than the rest of the material. The larger portion, called the *badan*, ('body'), takes up about two-thirds of the sarong length. The pattern of the *kepala* is worked into the design of the skirt.

Batik, a popular Southeast Asian handicraft is made of plain white cloth which is dyed in stages using wax to form a colour-resisting pattern. A compound of beeswax, beef fat and resins is melted and applied with a spouted instrument, called the *canting* (*tjanting*) in Javanese.

The Chinese *Peranakan* of Java developed a special style of batik for their own use

Two Penang Nyonyas with Burmese-style coiffure, wearing *baju panjang* with organdie prints. (Courtesy Dr. Khoo Joo Ee)

A Malacca Nyonya with 'bobbed' hair and handcrafted bead slippers. (Courtesy Amy Hamidon)

and for trade. The town of Pekalongan on the north coast of Java, known as Pasisir, is at the heart of the area's batik industry. Its entrepreneurs have been the most enterprising and progressive in Java. Batik factories, some employing hundreds of workers, catered for local tastes and the export market. Exports reached the Malay Peninsula, Thailand, Burma, South India and South China. Within Indonesia, Pasisir cloth was also sold in the eastern islands, Borneo and Sumatra.

The heyday of Pasisir batik was from the late nineteenth century till the Second World War.

Pasisir batik was significantly different from that of central Java; the former was colourful even before the advent of chemical dyes which produce brighter colours than those from plants. The strong colours gave way to those of pastel chemical dyes in the 1930s, when these shades were more popular. Besides pioneering chemical dyes, Pekalongan was also the first to use the block stamp. When this technique is used the whole process of batik-making is faster, but good Pekalongan batik was still laboriously hand-drawn, not block stamped. A good Pekalongan sarong length has narrow decorative edges and the *kepala* itself is also often bordered. Hand-drawn Pekalongan cloth was the first to be signed by the designers.

Chinese and European influences pervade this 'Chinese batik style'. Arabesques of creeping floral scrolls, or spiralling and meandering stalks with leaves and flowers, are standard patterns on the materials. There are some other recurring motifs, such as the bouquet, called *bukitan*, and pairs of lovebirds, which were introduced by the Europeans in Pasisir and were fashionable in the 1920s and 1930s. Stalks of flowers have butterflies, insects and birds surrounding them. This type of pattern is also seen in Chinese silk embroidery.

In addition to stalks of plants, the background can be filled with rice-grain or cobweb motifs. The number of colours used and the laborious patterning make such cloths real works of art, with a baroque effect that we see in some other crafts. *Batik Hokukai* developed from *batik Cina*. Both types were popular with the *Peranakan* communities of Pasisir, and Palembang and Medan in Sumatra, and in the Straits Settlements, but *Hokukai* batik was commissioned by the Japanese during their occupation of Southeast Asia from 1942 to 1945. The floral decoration is like millefiori: of all Pekalongan batik, *Hokukai* is the most elaborate. The design is almost always the *pagi-sore*, 'morning-evening', when it is an unsewn rectangular *kain panjang*, or long cloth. Two different patterns divide the long cloth in half and it can be folded in use

RIGHT: German organdie long dress with an added bodice lining. The diaper design, here embroidered with white thread, was a favourite.

FAR RIGHT: Later, colourful organdie prints became more popular than embroidered ones. (Collection Dr. Khoo Joo Ee, photos H. Lin Ho)

so as to reveal either pattern; a single sarong thus serves as two different ones. The sewn sarong had an additional strip of patchwork design in the central *kepala* panel. During the Japanese Occupation some Nyonya sold their precious Javanese batik, just as they did their jewellery, to buy food.

Prada, (Javanese for 'gilding'), is gilded cloth. When batik has been enhanced with gold leaf, it is usually used for ceremonial purposes. Even in seventeenth-century Java, *prada* cloth was prestigious and only the upper class wore it. The earliest type had gold streaks; later materials were floral. In central Javanese courts, *prada* garments were sacred and used only for the most auspicious events such as special court ceremonies, court dances and marriages. In Bali, statues of the gods are still clothed in silk *prada*, especially during temple festivals. For the Chinese on the north coast of

LEFT: Kebaya with embroidered front lapels.

BELOW: A kebaya of sheer robia material with cut-work embroidery. (Collection Dr. Khoo Joo Ee, photos H. Lin Ho)

213

The organdie was further starched to a high degree of stiffness. (Courtesy SCPA)

Java, a *prada* is a wedding gift. In the Peninsula, such lengths of gilded cloth are called *kain telipuk*.

Usually only the finest hand-drawn batik was chosen to be decorated with gold leaf. Such a piece would take anything from six months to a year to finish, with the gold leaf applied as the last step. On the north coast, gold dust was mixed with linseed oil and resin to ensure that it would adhere firmly to the cloth. In central Java, much the same method was used, except that albumen from egg white was the bonding agent mixed with the gold.

The *Peranakan* of Pasisir use batik in many more ways than those of the Malay Peninsula. On the whole, the Nyonya of the Peninsula have always worn the sarong. The Javanese of the interior tend to wear wrap-around long skirts whose ends are not sewn, known as *kain panjang*. However, the people of the north coast prefer the sewn-up sarong. In the Peninsula, a narrower and shorter unsewn length is called *kain lepas*, or unfettered cloth, and is worn by Malay women as a scarf, or *selendang*.

Western attire

For many Baba men, Western-style attire was the norm before the end of the nineteenth century, although those of earlier generations dressed in loose jackets and trousers. The first Western-influenced Babas wore European shoes, even patent leather ones, and straw hats. Old portraits show some of these men wearing waistcoats with brass buttons while others sport bow ties. Christian converts were likely to take to Western attire for different reasons from the affluent businessman who socialized with colonial officers and European entrepreneurs. The standard outfit for a male office worker was a white cotton shirt and trousers.

Although Western dress was not usual among the Nyonya, occasionally women of affluent families wore it as a sign of social status. The daughter of a wealthy Baba entertaining European guests with an after-dinner music recital was likely to be dressed in a Western gown rather than a sarong and blouse. However, Christian converts, whether Nyonya or later immigrant women, tended to wear Western clothes from the 1930s onwards.

The chignon

The Nyonya grew her hair to hip length before the days of bobs and permanent waves. She was almost always seen with her hair pinned up in variations of the chignon; only a deranged woman wore her hair loose in public. Hairdressing was such a long, drawn-out affair that the Nyonya only let her hair down at night when she went to bed. If she lay down for a nap during the day, she used a small, hard wooden or ceramic block to support her neck and save her hair-do.

The chignon of the Nyonya is a cross between the Burmese and Javanese hairstyles. The position of the bun on top of the head, and not behind the head, as the Malay style, and its decoration with a string of white flowers, is reminiscent of Burmese traditional coiffure. The Nyonya's hairstyle was also similar to that of Victorian ladies because of its broad flat shape. The styling of the hair around the brow, however, distinguished the Nyonya's chignon from that of her Victorian counterpart.

Daily hair care was a tedious affair. After the hair near the scalp was conditioned with wood resin, the long hair was combed into a tail. The top front section was pulled straight back while the hair on both sides was released slightly so that it curved at the

ABOVE LEFT: The 'bob'. (Courtesy Mrs. Ong Chong Keng)

ABOVE: A Penang Nyonya in western dress. (Courtesy Dr. Khoo Joo Ee)

temples. The tail was further released near the nape of the neck to create a slight protrusion, and coiled on top of the head. The protrusion near the nape resembled an aeroplane's tail. The curves flanking the temple looked like the wings, and this style was dubbed 'aeroplane chignon' or, more picturesquely, 'the swallow's nest with a tail'.

Theoretically, one giant hair pin inserted right across the axis of the circular bun was enough to hold the hair in place. To decorate the coiffure, however, the Malacca Nyonya usually wore a set of three to five hairpins while the Penang Nyonya wore five or more. The hairpins were graduated in length; the longest measured about 12 cm and was the first to be inserted, right in the centre directly above the nose. The next longest was inserted about 2.5 cm to the right, and so on. These hairpins were made of silver or of a gold and copper alloy, *suasa*; some were even studded with pearls and diamonds. They were unlike the pins used in China and generally different from those used by Malay women. Older women wore only one hairpin, while young girls wore at least three; the latter had more hair to hold in place and their hairstyles were more elaborate than those of their seniors. Younger Nyonya would begin by wearing at least three pins, while mature Nyonya might wear as many as nine. Such hairpins developed from chopstick-like wooden implements, to copper sticks resembling earbuds, and to crafted ornaments of silver and gold. A Nyonya might also use a comb in her hair, but not several small combs like her Malay counterparts. A different type of hairpin had flowers of metal foil fixed to it with a spring; the flowers vibrated

ABOVE: Member of the Penang smart set, dressed up in western style.
ABOVE RIGHT: The 'aeroplane' chignon. (Photos courtesy Asia House, Hong Kong)

OPPOSITE PAGE: A *batik cina*, made in a Chinese workshop in Pekalongan, north Java. Such sarongs were exported on a large scale to Singapore and the peninsula. (Collection Dr. Khoo Joo Ee, photo H. Lin Ho)

gently whenever the wearer moved her head.

Because the Nyonya combed her hair and pulled it into a tight knot on her head every day, her hairline receded quickly. Older Nyonya women used various methods to colour bald patches. The most popular was a piece of roasted candlenut or chestnut. On her dressing table she usually had a hairpiece in the form of a pony tail which she used to give her chignon the extra bulk it needed.

A garland of jasmine buds usually surrounded the Nyonya chignon. Young Nyonya had their tiara of buds interspersed with other small coloured flowers. The garland was strung in double or triple rows using parallel threads and needles so that the finished piece was broad enough to encircle and cover the sides of the high bun.

Younger Nyonya girls often wore two small buns, one on either side of the head. This was dubbed the 'telephone' style; the two buns were coiled from plaits and encircled by garlands of jasmine buds or some other small fragrant flowers. The front of the girls' hair was usually cut in a fringe. During the 1930s, young Nyonya 'bobbed' their hair and the permanent wave came into fashion.

ABOVE: A Singapore Nyonya with
her hair done in the everyday
style, without frills. The hairpins
used are of a plain 'earbud'
design, placed at right angles to
hold the flat bun. (Courtesy Ong
Siong Ngo)

RIGHT: Older generation Nyonya
used a hair comb. (Collection
Muzium Negara, Kuala Lumpur,
photo The Pepin Press)

Nyonya jewellery

Straits Chinese women believed in the conspicuous display of opulence, adorning themselves with jewellery — the more the better. Cartwright (1907:731) remarked that the Nyonya was 'resplendent in jewellery'. For daily wear the Nyonya would adorn her hair, ears, neck, chest, waist, arms, fingers and ankles. On festive occasions, she was bedecked from head to toe like a Christmas tree, with a glittering array of southern Chinese, Malay and European jewellery of gold, silver and precious stones.

During a wedding ceremony in bygone times, the bride's jewellery, along with luxurious fabrics and items of gold and silver, were actually laid out on dowry trays and displayed for the inspection of guests and onlookers. Some of the jewellery boxes used were shallow lacquer containers with decorative lids. The bride herself wore the biggest and heaviest piece of jewellery: a wonderfully elaborate wedding head-dress.

The older Nyonya often engaged Singhalese goldsmiths. originally from Sri Lanka, reputed to be the best in the business, to fashion the elaborate sets of jewellery required for their daughters' weddings. It was common practice for the goldsmiths to be summoned to the house in order to produce the commissioned jewellery under the Nyonya's strict supervision. Though the work could take several days, the shrewd matriarch would watch the whole procedure like a hawk.

Professional jewellers sometimes had their own jewellery collections for rental. Some of them hired out such sets to traditional Baba mistresses of ceremonies. The reputation and popularity of a mistress of ceremonies often depended on the quality and variety of her jewellery. Another source was the roving haberdasher who sold silver jewellery.

For the manufacture of Nyonya gold jewellery, the 20/21 carat gold which the Nyonya call *kim toon* was preferred. This was hard, yet malleable enough for decoration. Another favoured substance was the reddish gold alloy which the Malays call *suasa,* which gets its reddish colour from the copper content: this is nine carat gold; *suasa* is not to be confused with gold which is chemically stained bright red, orange or brownish red. Some of the Malay-type jewellery used by the Nyonya was made in a combination of metals. Both the Thais and the Malays of the northeastern states of the Peninsula believe in using three metals, namely gold, silver and copper, especially in protective amulets. Chinese goldsmiths were organized in guilds, and the jewellery

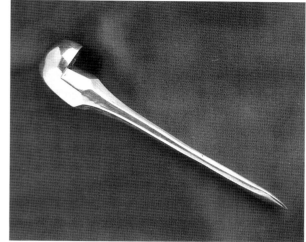

ABOVE: Some hairpins were enormous. Length 13.8 cm. (Courtesy Azah Aziz, photo H. Lin Ho)
LEFT: Children often wore long chains with a pendant. This double-sided gold pendant has Indian and Buddhist influences, indicated by the pair of peacocks and the lotus bloom. (Collection Dr. Khoo Joo Ee, photo H. Lin Ho)

crafted by them was hallmarked or stamped with the place or year of manufacture. In contrast, Straits Chinese silver bore no such marks and did not therefore reveal the purity of the metal. A reason for this could be that the silver used was often adulterated with nickel.

For the manufacture of both gold and silver Nyonya jewellery, the three most common decorative techniques used were repoussé, granulation and filigree. Repoussé is the technique of embossing the pattern in relief on to a thin sheet of metal by hammering out the design from the back; the metal sheet is held down on a bed of pitch or resin. The punching and grooving is done with a blunt-nosed tool, thus moving the metal without cutting or scraping it. Granulation, an ancient European (Etruscan) technique, is very time-consuming and laborious. To produce gold granules, averaging 1.5 mm in size is difficult enough; the tiny grains of molten metal have to be evenly hammered with a flat-tipped puncher to create a faceted effect. The granules are then fixed to an item of jewellery, and it is important that they are not discoloured by the solder or displaced during the process. A paste containing some form of copper salt is used to

OPPOSITE PAGE: A pair of convert-
ible earrings; the lower circular
portion is detachable and can be
worn as an earstud. Rose diamonds set in *suasa*, an alloy of
gold and copper. (Collection Dr.
Khoo Joo Ee, photo H. Lin Ho)

BELOW: Jewelley was the
Nyonya's social security, as she
had no professional earning
power. The standard ensemble
of jewellery must be seen on
formal portraits, such as this
one. Here, many of the jewels
were not worn when the picture
was taken, but painted in later.
(Courtesy Lily Khoo)

BELOW RIGHT: Early twentieth
century hand-coloured picture
of a Penang Nyonya, bedecked
with typical Straits Chinese jewellery. (Courtesy Prof. Dr. Cheah
Jin Seng)

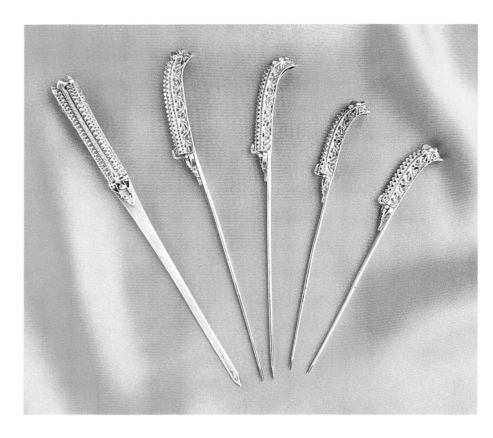

solder the granules. When copper and gold are mixed in the right proportions the alloy melts at a lower temperature (890° C) than the melting points of the two components. A tiny amount of copper is found as an impurity in ancient gold with granulation. This is the ever-so-thin layer of gold-copper alloy at the bottom of the granule. Filigree is a type of extremely delicate and decorative work in which the gold or silver is pulled into thin wires.

Diamonds were the most popular precious stones used for Nyonya jewellery. The best and most brilliant diamonds are called *berlian* in Malay; old cut diamonds glitter less than modern ones only because there are fewer facets to refract light. The parts of the diamond stone which are normally cut off are of lower quality; these so-called 'rose diamonds' known as *intan, batu Seylan* or *batu Yaacob* by the Malays and *suan phuay* (literally diamond crust or skin) by the Nyonya, were flat, and irregularly shaped. Because of this they had to be set in a box-setting without claws. Occasionally even less sparkling rough-cut industrial diamonds were used in some *keronsang* (brooches). Sometimes faceted gold pieces were used in a setting instead of gemstones.

Two types of gemstone setting, the box-setting and the open-back setting, lend themselves to the type of stones used in Nyonya jewellery. The box-setting is fashioned as follows: first a bezel (the metal frame that holds the stone) is formed from a separate strip, and then it is soldered onto the piece of jewellery. Gemstones with few flaws are set *à jour* to display them to full advantage. This is the open-back setting which allows light through the stone to maximize the effect of colour. However, with the exception of jade, the Nyonya did not take to coloured stones.

The Nyonya's fondness for gold jewellery was set aside during any period of mourning because this restricted the mourner's dress to a few sombre colours. The initial period of mourning was strictest, and the only jewellery permissible was pearls, because they connote tears. Pearls were usually set in silver and worn with silver accessories. This was followed by the 'blue period', during which the Nyonya could only wear clothes in shades of blue accompanied by blue glass costume jewellery. Lastly, during the 'green period' Nyonya women were supposed to wear jade jewellery, or soft greenstone or soapstone set in silver.

The Straits Chinese inherited their ancestors' feelings about animals and flowers having symbolic meanings, and the designs and motifs on Nyonya jewellery are a good example of this. A favourite design was the auspicious pair of the male dragon and female phoenix. The Chinese unicorn, *qilin*, was often worn as a symbol of wisdom, justice, success and overall good fortune. Also seen on jewellery was the butterfly, which signified wedded bliss, and the peony, which was predominantly a symbol of prosperity. The jewellery tended to be decorated in a baroque style, often mixing various motifs with little regard to unity of theme or style. Flowers of the four seasons could bloom side by side with emblems of the Taoist immortals and of scholarly accomplishments. Jewellerymaking was more a display of technique and ornamention than of design concepts. Very often pieces of jewellery were very fussy and included much filigree work, in keeping with late Qing styles.

Without exception, all Nyonya had their ears pierced so that they could wear dangling earrings which were too heavy to be borne by clips alone. On her wedding day the Nyonya would have diamonds cascading from ear lobe to shoulder. Some of the ear studs used by older Nyonya had formidably large stems, and their heavy earrings

A necklace and pendant, worked in the 'Malay arabesque' style of curlicules. The recurring three-pointed motif is often, erroneously, identifed as a pomegranate; it is, in fact, a tulip, which Singhalese goldsmiths copied from the Dutch and Portuguese. (Photo H. Lin Ho)

tended to produce enlarged holes in the lobes. At one time 'ear-clips' were fashionable; these clip-on earrings sometimes also had a pin for pierced ears. Those of the Indo-European paisley design accorded well with the shape of the ear.

The Nyonya usually wore gold necklaces of various lengths and thicknesses. For formal wear they were more like chokers, gold collars, or even bibs. Amulets, often in the form of a cylindrical locket, were worn, especially by the very young Nyonya, although Baba boys occasionally wore them too. The cylinder contained a rolled-up piece of paper with characters inscribed on it, which was sanctified by a temple priest. Other forms of amulet were sometimes worn by both sexes: if a child was sickly or seemed to be harassed by misfortunes, he or she might wear a 'blessed' amulet. A particularly potent protective amulet, which was also imbued with sympathetic magic, was one in the form of a fish-dragon. This recalls the carp leaping the dragon gates (see Architecture). Part of the amulet was a tiger's claw, which represented the protective aspect. (In rural China children wore bibs or cape-collars in the form of a tiger.) An especially timid and reticent child would need not only the protection of the strong fierce tiger, but also the spirit of the leaping carp to get through life and succeed.

To secure a jacket or blouse, two types of *kerongsang* (brooch) were used. The first was a set of three brooches, almost always circular, used for the *baju panjang*. The more elaborate designs usually featured a peach or heart-shaped *kerongsang ibu* (mother brooch) and two *kerongsang anak* (baby brooches). When the main brooch was very big and heavy, it was sewn onto the *baju panjang* when worn. Another design for such brooches had the main piece in the shape of a finger citrus (Citrus medica, which is shaped like fingers and also known as Buddha's hand) and the subsidiary ones as stylized pomegranates. The brooch for the long dress had no catch at the back; a front-fastening pin held it in place. The dress was pulled through the brooch and the pin passed through it leaving the point of the pin visible.

The second type of *kerongsang*, also consisting of three brooches, was worn with the modern Nyonya blouse or *kebaya*. The shapes were elongated rather than rounded and the individual brooches were joined together by ornamental chains to form a *kerongsang rantai* (chained brooch).

Cotton blouses had metal studbuttons. The stems of these flared out into a disc worn inside the blouse. The front of the stud, sometimes in the shape of a rosette, would be set with diamonds or glass. Later buttons were made from gold coins. A loop was soldered perpendicularly to the back of the coin and a split ring was passed through the loop to hold the button in place.

A typical belt was a flexible band composed of a network of several hundred interlocking silver rings or links, with a hook or hooks at the ends for attaching to the buckle. Alternatively, openwork pieces of a single design were joined by loops. The buckle itself was equipped with hooks. Still another form was silver wires twisted into thicker 'ropes' combined in parallel to the desired width. Such a belt fitted anyone.

Made in a somewhat similar style were the Victorian wire mesh purses which the Nyonya attached to the belt with a belt hook. (This could be used at other times to hang a bunch of keys on the belt.)

Traditionally, bangles and finger rings were always worn in pairs. Of the wide variety of bracelets and bangles, the inevitable charm bracelet was generally worn by children. Bangles were often designed like bamboo sections, or featured the ever popular

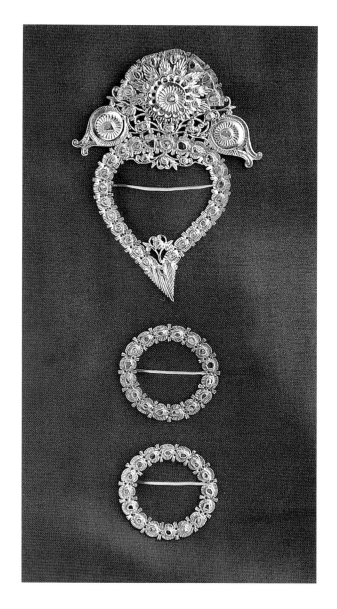

Kerongsang with rose-cut diamonds, called *intan*, set in *suasa*. The heart-shaped top piece is called *ibu* (Malay for mother), the two smaller ones *anak* (child). This variety was typical of Penang. (Photo H. Lin Ho)

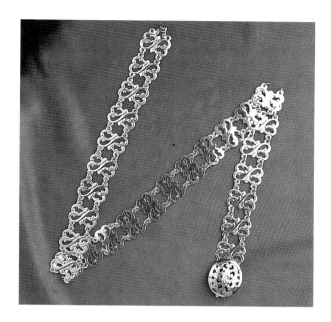

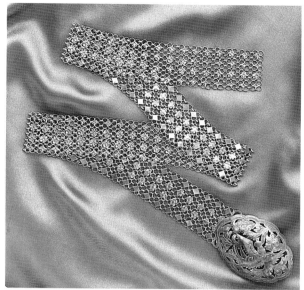

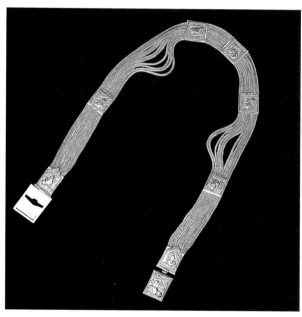

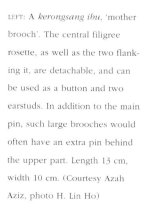

RIGHT: A silver belt hook. On the attached ring are a pair of bells, a finger or hand-shaped citrus fruit dubbed 'Buddha's hand', four small keys, a peach and a shell. (Courtesy David Chan)

OPPOSITE PAGE: A collection of silver belt hooks. (Courtesy David Chan)

RIGHT: A silver ogival-shaped buckle. In the centre is an image of the God of Prosperity on a horse. He is surrounded by the Eight Immortals. The outer register is decorated with zoomorphic creatures. 15 x 10 cm, 200 gm (Courtesy Prof. Dr. Cheah Jin Seng, photos H. Lin Ho)

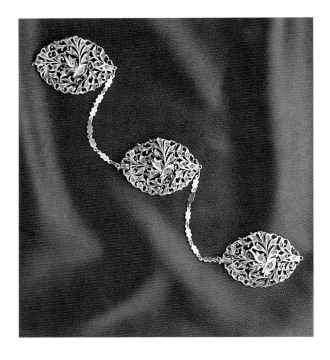

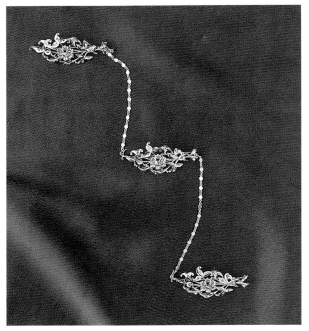

ABOVE: A set of *kerongsang* from Malacca, each is decorated with a stylized bird surrounded by foliage.

ABOVE RIGHT: A set of *kerongsang* for a *sarung kebaya* ensemble. Such *kerongsang* always consisted of three identical brooches, joined by a decorative chain. (Collection Dr. Khoo Joo Ee, photos H. Lin Ho)

OPPOSITE PAGE: A pair of gilt silver filigree dragon bangles. (Collection Dr. Khoo Joo Ee, photo H. Lin Ho)

BELOW: Two pairs of gold bangles showing popular zigzag designs; right, faceted globules and left, diamond shapes (*potong wajik* in Malay). (Photo H. Lin Ho)

dragon and phoenix. Some bangles composed of multiple strands twisted like ropes appear quite modern in design.

The bamboo design was also favoured for anklets, an item which distinguishes the Nyonya from her Chinese counterpart. Indian influence can be detected in the wearing of anklets and the fact that some of them featured peacocks instead of phoenixes. The anklets are hollow and made in two parts which are hinged. Usually, a Chinese hallmark was stamped between the hinges. The two parts were not always of equal length; some anklets were made in one-third and two-third parts which were joined. The anklet is secured by a screw which slots through two small loops protruding from each end. Some unusual anklets have amulet pieces attached, rather like charm bracelets. Older Nyonya wore anklets with their *baju panjang*, although during the transition between the *baju panjang* and the *kebaya*, the young Nyonya also still wore them. While silver and silver-plated anklets were commonly worn, gold ones were reserved for festive and auspicious occasions. Among the Malays, gold anklets were originally reserved for royalty.

A handkerchief ring with a large decorative handkerchief attached was part of the Nyonya's costume. She slipped the ring on a finger and swung the handkerchief as she walked. When she needed to use both her hands, she would slip the ring off and drape the handkerchief over her shoulder.

The import of machine-made gold jewellery at the beginning of the twentieth century led to the decline of the jewellery industry in the Malay Peninsula and Singapore. Some form of mechanization was also gradually introduced into the area, beginning around this time, so that local handcrafted jewellery from the modern period is not easily come by. Few original pieces of jewellery have survived the Second World War, when both gold and silver pieces were often stolen, sold or melted down. Lately, however, there has been a revival of interest in traditional designs for antique reproduction jewellery, from dangling earrings to quaint anklets.

LEFT: Two rings of a design popular among the Nyonya. On the left is a Burmese jade in the *potong wajik* cut. The type of ring on the right, with a cluster of diamonds set in a diamond shape, appears in practically all old pictures of mature Nyonyas and matriarchs. It is called *bujur kana*, which means oval shaped olive. Salted and glacéd olives are a common sweetmeat among both Malays and Straits Chinese. (Collection Dr. Khoo Joo Ee, photo H. Lin Ho)

RIGHT: A pair of anklets, showing Indian influence in their design. Instead of the usual phoenix, the terminals feature peacocks.
FAR RIGHT: Anklets in a bamboo design, with terminals in the form of lotus buds. These anklets consist of two pieces, joined by a hinge. The terminals are secured by screw clamps. (Collection Dr. Khoo Joo Ee, photos H. Lin Ho)

ABOVE: A silver purse, composed of small interlocking rings and prunus flower petals, held by a silver hook. 7.5 x 10 cm. (excluding hook). (Courtesy Prof. Dr. Cheah Jin Seng, photo H. Lin Ho)

Silver and other metalware

Silver, silver-plated, silver-gilt or gold-plated and other metal household artefacts are mostly wedding paraphernalia which were also used on other festive occasions. The best known of these items is the betel leaf set which comes in a variety and combination of materials (see also pages 66-70). While northern Baba-Nyonya are likely to have used sets of Thai manufacture, those in the South often possessed Indonesian ones. The two types from these neighbouring lands are both decorated with high relief repoussé work.

In a betel set, there are four containers, at least two of which are covered, and a pair of shears to slice the betel nut. The containers are of a size that is easily enclosed by the palm of the hand. The covered ones are for powdered gambier and a slaked lime preparation; the lime container has an inner bowl. To complete the set there is a miniature spatula for spreading the lime paste on the betel leaf. The container for the sliced betel may or may not be covered. The fourth lidless bowl is for shredded tobacco. Older Nyonya women claimed that chewing tobacco massaged the gums.

The hinge of the blades of Straits Chinese betel shears (unlike those from mainland Southeast Asia or India) is almost always of a bird or hobbyhorse design. The handles

of the shears are sometimes of solid silver but they may also be silver sheaths encasing an iron core.

The whole set is held on a tray, which is deep because it has to have high sides to keep the containers in place. The tray or basket holding the ingredients can be silver-gilt, or made of brass, cane or wood, which may be lacquered. Silver betel sets were reserved for festive or auspicious occasions. If the tray or box is made of wood, it usually has a drawer for storing the betel leaves built into its longer side. However, if the tray holding the containers is metal, it fits into a slightly larger tray, and the space between the two is used for storing betel leaves. Besides the betel leaves stored in these places, leaves for immediate use are placed in a flattish metal cone-shaped container which is almost always of open-work. The flaring portion of the cone holds the leaves, the cone standing on its apex which has been truncated to form a flat base. A mortar and pestle are not usually part of a betel set, unless it has been specially manufactured for the very elderly. The mortar, usually cylindrical, may have an outer layer of silver. The handle of the pestle may be similarly encased in silver, but the shaft is of iron and shaped like a screwdriver with a sharp cutting end so that the betel ingredients are actually shredded by its action in the cylindrical mortar.

Another common item in Straits Chinese homes was the enamelled metal 'tiffin carrier'. These food containers — consisting of a tier of receptacles — sometimes had greetings equivalent to *bon appetit* inscribed and gilded on the individual receptacles

Chinese export silver of the China Trade. (Courtesy Asia House, Hong Kong, photos Cheang Yik On)

which also had matching floral designs. Such items were probably commissioned, not from China but from Indonesia. Almost all available examples have wording in the older romanized Indonesian spelling. Considering the trade and family ties between the Straits Chinese and Indonesian Chinese *Peranakan,* it is not surprising to find evidence of the connection in artistic household handicrafts. In rural areas, Straits Chinese more assimilated with the Malay lifestyle possibly adopted the habit sometimes followed by Malays of communal eating from a large enamel tray.

A tea ceremony set, which is meant for serving a couple, consists of a tray to hold a pair of small round teapots, and a pair of teacups with accompanying covers, saucers and spoons. The traditional Chinese teacup is actually a bowl, i.e. it does not have a handle. The saucer holding the tea bowl may have a hole in the centre for the foot of the tea bowl to sit in. Alternatively the bowl and saucer may be manufactured as a single piece. Strictly speaking, one does not need a spoon for drinking tea. However, the tea served at a ceremony is almost always a sweet beverage of longan fruit or edible birds' nest, so that the spoon is needed to scoop up the solids.

A more intimate ceremony, usually occurring between men, is that of offering wine. Plum wine is generally drunk on such occasions. The wine ewer is normally of a slender, tall cylindrical form. The cup which accompanies the ewer may have a pair of handles.

Decorated handles were also a feature of the large hooks to hold up the net drapes of

LEFT: A silver *kamcheng*, with a pheasant in its principal panel. The shoulder of the jar carries bands of *ruyi* and *banji* motifs; the latter is echoed at the base of the body and on the protruding rim of the lid. The lid is topped by a peach knob. Height 8.3 cm, diameter 7.5 cm, 210 gm, Ta Hing shopmark. (Courtesy Tan Siok Choo, photo H. Lin Ho)

BELOW: A pair of 'tiffin carriers'. Southern Straits Chinese use the Malay term *tingkat* (steps, tiers), while in the north the Hokkien name *ua chan* is preferred. Height 19 cm, diameter 14.5 cm 1.5 kg each, Ta Hing shopmark. (Courtesy Dr. Chan Chin Cheung, photo H. Lin Ho)

LEFT: A silver wine ewer, part of a ceremonial set. The lobed ogival panel on the body features two phoenixes and a peony. Around the high neck are more ogival panels with Buddhist symbols. *Ruyi* lappets form a border register for the domed cover, which is topped by a lion. Height 16 cm, 600 gm, Ta Hing Shopmark. (Courtesy Tan Siok Choo, photo H. Lin Ho)

RIGHT: An ovoid silver *chepu*. The panels all feature phoenixes and peonies, and are set against a background of plaiting design. Height 15.2 cm, diameter 12 cm, 480 gm, Ta Hing shopmark. (Courtesy Prof. Dr. Cheah Jin Seng, photo H. Lin Ho)

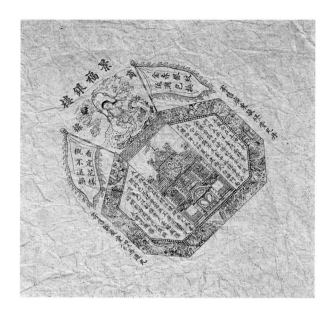

ABOVE: Wrapping paper bearing the label of Jin Fu silver and goldsmith shop in Shanghai. Many mainland Chinese smiths had agents in the Straits Settlements. (Courtesy Dr. Chan Chin Cheung, photo H. Lin Ho)

BELOW: A silver soap box. 12 x 9.3 cm, 300 gm, Ta Hing shopmark. (Courtesy Tan Siok Choo, photo H. Lin Ho)

one long side of a canopied bed. While some of these were of brass or even iron, the most elegant ones were of silver-gilt. The handle, normally the length of a hand's grasp, was often a flattish piece which lent itself to the repoussé type of ornamentation.

Another decorative item used around the wedding bed was the scent holder. Pairs of convex perforated silver pieces joined with links and clasps were used for containing some source of perfume, for example flower petals or shredded *pandanus* leaves. Several of these pouch-like containers were strung together with chains and hung from the canopy of the bridal bed. Pouches of later manufacture were sealed and no longer functioned as containers, thus becoming only decorative hangings.

Flat pieces of silver were used on the ends of pillows or bolsters. They had tiny holes around their edges so that they could be sewn on. The round, hexagonal or rectangular plates came in pairs and were patterned by embossing. Other plates, also with sewing holes but not of the above shapes, were used to face belt purses (see Embroidery).

The formal and ceremonial bridal handkerchief was also sometimes made from silver and its shape imitated that of cloth handkerchiefs. Even the scallops of lace-edged handkerchiefs were faithfully copied. The embroidered fabric version itself often had decorative silver tassels.

One of the customary gifts from the bride to the groom was a silver belt with an elaborate oval buckle. This was decorated with high relief designs and a multitude of auspicious motifs. Ceremonial chopsticks could be all metal, metal and wood, or a combination of silver and ebony. Sometimes a pair was linked by a chain at the upper end. Such chopsticks are used at the wedding couple's ceremonial first meal, or on offering altars.

Older generations of Babas sometimes used finger bowls when eating with their fingers. They were placed near each person and used to moisten the fingers before a meal or to rinse them at the end of it. Such bowls usually do not have a foot and are technically beakers. This form is common with Indian metalware. Large brass beakers usable as water dippers or basins are found in Nyonya kitchens. They are almost always of Indian manufacture. The Babas also used other Indian brassware, such as trays and vases.

All these items were almost always decorated by repoussé in the same fashion as Malay and Indonesian ware. Similar items were also used by Malays, but distinguishing Straits Chinese characteristics are to be seen in the general forms of pieces, in the quality of the metal, in the embossing or repoussé techniques themselves, and most obviously in the decorative motifs. Islamic constraints do not allow depiction of human or animal forms. Thus pieces for Malay clients had exclusively calligraphic or vegetal designs, while the Straits Chinese preferred symbolic decoration with many plant and animal forms. Modern Straits Chinese may choose less ornate and more restrained patterns.

Straits Chinese silver workmanship is akin to the Southeast Asian style. Most Straits Chinese silver has no assay marks; although shopmarks are sometimes seen. The Straits Chinese also used other gold, silver-gilt and silver household items made in south China. The main difference between articles made in south China and those manufactured in Southeast Asia is the technique. The former are usually chased, while the latter are almost always embossed or decorated with repoussé, although late Qing

works from China are also elaborately encrusted with heavy repoussé work.

In chased or traced work, the beaten metal sheet is decorated on the upper surface. The result is a low relief pattern, and because of this the bed of soft material on which the sheet is worked need only be wood or lead.

The silversmiths of Canton flourished as part of the important China Trade between China and Europe. Many of them were listed as jewellers, and as such were members of the Goldsmiths' Guild, which was second only in importance to the Bankers' Guild in the commercial life of Canton. A large proportion of these craftsmen were also carvers of ivory, mother-of-pearl and tortoiseshell, making items for the China Trade. The art of Chinese silversmithing, which first developed during the Tang Dynasty (AD 618-906), flowered again in the China Trade period which, in fact, may be considered the greatest period of achievement in the history of the Chinese silvermakers. (A direct result of the China Trade was the European adoption of Chinese decoration, termed *chinoiserie*, which reached its height in the eighteenth century. The trend started in England as early as the 1680s, some years before the English East India Company became established in Canton, but there was trade with China even before this.)

Silversmithing in Hong Kong is a continuation of the earlier Canton tradition. The well-known Hong Kong silversmith and jeweller Wang Hing, who was active in the last quarter of the nineteenth century and the first decades of the twentieth, never

ABOVE: A pair of silver *kamcheng*, with the phoenix in mirror image. Height 21.5 (including knob), diameter 20.5, 2 kg each, Ta Hing shopmark. (Courtesy Dr. Chan Chin Cheung, photo H. Lin Ho)

Eight-lobed, circular betel set, decorated with phoenixes, butterflies and peonies. The boxes and cups are similarly lobed and decorated. Diameter 24 cm, 1.3 kg, Ta Hing shopmark. (Courtesy Dr. Cheah Jin Seng, photo H. Lin Ho)

actually made any of the items that bear his mark. The Chinese characters on the punch merely indicate a shop. Some Straits Chinese pieces have similar shopmarks.

In China, silver was used throughout the Qing period but the items for the home market differed from those produced for Europe, and the silversmiths supplying the local market were not based in Canton.

Some wealthy Babas, besides using Straits Chinese and south Chinese silver for their own ceremonial use and when entertaining their Chinese business associates, also had special silver or gold-plated tea services and dishes for their Western guests. Such objects were not only a sign of wealth, but also of status.

Ceramics and glass

Crockery in a Straits Chinese kitchen used to be a mixture of Chinese and Japanese blue-and-white or brightly coloured pieces; some homes also used European ware. While the cheaper Chinese blue-and-white china was found in almost every household, the well-to-do families had European dinner services imported from Holland, England, Scotland, and later Germany.

The range of Chinese blue-and-white crockery used by the Babas has been given the group name of 'Kitchen Qing' (SEACS, 1981), and it formed part of China's ceramic trade (Khoo, J.E., 1991:13-18). Ming Dynasty blue-and-white ceramics have been found in almost every corner of the world, so much so that a 'Ming gap' (i.e. the absence of Ming ceramics) is conspicuous in any archaeological tabulation of Chinese export ceramics, since Ming made up the bulk of these exports. Blue-and-white crockery continued to be manufactured well into the Qing period. Kitchen Qing was considered to be rather rough-and-ready; dishes were churned out by the million then packed in tea leaves for their voyage to the Malay Archipelago, where the tea was trans-shipped to Europe. The ceramics which arrived thus, formed part of the Kitchen Qing collections of Straits Chinese homes.

Among the Straits Chinese, the blue-and-white ware was known as 'batik crockery'. Much of the elaborate decoration on ceramics is inspired by textile designs, and some of the earliest batik is monochrome indigo. The blue-and-white china was for daily use and together with European porcelain, it was about the only crockery available to supplement earthenware and metal utensils. Suggestions that the dishes, being blue-and-white, were used only in times of mourning are unfounded, although they would no doubt have been preferred to battered kitchen utensils of metal to contain food for ancestors placed on an altar. Kitchen Qing would also have been a natural choice for everyday use, since the Chinese generally prefer their food piping hot, and china is better for this purpose.

Blue-and-white china in the Nyonya kitchen ranged from very rough-and-ready dishes which were heavily potted and sketchily ornamented, to finer porcelain plates and bowls of which those with the sweet-pea motif were typical. This provincial southern

European ware, used by Straits Chinese in Penang. (Courtesy Penang Museum, photo Cheang Yik On)

Chinese crockery was mainly from the provinces of Guangdong and Fujian, particularly from the ports of Swatow (Shantou) and Amoy. Swatow is a trade name for a class of chinaware produced around Swatow; it is not a particular type of chinaware. The most common characteristic of the 'Kitchen Qing' china is grit on the bottom of the sturdy pieces. Designs were often drawn freehand. When the cobalt that was used in the colouring process was fired, it produced a range of hues from blues and purples to grey or even black.

A single fish painted in the well of a plate and surrounded by water weeds or eelgrass is common in Song ceramics. Such plates depicting fish have continued to be manufactured through the centuries to the present day, but an interesting point to note is that over the years the fish in its setting became simplified. On such plates in the nineteenth century, the fish is very big, filling up space on the surface, while its seaweed setting is almost non-existent; a few curving lines are supposed to evoke luxuriant seaweed and eelgrass.

Other common items are the rough, pitted, shallow bowls known as tin-miners' rice bowls. They have the double happiness character drawn among scrolling patterns. Such bowls have been found in sites as far afield as gold mines on America's Pacific coast.

There are also blue-and-white Dutch earthenware plates, which were decorated by stencil. The backs of the plates have the stamp 'Petrus Regout & Co., Maastricht'. Typical designs are the so-called sun-burst or chrysanthemum and the Sanskrit sacred syllable *om*. The chrysanthemum design is interspersed with scribbled calligraphy which has been interpreted as a degenerate form of the Arabic character for Allah. The *om* symbol, transferred into a Chinese character and stylized as a decorative design in Maastricht, has been dubbed the 'toothbrush motif'.

In a different class from the day-to-day crockery was a type of Chinese ceramics called 'Nyonyaware' (SEACS, 1981). The Nyonya themselves, however, call this colourful china 'Shanghai ware'. The association of Shanghai with things Chinese came about because the port of Shanghai was the leader in exporting fashionable *objets d'art* in the nineteenth century. Even the Shanghai tailors were considered to be superior, earning a good collective reputation in the same way that *amah che* servants had. The art goods exported from China were luxury items similar to those made for the European market in the eighteenth century and the *Bencharong* ceramics designed for the Thai court and nobility of the nineteenth century.

In the household of an extended Baba family, the crockery would include at least ten sets of Chinese tableware. There were also special sets for the tea ceremony at weddings. This essentially functional crockery was of the traditional Chinese designs. The coloured dishes were very varied but they were all decorated with the same kinds of pattern. Such imported ceramics also included vases and jars besides tableware and they were very often commissioned. They were decorated with motifs for happiness and good fortune because these pieces were meant for festive occasions. Two recurrent symbolic motifs are the phoenix and the peony, which take central place in the decorative design. The colourful enamel decorations on these ceramics are as elaborate and fanciful as the façades of shophouses and terrace houses. The colours used for these enamelled ceramics were pink, yellow, green, olive, brown and blue. Imperial yellow was very uncommon. Green was the most common background colour; in contrast to the earlier *famille verte* ceramics there is hardly any black,

LEFT: A *kamcheng* of coral red.
(Courtesy P.G. Lim, photo The
Pepin Press)

RIGHT: A *kamcheng* of deep blue
enamel, with an overglaze
design of birds, flowers and
scrolling tendrils. The cover is
topped by a standing *qilin*.
(Courtesy P.G. Lim, photo The
Pepin Press)

RIGHT BELOW: Three *kamcheng*,
each with a different design.
The ogival panel of the left jar
features a standing phoenix, on
the middle jar a phoenix in
flight, while on the right only
peonies decorate the jar.
(Courtesy Penang Museum,
photo Cheang Yik On)

Covered bowls decorated with phoenixes in flight and peonies on a white background, and an iron-red key-fret pattern on the rims. (Courtesy Penang Museum, photo Cheang Yik On)

because it is inappropriate for auspicious occasions. Less common than green are olive and brown, while blue is rare.

Nyonyaware items are now often seen as heirlooms; those of the *Tongzhi* period (1862-1874) are the oldest type, although there is the occasional *Daungkuang* forerunner. Most Nyonyaware was produced in the *Guangxu* period (1875-1909) and in the first decades of this century. The brightly coloured ceramics are like the late Qing enamelled porcelain of the *famille verte*, 'green family', *famille rose*, 'pink family' and *famille jaune*, 'yellow family' types.

The term *famille verte*, was coined by Jacquemart in the nineteenth century. Strictly speaking, it applies only to a variety of Qing dynasty translucent enamelled porcelain which has green as the predominant colour. Almost all Nyonyaware is of the opaque *famille rose* type. In China the pink shades ranging from light pink to crimson, which were originally pale and soft, were called 'foreign colours'. In about 1721 (towards the end of the Kangxi period, 1662-1722) a purplish rose colour, which had been invented by Andreas Cassius in Leiden, Holland around 1650, was introduced into China. The Dutch invention is linked to the Dutch East India Company, which traded in Chinese exports of ceramics and tea to Europe. The ceramic pigment known as 'The purple of Cassius' was used on Chinese export ceramics of later date than the older soft pink *famille rose* porcelain. Legeza (1972:lxxxi) pointed out that the exquisite, fresh, feminine delicacy of *famille rose* porcelain was spoilt by the demand from overseas for rich and garish decoration, finally degenerating into the murky salmon-pink of the early nineteenth century.

All literature on Nyonyaware claim that it was manufactured in the well-known ceramic producing town of Jingdezhen in Jiangxi province, yet no shards of Nyonyaware have been found there. The town was dominated by the imperial porcelain factory, which supplied chinaware to the court. In the neighbourhood of this great ceramics metropolis there were also many smaller kilns producing inferior porcelain for the West Asian and European markets. Apart from occasional imperial presents and looting upon the collapse of dynasties, Chinese fine porcelain had always remained in China. Even the lower grade porcelain exported to Persia and more inferior exports to Europe are, however, high grade porcelain compared with Nyonyaware, which is nowhere near the quality of porcelain manufactured in Jingdezhen. Porcelain which gives a sonorous ring when flicked lightly has to be fired to 1300-1400° C to acquire its hardness. Most Nyonyaware, which gives a dull thud when tapped, does not approach this quality.

The word porcelain is a European term to describe ceramic ware which has been fired at a high temperature, particularly the white and decorated white wares of Jingdezhen. Porcelain is hard, whitish, translucent and resonant. Marco Polo applied the term *porcellana* (derived from *porcelletta*, literally 'little pig' but also a name for cowrie shells) to describe the physical appearance of this particular ceramic material.

Jenyns (1971:83), in surveying south Chinese provincial kilns, stated that Dehua porcelain was also decorated in China in red or green enamel, to which yellow and purplish-red were sometimes added. This observation may indicate that Nyonyaware was manufactured in Dehua, 75 miles north of Amoy in Fujian province. Dehua is well

ABOVE: Nyonya ceramics of delicate palette, displaying a cross between *famille rose* and *kakiemon* styles. In the well of the plates, phoenixes sit perched on rocks, while Buddhist symbols line the rims. (Courtesy Penang museum, photo Cheang Yik On)

OVERLEAF LEFT: Plate decorated with a phoenix and a peony: the hallmark of Nyonyaware.
OVERLEAF RIGHT: Plate with a scallop rim; such plates were used for offerings. (Courtesy Baba Nyonya Heritage Museum, Malacca, photos H. Lin Ho)

ABOVE: Spoons and their matching rests, which can also be used as sauce dishes. Contrary to the widely accepted practice of using only chopsticks, food is actually supposed to be placed on a spoon and eaten from it.

OPPOSITE PAGE: Four-tiered ceramic food container, decorated with pheasants, peonies and prunus. The centre of the slightly domed lid features a carp in iron red and mauve. This piece is an example of Nyonyaware of Japanese manufacture. Height 31 cm, diameter 22 cm. (Courtesy Asia House, Hong Kong, photos Cheang Yik On)

known for its quality porcelain, but it usually produced only figurines. Its white porcelain is the original *blanc-de-chine* of the French, which displays a perfect marriage between the glaze and the body. While no Nyonyaware shards have surfaced from the southern provincial kilns, the nearest ceramic type to Nyonyaware is in fact the Swatow ceramics mentioned earlier. The frequently pitted body of Nyonyaware is similar to the coarse body of Swatow products, while the colours and motifs of Swatow ware are also similar to those of Nyonyaware. Ming polychrome, commonly known as the Swatow type, was produced in large quantities in Fujian during the sixteenth and early seventeenth centuries. The products of the factories of Swatow and Amoy are coarse porcelain. There are kilns between Swatow and Chaozhou Fu where there are beds of kaolin as well as more common clays.

Harrisson (1979:50) gave the example of a buff stoneware Jingdezhen dish of the mid-seventeenth century, which is more delicately potted than Swatow types even though the glaze is marred by pin-holes and cracks and has a tendency to peel. This shows that while some Jingdezhen ware may have the pin-holes in the glaze, as is characteristic of the Swatow type (which is more similar to Nyonyaware), Jingdezhen ware is distinguishable from Swatow and thus from Nyonyaware which, it has always been claimed, was made in Jingdezhen.

The phoenix, a characteristic Swatow motif, is always depicted standing on blue-and-white ware, but on polychrome ware the phoenix may be standing or flying. Most of the patterned area is filled with the large motif of the long-legged phoenix, standing in profile; the remaining space shows a background of bamboo and peonies.

Not all ceramics were decorated by brushwork: South China wares include examples of the printing or stamping block technique, which is not dissimilar to methods using cutout stencils for tracing patterns in other media, such as embroidery.

In assembly line mass production, pots are often thrown and fired in one place and decorated elsewhere. Even the application of enamel may be started in one factory and completed in another.

The so-called Japanese type of Nyonyaware has a fish-dragon motif in which the carp has wings attached near its neck. This ware, with a blue underglaze combined with enamelled decoration in the asymmetrical Japanese *kakiemon* style (see Glossary) may be of actual Japanese or of Dutch manufacture. The Petrus Regout Company of Maastricht may have been in competition with Nippon Koshitsu, or it could have filled the gap when supply from the latter ceased. The fashionable European houses which

A wine warmer, with the external form of a *himcheng* (see page 252). Height 16.5 cm, diameter 14 cm. (Courtesy the late Ho Hong Seng, photo Cheang Yik On)

ordered large dinner services of Chinese porcelain did so through the East India Companies, of which the Dutch one was the main carrier, with a supply from the port of Nagasaki. The company transported Chinese ceramics through Nagasaki, but during political disturbances in China in the seventeenth century, actual Japanese ceramics were exported for a while. Similarly some Nyonyaware which was made for the Straits Chinese in the nineteenth and early twentieth centuries was of Japanese manufacture.

In Europe, at the end of the eighteenth century, a new material became popular. This was bone china, made from a mixture of traditional porcelain ingredients and calcined bone ash, which was formulated in England. Bone china is pure white, translucent, strong, and was relatively cheap to produce because of the discovery of a plentiful supply of china clay in Cornwall. Of later European ceramics, Meissen porcelain, especially dinner-table ware, became popular in the early decades of this century. Coffee and tea sets from Germany sometimes have appliqued floral designs with colourful glazes. Continental and English (mostly Victorian) ceramic figures were used as candle stands or simply for decoration. Examples of all these styles found their way into Baba houses.

The chandelier was a statement of one's opulence. In the European-style villas of the Straits Chinese, these Italian cut-glass creations were common. There were also Italian cut-glass wine glasses and decanters especially for European guests.

RIGHT TOP: A circular *kwa kee* (Hokkien: water melon seed) box with domed lid, painted with peonies against a green background. The inside of the five compartments is decorated with flowers of the four seasons. Height 8 cm, diameter 13.5 cm. (Courtesy Prof. Dr. Cheah Jin Seng, photo H. Lin Ho)

RIGHT MIDDLE: A *famille rose* soap box. (Courtesy Penang Museum, photo Cheang Yik On)

RIGHT BELOW: A *chepu* with an 'in and out' design (decorated inside and outside). Height 16.5 cm, diameter 12.7 cm. (Courtesy Prof. Dr. Cheah Jin Seng, photo H. Lin Ho)

ABOVE: This form of covered jar is called *chepu* (or *chupu*; the Malay word *cepu* means 'metal box') by southern Baba, while the northerners call it *himcheng*. Although similar in shape to *kamcheng*, *chepu* are normally not as big as some larger *kamcheng*. (Courtesy the Baba Nyonya Heritage Museum, Malacca, photo H. Lin Ho)

RIGHT: A coral red *chepu*, decorated with fruits and ogival panels with peonies in white reserve. Height 16.5 cm, diameter 18.3 cm. (Courtesy Prof. Dr. Cheah Jin Seng, photo H. Lin Ho)

LEFT: Ceramic stool in the shape of a barrel, decorated in enamel colours on an ochre-yellow background. The overlapping Chinese coin motif is repeated on the seat. (Courtesy P.G. Lim, photo The Pepin Press)

RIGHT: A pair of balustrade-shaped vases. The turquoise shade is a variation of the green base type of Straits Chinese ceramics. (Courtesy Penang Museum, photo Cheang Yik On)

RIGHT: A tea set with two globular teapots and matching cups. This set is meant for two persons; each would have one pot and two cups, one cup for decanting and cooling, and one to sip from. (Courtesy David Chan, photo H. Lin Ho)

BELOW: A tall cylindrical teapot in *famille rose* on a lime-green base. On one side of the pot a phoenix stands on rocks next to a peony in full bloom. The other side features a phoenix in flight. (Collection Dr. Khoo Joo Ee, photos H. Lin Ho)

RIGHT: Two small globular teapots in *famille rose* on a green background. Height 8.5 cm, diameter 9.5 cm.

BELOW: Tea tray with four lobes, decorated with peonies in shades of aubergine and mauve against a green background. 26.5 x 21.5 cm. (Courtesy Ong Siew See, photos Cheang Yik On)

RIGHT: Two pear-shaped teapots, and a tray with a smaller, globular teapot and four matching cups. (Courtesy Penang Museum, photo Cheang Yik On)

Literature

Peranakan publications

In the late nineteenth century, much *Peranakan* literature was produced, including works by Chinese *Peranakan* in Java and Sumatra. The communities published their own newspapers documenting their daily activities and lifestyle. At one time there was a movement against the queue. A pamphlet entitled 'The Story of the Queue', published in Singapore in 1899 in colloquial Malay, pointed out that the pigtail was not a Chinese custom or tradition. It was imposed on the Chinese by their foreign overlords the Manchu, who ruled as the Qing Dynasty (1644-1911).

A Chinese-Malay dictionary by a Javanese Chinese *Peranakan* which appeared in 1878 is unusual in that it is of double-leafed pages, which is the traditional Chinese book format.

The Straits Chinese Magazine was published in Singapore between the years 1897 and 1907 under the editorship of two Queen's Scholars there. Both were critics of Baba culture. Apart from literary essays, the magazine produced a wide range of articles on numerous other subjects. A typical edition contained verses, correspondence, reports of current affairs and essays on education, ethics, politics, religion and science. The magazine was advertised as 'a quarterly journal of oriental and occidental culture', but there was a clear indication of a bias toward anglicized literature. It also reported on the programmes of literary circles in the Straits Settlements; there were more activities of this type in Singapore than elsewhere in the Straits. The literary groups included the Anglo Chinese School Literary Society and the Chinese Christian Association, which also staged readings of plays, including Shakespeare's. Judging from the numerous societies with a literary interest, such as the Straits Chinese Recreation Club, the Straits Chinese-British Association, the Straits Chinese Reading Club and the Straits Chinese Literary Association, there was a considerable awareness of literature within the Baba community. While some of these organizations were mainly Baba concerns, others of a Pan-Chinese character allowed for the Baba to interact with the wider Chinese community. The number of literary essays gradually dwindled and social and political commentaries increased.

The majority of the *Peranakan* works published in the nineteenth century in Singapore were translations of old Chinese epics, in Romanized Baba Malay. The Indonesian Chinese *Peranakan* had started such translations and in fact the earliest translations in the Straits Settlements were re-translations of works published in Java.

The biggest undertaking of this type of literature in Malay was a translation of the famous fourteenth century epic, *Sam Kok*, 'The Romance of the Three Kingdoms', by Batu Gantong, the pen name of Chan Kim Boon, published in thirty volumes. Chan Kim Boon, a Baba whose father was a businessman from Sumatra, was born in Penang in 1851. While attending an English-medium school in Penang, he was also tutored in Chinese at home. His pen name is, in fact, the name of a cemetery in Penang; his rationale for adopting the name was that he would eventually be there.

'The Three Kingdoms' was brought out as a profusely illustrated series. Besides anecdotes about Chinese culture, Chan inserted jokes and even a caricature of his illustrator. The series also published readers' letters in Chinese, Malay and English. Finally, Chan even included a portrait of himself. The books were only four inches by six-and-a-half in size and they contained between a 100 and a 170 pages. Longer stories were

Translation of a Chinese classic, *Kou Chey Tian* (Monkey), in Baba-style Malay. (Collection Dr. Khoo Joo Ee, photo The Pepin Press)

published in series, with the page numbering continuing from one book to the next. Illustrations, prefaces, biographies, commentaries and readers' letters had no page numbers. The small, handy volumes were similar to the British 'Penny Dreadfuls' and they were also circulated on loan. In the early twentieth century, when a good command of the English language was a prerequisite for better job opportunities, this series in Romanized Malay lost popularity.

There is also a translation of Jules Verne's 'Around the World in Eighty Days', entitled *Hikayat Fileas Fogg*. (*Hikayat* is Malay for ancient story or biography.)

One result of the Christian missionary activity mentioned in Chapter II was that some religious poems were composed in Malay by the Christian Babas. Similarly, religious services for Chinese *Peranakan* were conducted in Malay, and Christian hymns were also translated into the language. The early nineteenth century missionary publications were printed in Singapore.

Further literary works such as novels were written in Malay by Chinese *Peranakan* in Java; until very recently, there were no such creative works from the Straits Settlements.

Translations into Baba-style
Malay of Chinese classics. The
most famous of these works was
a thirty-volume set of the epic
Romance of the Three Kingdoms
or *Sam Kok*. (Collection Dr.
Khoo Joo Ee, photo The Pepin
Press)

A compilation of Baba *pantun*, meant to be sung. (Collection Dr. Khoo Joo Ee, photo The Pepin Press)

The *pantun*

The *pantun* is a particular style of Malay verse which often tells a story or is recited as a riddle. Using rhyming couplets and quatrains, it is usually presented in a question and answer style and can become a performance by two people. *Pantuns* lend themselves to an impromptu style and one of their purposes is to bring out some quick-witted repartee between the performers. Throughout Malay-speaking Southeast Asia the pantun has long been a medium of social interaction between peoples of varied ethnic backgrounds. Literary compositions of this type originated from across the Straits in Sumatra and from the adjoining Riau Archipelago near Singapore.

There are several types of *pantun*; in the simplest of these, the second couplet answers the question of the first in an open direct manner. A metaphorical *pantun* is more elusive, to the extent that it has an unexpressed, confidential meaning known only to the poet's close circle of friends. Proverbs are often incorporated in the verses.

The imagery conjured up in poetry such as pantuns, though sometimes elusive as it is in other art forms, gives artistic 'licence' to express the sensitive, prohibited or forbidden under the guise of frivolity. Perhaps this is why it became such a popular form of entertainment and has remained so till the present day.

The Malacca Baba, in particular, practised the art of reciting *pantuns*, which certainly

263

requires a command of more than just colloquial Malay, although simple verses could have been learned by rote. In aspiring to compose Malay *pantuns*, the Babas were aiming at a more refined use of the language. Composing poems in Malay was apparently quite beyond the Penang Nyonya, who spoke Malayanized Hokkien. Instead, they composed homely Hokkien rhymes and short songs. The Malacca Nyonya, who sometimes sang *pantuns* in a similar manner, may have composed these Malay verses herself, or it could simply be that she memorized them.

Pantuns had a universal appeal; even Chinese *Peranakan* traders learned the art from the Malays, but while their Malay counterparts simply enjoyed creating poems, Baba *pantun* practitioners tended to want to discuss and analyse the verses; sometimes this reduced spontaneity.

Performing arts

The *pantun* and *Dongdang Sayang*

When *pantuns* were sung in a certain manner they were given the name *Dongdang Sayang*. Dengdang or *dongdang*, meaning song or chorus, imply a poem that is sung. *Dongdang Sayang*, or love poems, are rendered in rounds of quick repartee between two singers or groups of singers. The *Dongdang Sayang* style originated in Malacca and eventually spread to Penang, Singapore, and Sarawak. It is one of the most elaborate forms of *pantun* singing. It is accompanied by the music of a violin, a gong and drums.

Dongdang Sayang was very popular with the Babas in the early 1900s. At informal family parties, perhaps on the verandah of a house, Nyonya women joined in the sung debate. Gatherings such as these soon attracted transvestites who dressed up as Nyonyas. After some time, groups, in the style of wandering minstrels, travelled round in buses serenading the residents of a neighbourhood. The singers used well-known love songs with which to begin 'duels' of quick repartee. Their wits were tested when they had to sing impromptu verses. As the *Dongdang Sayang* developed into cultural entertainment, a flute or an accordion was added to the accompanying band. In Singapore, Sumatra and Riau *Dongdang Sayang* is now known as *Gunong Sayang*.

Eberhard (1968:118-122), in his study of the local cultures of South China, talks of alternating love songs at Spring and Summer festivals. Two groups of singers, usually one of men and the other of women, sing improvised verses alternately as a pre-marriage courting ritual. Such improvised love songs derived from work songs sung by people while labouring in the fields. Presumably the earliest Straits Chinese would have had some memory of such songs.

A *Penang Dongdang Sayang* band in attendance at, say, a party, would consist of two drummers, an accordionist, a violinist and a gong player. Most of the musicians would be Malay, except for the gong player who might be Chinese or Indian. A round of songs sung by those present could combine the three languages of Malay, Mandarin and Hokkien. A Chinese tune would sometimes be accompanied by a regular Malay beat on the drums. A transvestite often performed a popular Siamese dance while people in the party would clap and join him in a similar Malay dance. Then the *Dongdang Sayang* band would perhaps decide to play an excerpt from a popular classic, with the violinist accompanying the melody, and using Arab quarter tones, while the Malay drum-beat kept up the *basso continuo*. To round off this Baba-style entertainment, the revellers might take up some English refrain, or waltz to the Blue Danube: even that could suddenly change tempo to a Latin American beat.

Boria

Before the advent of the cabaret and the cinema, minstrel groups provided entertainment. One particular type was the *boria*, which was a popular form of theatre in Penang, especially with people of southern Indian Muslim origin. A *boria* group comprised amateur musicians and singers who performed in both Malay and English, sometimes even dressing up as black and white minstrels. Both the Red and White Flag societies had their own *boria* troupes which entertained the neighbourhood, especially during the Muslim New Year, *Awal Muharram*. At the end of the ten-day long celebration, the two troupes from the rival factions would traditionally enter into a skirmish.

Singing was only part of a *boria* performance; it usually began with a comic sketch, which was followed by a song and dance routine. The sketch was usually a farce, a caricatured mimicry of the sponsors of the show, who might be Arabs, Baba Chinese, or sometimes Europeans. While the Babas did not participate in the sketch, they may have joined in the song sequence, whether or not they were the sponsors of a particular performance.

The *boria* was brought to Penang by Muslim Indians from Madras, and the introductory sketch originally had a religious context, and referred to the schism between *Shi'a* and *Sunni* Muslims. As a new generation of Malayanized Indian Muslims emerged, i.e. *Jawi Pekan* or *Jawi Peranakan*, who were the offspring of Indians and their Malay wives, the *boria* was secularized. (As the *Jawi Peranak*an were urban dwellers, they were sometimes called *Jawi Pekan*; *pekan* being Malay for 'town'.)

Bangsawan

In the art of *bangsawan* a musical drama unfolds a well-known legend with much singing and minimal spoken dialogue, so that the *bangsawan* is usually described as a type of opera. Originally it was called *wayang Parsi* (Parsi theatre or Persian show) because that was the name for this type of entertainment in India, where it had been popular since the eighteenth century.

In the late nineteenth century, the Parsi theatre visited Penang, where *bangsawan* soon became popular with mixed crowds of Malays, Chinese, Tamils and the Indian *sepoys* of the armed forces stationed on the island. This popularity was gained despite the fact that performances used to be staged in the Hindustani language, recounting stories from India and West Asia.

The Babas who patronized this type of opera were called *Baba Bangsawan* by their Indian Muslim friends. These Malay-speaking Straits Chinese later formed their own *bangsawan* groups. Among these were the *Baba Bangsawan* and the Chinese Amateur Dramatic Association, which staged both Chinese and Malay plays.

When the novelty of the Parsi theatre wore off, a local Indian Muslim bought up the props and costumes and established a theatre group which became the *bangsawan* of Malaya (and later of Malaysia). For the first performances this group gave, the stories, although Malay, tended to be obvious adaptations from the repertoire of the Parsi theatre. The actors wore the Parsi costumes and were accompanied by Indian music. The word *bangsawan* in Malay connotes nobility or aristocracy, and the *bangsawan* theatre turned to stories about the Malay royalty and gentry. The lifestyles of the fashionable rich were also depicted. Comedians with bawdy jokes and song-and-dance routines afforded comic relief.

This pioneer troupe from Penang toured the Peninsula and went as far as Java. Penang remained the principal base for other touring groups and for a period of time it was the trend-setting place, the leader in the development of the theatre. Until just before the Second World War, professional troupes traversed the Peninsula in convoys of buses, and plays were staged by both Malayan and Indonesian performers. The troupes were often owned by bigger business concerns. In Penang, *Baba Bangsawan* supporters used to sponsor such plays.

An average *bangsawan* troupe would consist of about fifty people. A talented, good-looking hero or heroine was essential for the troupe's reputation. The supporting cast was usually multi racial, including Malay, Baba, Indian and even Filipino actors. As with other kinds of theatre in that era, women were excluded. Female roles were played by effeminate-looking males or transvestites, although at a later date some female prostitutes were permitted to take to the stage. Originally *bangsawan* theatre was performed on temporary wooden stages in open public places, but it soon moved to indoor stages. School halls or community centres were leased to troupes. Finally, amusement parks built *bangsawan* theatres which remained active till the Second World War.

Classical theatre such as the Indian *jatra* and the Chinese opera influenced the development of the *bangsawan* style, which resembled the Italian *commedia dell'arte*. Some of the operas also took their themes from Indian, Chinese, Indonesian and Thai stories. Generally, the historical setting of a drama was respected in the stage sets, music and costumes. Western plays, including those of Shakespeare, were freely adapted. In 1918, Muslim students of the Penang Free School staged a Malay *bangsawan* version of Shakespare's 'A Midsummer Night's Dream'.

Epilogue: the Straits Chinese Today

The Chinese have always had problems regarding unity and leadership. As we have seen, overseas Chinese communities generally divide themselves into groups according to such things as dialect, place of birth, education, guild or secret society affiliation, occupation and political alignment. The Straits Chinese, like the rest of the Chinese in Malaysia, have never put up a united front. However, in Penang there has always been more interaction between the Baba and non-Baba Chinese than in Malacca or Singapore. The fact that the Penang Babas speak more Hokkien than Baba Malay illustrates this point. The main difference between the Baba and non-Baba groups is that the former was a settled urban community while the latter still consisted of struggling immigrants.

There is also among the Straits Chinese a large group who are partly Baba but who do not speak the Baba patois. The Babas still operate in 'concentric circles', largely keeping to their own group with which they identify on the subjects of lineage, food and, to a lesser extent, some cultural practices and dress. Babas feel close to their Chinese heritage when they join the wider Chinese community for religious festivals.

The educated Babas were keen to modernize and adapt their culture to fit in with the outside world and western ways. However, their élite position made them preserve traditions to keep their status; thus they were paradoxically both *avant-garde* and stagnant.

Features of the Baba culture like *Dondang Sayang*, Malay-style cuisine and clothes, and traditional weddings are relatively private (see The Arts, Everyday Life and Ceremonies). The Babas' social clubs and associations are more open and public (see Everyday Life).

The history of the Babas started not with their local birth, but with their socio-political maturity as an important new entity in the local community. Of their cultivated lifestyle, their language, dress and type of cuisine live on.

The Depression beginning in 1929, and the Japanese Occupation of Malaya from 1941 to 1945, put an end to much of the traditional lifestyle of the Babas. The urban Baba-Nyonya were humbled, and wartime hardships taught them self-reliance, with the result that they adapted to modern society. Since the war, Nyonyas have increasingly attended English schools, as if to prepare themselves for future roles outside the household (see Everyday Life). With other ways of seeing the world outside the four walls of the house, the *Chap Goh Meh* parades (see Festivals) were no longer eagerly

looked forward to. The Nyonyas, forced out of their cloisters to work outside their homes, are no longer secluded. Neither are they protected by a retinue of servants in a large household with an extended family. It is acceptable for them to go out shopping and socializing alone. Older Nyonyas now wear that short inner dress, which is a long sleeved blouse over which a long organdie tunic is donned, in public (see The Arts, Costumes). This casual wear, which previously had to be made of plain white cotton, is now often seen in a floral material, even though it clashes with the sarong worn with it, which is also floral.

There have also been changes in marriage customs. Beaded slippers are no longer made as wedding gifts, and as elaborate ceremonies became unaffordable, the reformed style of wedding gained popularity as long ago as the 1930s, being cheaper and more convenient.

Western education lays more stress on conjugal love than filial piety, and inculcates the ideal of the husband-wife-and-children unit; this is quite different from the Chinese traditional practice of living in large family groups. The consequence of adhering to these western values is the breaking up of the large group which used to include aged parents or grandparents and a host of kinsfolk. When this happens, as it still often does, the resulting smaller families are less likely to continue the ancestral cult and to observe family traditions.

Younger generations of Babas have been pressured by the demands of larger social groups and caught up in political developments which were beyond their power to control. The most significant change was the end of colonialism and the achievement of independence. In spite of encouraging immigration when the Straits Settlements were first established, the British regarded the Straits Chinese as sojourners even though many had chosen to stay. As already recounted, social organization, especially of commerce and labour, had been dominated by the secret societies. The British Government had found difficulty in handling these societies and had courted the Babas as allies. It was upon the prohibition of the secret societies in 1890, that 'Babaness' was publicly discussed. Throughout the nineteenth century, Baba identity had always been present, although it was more obvious in Malacca; in Penang and Singapore it developed slightly later, during the second half of the century.

With China being in the throes of disorientation as she was prised open by Europe and America, the majority of Straits Chinese knew that the Straits Settlements were by far the safest haven. However, even before independence when the Guomintang was active, the Babas found their privileged position being weakened. This contributed to erosion of the Baba identity which, by virtue of being evolved from an English-speaking group, was a product of British colonialism. The articulate Babas had pushed their British rights rather far and were headed for disillusionment, because the reforms they wanted were not clearly understood. Getting into the civil service seems to have been one of the main reforms they desired. It is doubtful that citizenship and its accompanying rights were valued at that time. Forfeiting part of their Chinese heritage was recognized and accepted although it had been awkward in confrontational situations between Baba and *Sinkhek* groups.

Large-scale immigration of Chinese women from the turn of the century had produced a generation of local-born Chinese to whom the Baba society became increasingly distant and even irrelevant. Beginning in the 1920s, two decades before the Second World War, there was tremendous growth of both Chinese schools and a lively

OPPOSITE PAGE: The three traditional ceramic figures symbolizing, from left to right, prosperity, success and longevity. They are still very often found in Chinese homes, both Baba and non-Baba. Height 62 cm. (Courtesy Ong Siew See, photo Cheang Yik On)

271

Chinese press. In the Chinese schools there was an increase in the numbers of local-born students from wealthy families who thought that they provided a superior education. Although they considered Malaya their home, such families committed their wealth and influence to developing Chinese cultural institutions. Post World War II Straits Chinese are very different from those of the previous generation.

As the term Baba has colonial connotations and the expression Straits (-born) Chinese is anachronistic because the Straits Settlements no longer exist as a political unit, *Peranakan* might seem to be a preferable label for the Straits Chinese. In terms of citizenship in present-day political entities, to be locally born or a *Peranakan*, becomes mandatory. Today, for the Babas, who are now effectively absorbed by the larger Chinese community, such definitions may be irrelevant.

Although '*Peranakanism*' was revived in Singapore in the late 1970s, the term is misleading because of its ambiguity and the confusion it causes among the Straits Chinese and other locally-born groups. Does it represent a deliberate open-door stance to recruit Sarawak, Javanese and Sumatran Chinese *Peranakan* into the fold for solidarity? The fact is that the term *Peranakan* is used less in the north or in private or non-political situations. In the Peninsula, Baba-Nyonya labels are still very prevalent: even the Malays continue to use these terms. The proponents of contemporary projects for the conservation of urban centres rhapsodize about the Baba shophouse and terrace house, albeit putting culture on parade for the tourist dollar. Straits-style pre-war buildings are still to be found in some areas. They are fine examples of the architecture of those times, but sometimes advertisements, for example for Colonel Saunders and Kentucky Fried Chicken have usurped the pediment and belfry of once handsome Anglo-Indian style mansions; it seems an affront.

The Straits Chinese combined Chinese and Malay cultures in such aspects as language, dress, type of cuisine and occupation. However, this synthesis was always a fragile one, with the Straits Chinese striving to assert their own identity as genuine indigenous people of Malaysia and Singapore. They drew on several ethnic traditions yet transcended them with something that was a new creation. The syncretism achieved by the Babas, fragile though it was, went beyond the kind of political coalition which exists between the different racial groups in present-day Malaysia.

Abbreviations

BEFEO   Bulletin de l'École Française d'Extrême Orient
BKI   Bijdragen tot de Taal-, Land- en Volkenkunde, uitgegeven door het Koninklijk Instituut
ISEAS   Institute of Southeast Asian Studies, Singapore
JIAEA   Journal of the Indian Archipelago and East Asia
(J)MBRAS   (Journal of the) Malayan/Malaysian Branch of the Royal Asiatic Society
JSBRAS   Journal of the Straits Branch of the Royal Asiatic Society
JSEAH/S   Journal of Southeast Asian History/Studies
JSSS   Journal of the South Seas Society
SCPA   State Chinese (Penang) Association
SEACS   South East Asian Ceramic Society

Abdurachman, P.R., *Pameran batik corak Cina*, Jakarta, Museum Tekstil 1977

Abdurachman, P.R., *Cerbon*, Jakarta, Sinar Harapan 1982

Abu Bakar, Syed, 'The Malay Boat Launching Ceremony', *JMBRAS* vol.24, pt.1, Feb. 1951:181-83

Ahern, E.M., *The Cult of the Dead in a Chinese Village*, Stanford University Press 1973

Aijmer, G., 'The Dragon Boat Festival in the Hu-nan and Hu-peh Plains: a Study of the Ceremonialism of the Transplanting of Rice', *Ethnos Monograph* 9, 1964

Aijmer, G., 'A Structural Approach to Chinese Ancestor Worship', *BKI* vol.124, 1968:91-98

Allom, T., *China, in a Series of Views, Displaying the Scenery, Architecture and Social Habits of that Ancient Empire*, London, Fisher, Son and Co. 1843

An Chih-min, 'Kan-lan shih chien-chu ti k'ao-ku yen-chiu' (Archaeological research into buildings of the kan-lan style), *K'ao-ku Hsueh-pao*, 1963:65-85

Ancient Architecture in Beijing, Beijing, Arts and Photography Publishing House 1984

Andaya, B.W. and L.Y. Andaya, *A History of Malaysia*, Houndmills, Macmillan 1982, repr. 1985, 1986

Anderson, J., *Acheen and the Ports on the North and East Coasts of Sumatra*, London, W.H. Allen 1840, Oxford University Press 1971

Arasaratnam, S., *Merchants, Companies and Commerce on the Coromandel Coast 1650-1740*, Delhi, Oxford University Press 1986

Arensmeyer, E.C., *British Merchant Enterprise and the Chinese Coolie Trade 1850-1874*, Ph.D. thesis, University of Hawaii 1979

Arkell, A.J., 'Cambay and the Bead Trade', *Antiquity* 10, 1936:299-305

Avitabile, G., *Von Schatz der Drachen/From the Dragon's Treasure*, London, Bamboo Publishing 1987

Ayers, J., *Oriental Art in the Victoria and Albert Museum*, London 1983

Baker, M. and M. Lunt, *Blue and White: the Cotton Embroideries of Rural China*, London, Sidgwick and Jackson 1978

Ball, J. Dyer, *Things Chinese*, Hong Kong, Kelly and Walsh 1903

Ball, K.M., *Decorative Motives of Oriental Art*, New York, Hacker Art Books 1927, repr. 1969

Bassett, D.K., 'European Influence in the Malay Peninsula', *JMBRAS* vol.33, pt.3, 1960:9-34

Bassett, D.K., 'The British Country Trader and Sea Captain in South East Asia in Seventeenth and Eighteenth Century', *Journal of the Historical Society* vol.1, no.2, 1961:9-14

Bassett, D.K., 'British Commercial and Strategic Interest in the Malay Peninsula During the Late Eighteenth Century', Bastin, J. and R. Roolvink (eds.), *Malayan and Indonesian Studies*, Oxford, Clarendon Press 1964:122-40

Bastin, J. and C.A. Gibson-Hill, 'Five Early Watercolour Sketches of Penang and Malacca', *JMBRAS* vol.31, pt.1, 1958:163-71

Bastin, J. and P. Rohatgi, *Prints of Southeast Asia in the India Office Library*, London, Her Majesty's Stationery Office 1979

Beamish, J., *A History of Singapore Architecture: the Making of a City*, Singapore, Graham Brash 1985

Begbie, P.J., *The Malayan Peninsula Embracing its History, Manners and Customs of the Inhabitants, Politics, Natural History from its Earliest Records*, Madras, Veperey Mission Press 1834, repr. Kuala Lumpur, Oxford University Press 1967

Benham, F.C., *Report on the Trade of Penang*, Kuala Lumpur, Govt. Printer 1948

Berendsen, A., *Tiles: a General History*, London, Faber and Faber 1967

Berliner, N.Z., *Chinese Folk Art*, New York, Little, Brown and Co. 1986

Beurdeley, M., *Chinese Furniture*, Tokyo, Kodansha 1979

Beurdeley, M. and G. Raindre, *Qing Porcelain: famille vert, famille rose*, London, Thames and Hudson 1987

Bielenstein, H., 'The Chinese Colonization of Fukien Until the End of T'ang', S. Egerod and E. Glahn (eds.), *Studia Serica Bernhard Karlgren Dedicata*, Copenhagen, E. Munksgaard 1959:108-11

Bird, I.L., *The Golden Chersonese: and the Way Thither*, London, J. Murray 1883, repr. Kuala Lumpur, Oxford University Press 1982

Bishop, C.W., 'Long Houses and Dragon Boats', *Antiquity* vol.12, 1938:411-24

Bland, R.N., 'Malacca Lace', *JSBRAS* vol.45, 1906:273-77

Blagden, C.O., 'Minangkabau Custom — Malacca', *JMBRAS* vol.8, pt.2, 1930:307-13

Blusse, L., 'Chinese Trade in Batavia During the Days of the V.O.C.', *Archipel* no.18, 1979:195-214

Blythe, W.L., 'Historical Sketch of Chinese Labour in Malaya', *JMBRAS* vol.20, pt.1, 1947:111-14

Blythe, W.L., *The Impact of Chinese Secret Societies in Malaya: a Historical Study*, London, Oxford University Press for the Royal Institute of Internal Affairs 1969

Bonney, R., 'Francis Light, the Nonya and Penang', *Jernal Sejarah* vol.3, 1964/65:31-35

Boville, E.W., 'The Shipping Interests of the Honourable East India Company', *The Mariner's Mirror* vol. 36/3, 1950:244-62

Boyd, A., *Chinese Architecture and Town Planning 1500 BC-AD 1911*, London, A. Tiranti 1962

Braddell, R., *The Lights of Singapore*, London, Methuen 1934, repr. Kuala Lumpur, Oxford University Press 1982

Brandon, J.R., *Theatre in Southeast Asia*, Harvard University Press 1967

Brown, H.M., *The South Indian Community and the Evolution of the Jawi Peranakan in Penang up to 1948*, unpub. MA thesis University of Malaya 1977

Buckley, C.B., *An Anecdotal History of Old Times in Singapore, 1819-1867*, Singapore, Fraser and Neave 1902, University of Malaya Press 1965, Oxford University Press 1984

Burkhardt, V.R., *Chinese Creeds and Customs: a Compilation of the Best-selling Trilogy*, Hong Kong, South China Morning Press 1982

Butcher, J.G., *The British in Malaya 1880-1941: the Social History of a European Community in Colonial South-East Asia*, Kuala Lumpur, Oxford University Press 1979

Byrd, C.K., *Early Printing in the Straits Settlements 1806-1858*, Singapore National Library 1970

Cameron, J., *Our Tropical Possessions in Malayan India: Being a Descriptive Account of Singapore, Penang, Province Wellesley and Malacca*, London, Smith, Elder and Co. 1865, repr. Kuala Lumpur, Oxford University Press 1965

Cammann, S., 'Origins of the Court and Official Robes of the Ch'ing Dynasty', *Artibus Asiae* vol.12, 1949:189-201

Cammann, S., *China's Dragon Robes*, New York, Ronald Press 1952

Cammann, S., *Chinese Mandarin Squares*, University of Pennsylvania University Museum Bulletin vol.17, no.3, 1953

Cammann, S., 'Embroidery Techniques in Old China', *Archives of the Chinese Art Society of America* vol.16, 1957:16-39

Cammann, S., 'Ch'ing Dynasty Mandarin Squares', *Ornament* 4, no.1, 1979:25-9

Chai Hon Chan, *The Development of British Malaya 1896-1909*, Kuala Lumpur, Oxford University Press 1964, 1967

Chang, Q., *Memories of a Nonya*, Singapore, Eastern Universities Press 1981

Changing Identities of the Southeast Asian Chinese since World War II, Cushman, J. and G. Wang (eds.), Hong Kong University Press 1988

Ch'en, J. and N. Tarling, *Studies in the Social History of China and South-east Asia*, Cambridge University Press 1970

Cheng Te-k'un, *Jade Flowers and Floral Patterns in Chinese Decorative Art*, Hong Kong Chinese University 1969

Cheng Te-k'un, *Studies in Chinese Art*, Hong Kong Chinese University 1983

Cheng U Wen, 'Opium in the Straits Settlements 1867-1910', *JSEAH* vol.2, pt.1, 1961:52-75

Cheo Kim Ban, *A Baba Wedding*, Singapore, Eastern Universities Press 1983

Chia, F., *The Babas*, Singapore, Times Books International 1980

Chia, F., *Ala Sayang*, Singapore, Eastern Universities Press 1983

Chia, F., *Reminiscences*, Singapore, Magro International 1984

Chia Kim Teck, *Panton dondang sayang baba baba pranakan*, Malacca, Tan Seng Poh, 1950

Chiang Hai-ding, *A History of Straits Settlements Foreign Trade 1870-1915*, Ph.D. thesis, Canberra, Australian National University 1963

Chin Kee Onn, *Twilight of the Nonyas*, Kuala Lumpur, Aspatra Quest 1984

Chinatown: an Album of a Singapore Community, Singapore, Times Books International 1983

Chinese Arts and Crafts, New York, Alpine Fine Arts Collection 1983

The Chinese in Indonesia, J.A.C. Mackie (ed.), Singapore, Heinemann 1976

Chinese Export Porcelain: an Historical Survey, New York, Universe Books 1977

The Chinese in Penang: a Pictorial Documentation, Penang Chinese Town Hall 1987

The Chinese in Southeast Asia, 2 vols., L.A.P. Gosling and Y.C. Lim (eds.), Singapore, Maruzen Asia 1983

Chong Lee Ngoh, 'The History of Kongsis in Penang', *Malaysia in History* vol.16/1, June 1973:16-19

Chu Tee Seng, 'The Singapore Chinese Protectorate 1900-1941', *JSEAH* vol.16, pt.1, June 1973:16-9

Chung Young Y., *The Art of Oriental Embroidery: History, Aesthetics and Techniques*, London, Bell and Hyman 1980, New York, Charles Scribner's Sons 1983

Clammer, J.R., 'Overseas Chinese Assimilation and Resinification: a Malaysian Case Study', *Southeast Asian Journal of Social Sciences* 3/2, 1975:9-23

Clammer, J.R., *Straits Chinese Society*, Singapore University Press 1980

Clothings and Ornaments of China's Miao People, Beijing, The Nationality Press 1985

Coatalen, P.J., *The Decorated Boats of Kelantan: an Essay on Symbolism*, Penang, Universiti Sains Malaysia 1982

Collis, M., *Foreign Mud*, Singapore, Graham Brash 1980

Comber, L., *Chinese Ancestor Worship in Malaya*, Singapore, D. Moore 1954, 1963

Comber, L., *Chinese Magic and Superstitions in Malaya*, Singapore, Eastern Universities Press 1955, 1969

Comber, L., *Chinese Temples in Singapore*, Singapore, Eastern Universities Press 1958

Comber, L., *Chinese Secret Societies in Malaya: a Survey of the Triad Society from 1800-1900*, New York, Locust Valley 1959

Comber, L., *The Traditional Mysteries of Chinese Secret Societies in Malaya*, Singapore, D. Moore for Eastern Universities Press 1961

Conner, P., *The China Trade 1600-1860*, Brighton Art Gallery and Museums 1986

Cormack, J.G., *Chinese Birthday, Wedding, Funeral and Other Customs*, Peking, China Booksellers 1927

Coppel, C.A., 'Mapping the Peranakan Chinese in Indonesia', *Papers on Far Eastern History* 8, 1973:143-67

Costumes of the Minority Peoples of China, Kyoto, Binobi 1982

Cowan, C.D., 'Early Penang and the Rise of Singapore, 1805-1832', *JMBRAS* vol.23, pt.2, 1949:1-210

Cowan, C.D., *Nineteenth Century Malaya: the Origins of British Control*, London, Oxford University Press 1961

Crissman, L.W., 'The Segmentary Structure of Urban Overseas Chinese Communities', *Man* 2, 1967:185-204

Crossman, C.L., *The China Trade: Export Paintings, Furniture, Silver and Other Objects*, Princeton, The Pyne Press 1972

Crow, C., *Handbook for China*, Shanghai, Carl Crow 1925, repr. Hong Kong, Oxford University Press 1984

Culture: Man's Adaptive Dimension, M.F. Ashley Montagu (ed.), London, Oxford University Press 1968

Cushman, J.W., *Family and State: the Formation of a Sino-Thai Tin Mining Dynasty 1797-1932*, Singapore, Oxford University Press 1990

d'Addetta, *Treasury of Chinese Design Motifs*, New York, Dover 1981

Damais, L.C., 'A propos des couleurs symboliques des points cardinaux', *BEFEO* vol.56, 1969:75-118

David, Lady S., *Illustrated Catalogue of Ch'ing Enamelled Wares in the Percival David Foundation of Chinese Art*, London 1973

Davies, D., *Old Penang*, Singapore, D. Moore 1956

Ding Choo Ming, 'An Introduction to the Indonesian Peranakan Literature in the Library of the Universiti Kebangsaan Malaysia', *JMBRAS* vol.51, pt.1, 1978

Dixon, R. and S. Muthesius, *Victorian Architecture*, London, Thames and Hudson 1978, 1991

Dodwell, C., *A Traveller in China*, London, Hodder and Stoughton 1985

Dogget, M., *Characters of Light: Early Buildings of Singapore*, Singapore, D. Moore 1985

Doolittle, J., *Social Life of the Chinese*, 2 vols., New York, Harper and Brother 1895, repr. Singapore, Graham Brash 1986

Dubin, L.S., *The History of Beads from 30,000 BC to the Present*, New York, Harry N.Abrams/London, Thames and Hudson 1987

Duyvendak, J.L.L., 'Chinese in the Dutch East Indies', *Chinese Social and Political Science Review*, Peking, vol.11, 1927:1-15

Dye, D.S., *Chinese Lattice Design*, Harvard University Press 1937, 1949, repr. New York, Dover 1974

Eberhard, W., *Chinese Festivals*, New York, H. Schumann 1952

Eberhard, W., *A History of China*, London, Routledge and Kegan Paul 1960

Eberhard, W., *The Local Cultures of South and East China*, Leiden, E.J. Brill 1968

Ecke, G., *Chinese Domestic Furniture*, Hong Kong University Press 1962

Edkins, J., 'Chinese Architecture', *Journal of the China Branch Royal Asiatic Society*, n.s. vol.24, 1890:253-88

Edwards, N., *The Singapore House and Residential Life 1819-1939*, Singapore, Oxford University Press 1991

Elliot, A.J.A., 'Chinese Spirit-medium Cults in Singapore', *JMBRAS* vol.29, pt.1, 1956:214-19, Singapore, D. Moore 1964

Elliot, I.M., *Batik, Fabled Cloth of Java*, New York, Clarkson N. Potter 1984

Eng-Lee Seok Chee, *Festive Expressions: Nyonya Beadwork and Embroidery*, Singapore National Museum 1989

English Cabinets, London, Victoria and Albert Museum 1972

English Porcelain, 1745-1850, R.J. Charleston (ed.), London, E. Benn 1965

Erickson, J.M., *The Universal Bead*, New York, W.W. Norton 1969

The Ethnic Chinese in the ASEAN States, L. Suryadinata (ed.), Singapore, ISEAS 1989

Evans, J., *A History of Jewellery, 1100-1870*, London, Faber and Faber 1953, 1970

Evers, H.D., 'Differing Concepts of Settlement Patterns: the Malay and Chinese in Malaysia', *Ekistics* 263, Oct. 1977:220-25

Ezerman, J.L.J.F., *Beschrijving van den Koan Iem-temple Tiao-kak sie te Cheribon*, KGKW, Populair-Wetenschappelijke serie 2, n.d.

The Face of China as Seen by Photographers and Travellers, 1860-1922, London, Gordon Fraser 1978

Falconer, J., *A Vision of the Past: a History of Early Photography in Singapore and Malaya*, Singapore, Times Edition 1987

Feller, J.Q., *The Canton Famille Rose Porcelains: Chinese Export Porcelain in the 19th Century*, Salem, Peabody Museum 1982

Fitzgerald, C.P., *The Southern Expansion of the Chinese People*, London, Barrie and Jenkins 1972

Fitzgerald, C.P., *China, a Short Cultural History*, London, Barrie and Jenkins 1976

Fletcher, B., *A History of Architecture*, London University Athlone Press 18th edition 1975

Flower, R., *Raffles: the Story of Singapore*, Singapore, Eastern Universities Press 1984

Forbes, D., *The Heart of Malaya*, London, Hale 1966

Forbes, H.A.C., et al, *Chinese Export Silver 1785 to 1855*, Mass., Milton 1975

Forrest, R.A.D., *The Chinese Language*, London, Faber and Faber 1948

Francis Jr., P., *The Story of Venetian Beads*, New York, Lapis Route 1979

Francis Jr., P., *The Czech Bead Story*, New York, Lapis Route 1979

Francis Jr., P., *Chinese Glass Beads: a Review of the Evidence*, New York Ctr. for Bead Research 1986

Franke, W., 'Some Remarks on the "Three-in-one" Doctrine and its Manifestations in Singapore and Malaysia', *Oriens Extremus* 19, 1972:121-29

Franke, W. and Ch'en Tieh Fan, *Chinese Epigraphic Materials in Malaysia*, 3 vols., Kuala Lumpur, University of Malaya Press 1982-87

Freedman, M., *Lineage Organization in Southeastern China*, London University Athlone Press 1958, 1966, 1970

Freedman, M., *Chinese Lineage and Society: Fukien and Kuantung*, London University Athlone Press 1958, 1965, 1970

Freedman, M., 'Chinese Kinship and Marriage in Singapore', *JSEAH* vol.3, pt.2, 1962:65-73

Freedman, M., *The Study of Chinese Society: Essays of Maurice Freedman*, G.W. Skinner (ed.), Stanford University Press 1979

Fregnac, C., *Jewellery from the Renaissance to Art Noveau*, London, Octopus Bks. 1965

Gallop, A. Teh, 'Early Malay Printing, an Introduction to the British Library Collection', *JMBRAS* vol.63, pt.1, 1990:85-124

Gardner, B., *The East India Company: a History, London*, R. Hart-Davies 1971

Garner, H.M., *Chinese Lacquer*, London, Faber and Faber 1979

Gaw, K., *Superior Servants: the Legendary Cantonese Amahs of the Far East*, Singapore, Oxford University Press 1988, 1991

Gibson-Hill, C.A., 'Six Wooden Images in the Cheng Hoon Teng, Malacca', *JMBRAS* vol.28, pt.1, 1955:173-79

Gibson-Hill, C.A., 'The Fortification of Bukit Cina, Malacca', *JMBRAS* vol.29, pt.3, 1956:166

Gittinger, M.S., *A Study of the Ship Cloths of South Sumatra: Their Design and Usage*, Ph.D. thesis Columbia University 1972

Ghulam Sarwar Yousof, *Ceremonial and Decorative Crafts of Penang*, Penang Museum 1986

Godley, M.R., 'The Late Ch'ing Courtship of the Chinese in Southeast Asia', *Journal of Asian Studies* vol.34, pt.2, 1975:361-85

Godley, M.R., *The Mandarin Capitalists from Nanyang: Overseas Chinese Enterprise and the Modernization of China 1893-1911*, Cambridge University Press 1981

Goh Thean Chye, *An Introduction to Malay Pantuns*, Kuala Lumpur, University of Malaya Press 1980

Goidsenhoven, J. van, *La famille rose*, Brussels, Laconti S.A. 1973

Gombrich, E.H., *In Search of Cultural History*, Oxford, Clarendon Press 1974

Goodrich, L.C., *A Short History of the Chinese People*, London, George Allen and Unwin 1969

Gostelow, M., *Embroidery: Traditional Designs, Techniques and Patterns from All Over the World*, London, Cavendish House 1982

Graham, T., 'Historical Sketch of Penang in 1794', J. Bastin (ed.), *JMBRAS* vol.32, pt.1, 1959:1-32b, *MBRAS* repr. 4, 1977:286-310

Granet, M., *Festivals and Songs of Ancient China*, London, G. Routledge 1932

Gregory, M., *China Trade Paintings and Other Pictures Relating to the Far East*, London, Green and Co. 1982

Gregory, M., *Canton and the China Trade*, London, Green and Co. 1986

Grimberg, M.L., *Some Games of Asia*, Singapore, Asia Pacific Press 1974

Groot, J.J.M. de, 'Les fêtes annuellement celebrées à émoui: études concernant la religion populaire des chinois', *Annales du Musée Guimet* vol.11-12, 1886

A Guide to Manuscripts and Documents in the British Isles Relating to the Far East, compiled by N. Matthews and M.D. Wainwright, J.D. Pearson (ed.), Oxford, Oxford University Press 1977

Gullick, J.M., *Indigenous Political Systems of Western Malaya*, London University Athlone Press 1958

Gwee Thian Hock, *A Nonya Mosaic: My Mother's Childhood*, Singapore, Times Books International, 1985

Gyllensvard, B., *Chinese Gold and Silver in the Carl Kempe Collection*, Stockholm, Nardisk Rotogravr 1953

Hall-Jones, J., *The Thomson Paintings: Mid-nineteenth Century Paintings of the Straits Settlements and Malaya*, Singapore, Oxford University Press 1983

Hall-Jones, J. and C. Hooi, *An Early Surveyor in Singapore, John Turnbull Thomson in Singapore 1841-53*, Singapore National Museum 1979

Hallgren, C., *Morally United and Politically Divided; the Chinese Community of Penang*, Ph.D. thesis, University of Stockholm 1986

Halson, E., *Peking Opera*, Hong Kong, Oxford University Press 1982

Hamilton, A.W., 'The Boria', *JSBRAS*, vol.82, Sept. 1920:139-44

Hamilton, A.W., 'Chinese Loan-words in Malay', *JMBRAS* vol.2, pt.1, June 1924:48-56

Hamilton, A.W., 'Penang Malay', *JSBRAS* vol. 85, Mar. 1922:67-96, *JMBRAS* vol.3, pt.3, Dec. 1925:56

Hamlin, T., *Architecture Through the Ages*, New York, G.P. Putman's Sons 1953

Hancock, T.H.H., *Coleman's Singapore*, MBRAS monograph no.15, 1986

Hao Yen-p'ing, *The Comprador in Nineteenth Century China: Bridge Between East and West*, Cambridge, Mass. 1970

Hare, G.T., 'The Game of Chap-ji-ki', *JSBRAS* vol.31, July 1898:63-71

Harlow, V.T. and F. Madden, *British Colonial Developments 1774-1834*, Oxford, Clarendon Press 1953

Harrisson, B., 'Trade in the Straits of Malacca in 1785', *JMBRAS* vol.26, pt.1, July 1953:56-62

Harrisson, B, *Swatow in Het Princessehof*, Leeuwarden, Gemeentelijk Museum Het Princessehof 1979

Harrisson, T., 'The Great Cave, Sarawak: a Ship of the Dead Cult and Related Rock Paintings', *Archaeological Newsletter* vol.6, no.9, 1958:199-203

Haughton, H.T., 'Native Names of Streets in Singapore', *JSBRAS* vol.23, June 1891

Haughton, H.T., 'Boriah', *JSBRAS* vol.30, July 1897:312-13

Hawley, W.M., *Chinese Folk Designs*, Toronto, General Publishing Company 1949, New York, Dover Publications 1971

Hentze, C., *Chinese Tomb Figures: a Study of the Beliefs and Folklore of Ancient China*, London, E. Goldston 1928

Higgins, A., *Java, with a Note Concerning the Islands of Penang and Singapore*, Boston, Raymond and Whitcomb 1909

Hill, A.H., 'Kelantan Silverwork', *JMBRAS* vol.24, 1951:99-108

Hilton, R.N., 'The Basic Malay House', *JMBRAS* vol.29, 1956:134-55

History and Development of Ancient Chinese Architecture, Beijing, Science Press 1986

History, Lore and Legend: Shiwan Pottery Figures, Hong Kong Urban Council 1986

History of Penang: a Selected and Annotated Bibliography, compiled by J. Tan Poh Choo, Penang, Universiti Sains Malaysia 1991

Ho, R., *Rainbow Round My Shoulder*, Singapore, Eastern Universities Press 1975

Ho Wing Meng, *Straits Chinese Silver*, Singapore, University Education Press 1976

Ho Wing Meng, *Straits Chinese Porcelain: a Collector's Guide*, Singapore, Times Books International 1983

Ho Wing Meng, *Straits Chinese Silver: a Collector's Guide*, Singapore, Times Books International 1984

Ho Wing Meng, *Straits Chinese Beadwork and Embroidery*, Singapore, Times Books International 1987

Honour, H., *Chinoiserie: the Vision of Cathay*, London, John Murray 1961

Hooi, C., 'Whampao and his Country House', *Malaysia in History* vol.10, pt.1, 1965:21-25

Horn, P., *The Rise and Fall of the Victorian Servant*, Gloucester, A. Sutton Pub. 1986

The House in East and Southeast Asia, K.G. Izikowitz and P. Sorensen (eds.), London, Curzon Press 1982

Howe, S.E., *In Quest of Spices*, London, Herbert Jenkins 1946

Hymes, D., *Pidginization and Creolization of Languages*, Cambridge University Press 1977

Imperial China: Photographs 1850-1912, Canberra, Australian National University 1980

Imperial Porcelain of the Yongle and Xuande Periods Excavated from the Site of the Ming Imperial Factory at Jingdezhen, Hong Kong, Urban Council 1989

Impey, O., *Chinoiserie: the Impact of Oriental Styles on Western Art and Decoration*, London, Oxford University Press 1979

Indonesia: Images of the Past, Singapore, Times Editions 1987

Irons, N.J., *Silver and Carving of the Old China Trade*, London, House of Fans and Hong Kong, Kaiserreich Kunst 1983

Jackson, J.C., *Planters and Speculators: Chinese and European Enterprise in Malaya 1786-1921*, Kuala Lumpur, University of Malaya Press 1968

Jackson, J.L., 'The Chinatowns of South East Asia', *Pacific View-point* vol.16, pt.1, May 1975:45-77

Jacob, G. and Jensen, H., *Das Chinesische Schattentheater*, Stuttgart, W. Kohlhammer 1933

Jarry, M., *Chinoiserie: Chinese Influence on European Decorative Art 17th and 18th Centuries*, New York, The Vendome Press/London, Sotheby Pubs. 1981

Jenyns, R.S., *Later Chinese Porcelain: the Ch'ing Dynasty (1644-1912)*, London, Faber and Faber 1951, 1971

Jenyns, R.S., *Chinese Art: the Minor Arts*, London, Oldbourne Press 1963

Jones, O., *Chinese Design and Pattern in Full Colour*, New York Dover 1981

Jones, O., *The Grammar of Ornament: Illustrated by Examples from Various Styles of Ornament*, New York, Van Nostrand Reinhold 1982

Jourdain, M. and R.S. Jenyns, *Chinese Export Art in the Eighteenth Century*, London, Country Life 1950

Keynon-Kies, C., *Collecting Victorian Staffordshire Figures*, Antique Pubs 1990

Khoo Joo Ee, 'An Approach to the Search for Identity', *Architecture and Identity*, Singapore, Concept Media for The Aga Khan Award for Architecture 1983:78-85

Khoo Joo Ee, 'Cloves, Nutmeg, Pepper, Cinnamon: the Life of Spice', *The UNESCO Courier*, June 1984:20-1

Khoo Joo Ee, 'The Romance of the Nyonya', *Pulau Pinang* vol.2, no.6 1990:17-20

Khoo Joo Ee, 'Nyonya Jewellery', *Pulau Pinang* vol.3, no.1, 1991:4-7

Khoo Joo Ee, *Kendi, Pouring Vessels in the University of Malaya Collection*, Singapore, Oxford University Press 1991

Khoo Kay Kim, 'Keterlibatan Orang-orang Melayu dalam persatuan-persatuan sulit', *Jernal Sejarah* 14, 1976/77:63-9

King, A.D., *The Bungalow*, London, Routledge and Kegan Paul 1984

Knapp, R.G., *China's Traditional Rural Architecture*, University of Hawaii 1986

Kohl, D.G., *Chinese Architecture in the Straits Settlements and Western Malaya: Temples, Kongsis and Houses*, Kuala Lumpur, Heinemann 1984

Koleksi Sastera Peranakan dalam Pegangan Perpustakaan Universiti Malaya, Kuala Lumpur, University of Malaya Library 1979

Kon, S., *Emily of Emerald Hill*, Singapore, Macmillan 1989

Kuchler, J., 'Penang's Chinese Population', *Asian Studies* 3, 1965:435-58

Kwee, J.B., *Chinese Malay Literature of the Peranakan Chinese in Indonesia 1880-1942*, Ph.D. thesis, University of Auckland, 1978

Lai Ah Eng, *Peasants, Proletarians and Prostitutes*, ISEAS 1986

Latsch, M-L., *Chinese Traditional Festivals*, Beijing, New World Press 1984

Law, J. and B.E. Ward, *Chinese Festivals in Hong Kong*, Hong Kong, South China Morning Post 1982

Lebra, J. and J. Paulson, *Chinese Women in Southeast Asia*, Singapore, Times International 1980

Lee Kip Lin, *Emerald Hill: the Story of a Street in Words and Pictures*, Singapore National Museum 1984

Lee Poh Ping, *Chinese Society in Nineteenth and Early Twentieth Century Singapore: a Socio-economic Analysis*, Kuala Lumpur/New York, Oxford University Press 1978

Liang Ssu-ch'eng, *A Pictorial History of Chinese Architecture*, Massachusettes Institute of Technology Press 1984

Lim Chong Keat, *Penang Views 1770-1860*, Singapore, Summer Times Publishing 1986

Lim, J., *Sold for Silver: an Autobiography*, Singapore, Oxford University Press 1985

Lim Jee Yuan, *The Malay House*, Penang, Institut Masyarakat 1987

Lim U.W., 'Opium in the Straits Settlements', JSEAH vol.2, pt.1, Mar. 1961:52-75

Lim S.H. Jon, 'The "Shophouse Rafflesia": an Outline of its Malaysian Pedigree and its Subsequent Diffusion in Asia', JMBRAS vol.66, pt.1, 1993:47-66

Ling Roth, H., *Oriental Silverwork, Malay and Chinese*, London, Truslove and Hanson 1910, repr. Kuala Lumpur, University of Malaya Press 1966

Lip, E., *Chinese Geomancy*, Singapore, Times Books International 1979

Lip, E., *Chinese Temple Architecture in Singapore*, Singapore University Press 1983

Lo Man Yuk, 'Chinese Names of Streets in Penang', *JSBRAS* vol.33, 1900:197-246

Loeb, E.M. and O.M. Broek, 'Social Organisation and the Long House in Southeast Asia', *American Anthropologist* vol.49, 1947:414-25

Lombard-Salmon, C., 'Un Chinois à Java (1727-1736)', *BEFEO* vol.59, 1972:279-318

Lombard-Salmon, C., 'À propose de quelques cultes chinois particuliers à Java', *Arts Asiatiques* 26, 1973:243-64

Lombard-Salmon, C., 'À propose de quelques tombes chinoises d'Indonesie des XVIIe et XVIIIe siècles', *Archipel* no.12, 1976: 207-218

Low, J., *The British Settlement of Penang*, Singapore, Free Press 1836, repr. Singapore, Oxford University Press 1972

Lu Hua and Ma Chiang, *Traditional Chinese Textile Designs in Full Colour*, Peking, People's Art Publishing House 1957, New York, Dover 1980

Lu Pu, *Designs of Chinese Indigo Batik*, Beijing, New World Press and New York, Lee Publishers Group 1981

MacDonald, M., 'Malacca Buildings', *JMBRAS* vol.12, pt.2, Aug. 1934:27-37

Mailey, J., *Chinese Silk Tapestry: K'o-ssu*, New York, China Institute in America 1971

Mak Lau Fong, *The Emergence and Persistence of Chinese Secret Societies in Singapore and Peninsular Malaysia*, Ph.D. thesis, University of Waterloo 1977

Malaya, a Retrospect of the Country through Postcards, Petaling Jaya, Star Publications 1983

Malaysian Architectural Heritage Survey: a Handbook, monograph Heritage of Malaysia Trust 1985

Maxwell, P.B., 'The Law of England in Penang, Malacca and Singapore', *JIAEA* vol.3, 1859:26-55

Maxwell, R., *Textiles of Southeast Asia: Tradition, Trade and Transformation*, Melbourne, Oxford University Press 1990

McTaggart, W.D., *The Distribution of Ethnic Groups in Georgetown*, Penang 1966, Kuala Lumpur, University of Malaya 1966

Melaka: the Transformation of a Malay Capital, 1400-1980, K.S. Sandhu and P. Wheatley (eds.), Kuala Lumpur, Oxford University Press 1983

Mialaret, J.P., *Passing through Singapore*, Singapore, Graham Brash 1986

Miksic, J.N., 'Archaeology and Palaeogeography in the Straits of Malacca', *Economic Exchange and Social Interaction in Southeast Asia*, K.L. Hutterer (ed.), University of Michigan 1977:55-75

Miller, H., *A Short History of Malaysia*, New York, Praeger 1965

Miller, R., *The East Indiamen*, New Jersey, Times-Life Books 1980

Mills, L.A., 'British Malaya 1824-67', *JMBRAS* vol.3, pt.2, 1925:1-339, vol.33, pt.3, 1960:5-320, repr. Kuala Lumpur, Oxford University Press 1966, New York, AMS Press 1971

Mohd. Kassim Ali, *Gold Jewellery and Ornaments in the Collection of Muzium Negara*, Kuala Lumpur, Persatuan Muzium Malaysia 1988

Mohtar Md. Dom, *Malay Wedding Customs*, Kuala Lumpur, Federal Publications 1979

Moore, D. and J. Moore, *The First 150 Years of Singapore*, Singapore, D. Moore 1969

Moorehead, F.J., *A History of Malaya and Her Neighbours*, London, Longman, Green and Coy 1957

Morris, E.T., *The Gardens of China: History, Art and Meanings*, New York, Charles Scribner's Sons 1983

Munsterberg, H., *Mingei: Folk Arts of Japan*, New York, The Asia Society 1965

Nagata, J., *Malaysian Mosaic: Perspectives from a Poly-ethnic Society*, Vancouver, University of British Columbia Press 1979

Newbold, T.J., *Political and Statistical Account of the British Settlements in the Straits of Malacca*, Kuala Lumpur, Oxford University Press 1971

Ng Chin Keong, *Trade and Society: the Amoy Network on the China Coast 1683-1735*, National University of Singapore 1983

Ng, D., *Malaya, Lifestyles 1900-1930*, Kuala Lumpur, Fajar Bakti 1989

Ng Siew Yoong, 'The Chinese Protectorate in Singapore, 1877-1900', *JSEAH* vol.2, pt.1, 1961:76-99

Nguyen van Huyen, *Introduction à l'étude de l'habitation sur pilotis dans l'Asie du Sud-est*, Paris, Librairie Orientaliste Paul Geuthner 1934

Olson, E., *The Chinese of Malaya: a Study of an Immigrant Group as a Field for Mission Work*, MA thesis, University of Chicago 1932

Omar Farouk Sheik Ahmad, 'The Arabs in Penang' *Malaysia in History* vol.21, pt.2, Dec.1978:1-16

Ooi, D., *A Study of the English-speaking Chinese of Penang, 1900-1941*, unpub. MA thesis, Kuala Lumpur, University of Malaya, 1967

Osgood, C., *Village Life in Old China*, New York, Ronald Press 1963

Othman Mohd. Yatim and Raiha Mohd. Saud, *Baba and Nonya Heritage at the Muzium Negara*, Kuala Lumpur National Museum 1986

Parkinson, C.N., 'The Homes of Malaya', *Malaya in History* vol.2, pt.2, Dec.1955:123-30

Pastel Portraits, Singapore's Architectural Heritage, Singapore, The Singapore Coordinating Committee 1984

The Penang Riots 1867, Penang Historical Society 1955

Penang: The City and Suburbs in the Early Twentieth Century, Penang Museum 1986

Penang: Past and Present, 1786-1963, Penang City Council 1966

Penang Through Old Picture Postcards, Penang Museum 1986

Philips, C.H., *The East India Company, 1784-1834*, London, Barnes and Noble 1961

Phillips, G., 'Two Medieval Fuh-kien Trading Ports: Chuan-chow and Chang-chow', *T'oung Pao* vol.6, 1895:449-65, vol.7, 1896: 223-40

Pintado, M.J., *A Stroll Through Ancient Malacca*, Johore Bahru, Gan Seng 1980

Pinto, M.H.M. and M.C.C. Moura, *Portugal and the East through Embroidery*, Washington D.C., International Exhibitions Foundation 1981

Pires, T., *The Suma Oriental of Tome Pires and the Book of Francisco Rodriques*, A. Cortesao (ed.), Cambridge University Press for the Hakluyt Society 1944

Png Poh Seng, 'The Kuomintang in Malaya, 1912-1941', *JSEAH* vol.2, pt.1, 1961:1-32

Png Poh Seng, 'The Straits Chinese in Singapore: a Case of Local Identity and Sino-cultural Accommodation', *JSEAH* vol.10, no.1, 1969:95-114

Poh, T., *Gods and Deities in Popular Chinese Worship*, Penang, T. Poh 1973

Poh, T., *Chinese Temples in Penang*, Penang 1978

Posener, J., 'House Traditions in Malaya', *Architectural Review* vol.130, Oct. 1961:280-83

Precious Cargo: Objects of the China Trade, New York, The Chinese Porcelain Co. 1985

Proceedings of the Committee Appointed by His Excellency the Governor to Report on Matters Concerning Chinese Marriages, Singapore Government Printers Office 1926

Purcell, V., 'Chinese Settlement in Malacca', *JMBRAS* vol.20, pt.1, 1947:115-125; *MBRAS* repr. no.4, 1977:131-41

Purcell, V., *The Chinese in Malaya*, Kuala Lumpur, Oxford University Press 1948, 1967, 1978

Purcell, V., *The Chinese in Southeast Asia*, Royal Institute of International Affairs, 1951, 1965, Kuala Lumpur, Oxford University Press 1966, 1981

Raadt-Apell, M.J., *De Batikkerij van Zuylen te Pekalongan*, Zutphen, Terra 1980

Rahmah Bujang, *Boria: a Form of Malay Theatre*, ISEAS 1987

Rapoport, A., *House Form and Culture*, New Jersey, Prentice-Hall 1969

Rutter, O., *The Pirate Wind: Tales of the Sea-robbers of Malaya*, Singapore, Oxford University Press 1986

Ryan, N.J., *The Cultural Heritage of Malaya*, Kuala Lumpur, Longman 1971, 1975

SEACS, *Nonya Ware and Kitchen Ch'ing: Ceremonial and Domestic Pottery of the 19th-20th Centuries Commonly Found in Malaysia*, Kuala Lumpur, Oxford University Press for SEACS 1981

Salmon, C., *Literature in Malay by the Chinese of Indonesia: a Provisional Annotated Bibliography*, Paris, *Études Insulindiennes-Archipel* 3, 1981

Salmon, C. and D. Lombard, *Les Chinois de Jakarta: temples et vie collective*, Paris 1977 (Cahier d'Archipel 6)

Santa Maria, L., 'Linguistic Relations Between China and the Malay-Indonesian World', *East and West*, n.s. 24, 1974:365-79

Sardesai, D.R., *British Trade and Expansion in Southeast Asia 1830-1914*, New Delhi, Allied Publishers 1977

Savidge, J., *This is Hong Kong: Temples*, Hong Kong Government Printers 1979

Schafer, E.H., The Empire of Min, Tokyo, C.E. Tuttle 1974

Schafer, E.H., The Vermilion Bird, University of California 1967

Scholland, F.S., 'Temple Rooftop Styles in Overseas Chinese Communities', *Chinese Society Bulletin* 1976/77:7-10

Scott, J., 'The Settlement of Penang', *JMBRAS* vol.28, pt.1, 1955:37-51

Sejarah Melayu: or Malay Annals, tr. Brown, C.C., Kuala Lumpur, Oxford University Press 1970, 1976

Semple, E.G., *Singapore Religions*, Singapore, Methodist Publishing House 1927

Seyd, M., *Introducing Beads*, London, B.T. Batsford 1973

Shellabear, W.G., 'Baba Malay: an Introduction to the Language of the Straits-born Chinese', *JSBRAS* vol.65, 1913:49-59, *MBRAS* repr. no.4, 1977:36-46

Sheppard, M.C., 'Emperor Yung Lo and Admiral Cheng Ho', *Malaya in History* vol.3, pt.2, July 1957:114-5

Sheppard, M.C., 'Malacca in the Time of Cheng Ho', *Malaya in History* vol.4, pt.1, Jan 1958:18-9

Sheppard, M.C., 'The Penang Boria: a Fragment of Malayan Musical History', *Malaya in History* vol.10, pt.1, Apr.1965:39-41

Sickman, L. and Soper, A., *The Art and Architecture of China*, Harmondsworth, Middlesex, Penguin Books 1956, 1971

Sidhu, J.S., 'Sir Cecil Clementi and the Kuomintang in Malaya', *Malaysia in History* vol.9, pts. 1 and 2, 1965:18-21

Sim, K., *Flowers in the Sun*, Singapore, Eastern Universities Press 1982

Simmonds, E.H.S., 'Francis Light and the Ladies of Thalang', *JMBRAS* vol.38, pt.2, 1966:213-28

Singam, S. Durai Raja, *Malayan Street Names*, Ipoh, Mercantile Press 1939

Singapore Historical Postcards from the National Archives Collection, Singapore, Times Editions, 1987

Siti Zainon Ismail, *Konsep pakaian cara Melayu: satu kajian analis budaya benda*, unpub. Ph.D. thesis, University of Malaya 1991

Skeat, W.W. and H.N. Ridley, 'The Orang Laut of Singapore', *JSBRAS* vol.33, Jan. 1900:247-250

Skinner, G.W., 'Java's Chinese Minority: Continuity and Change', *Journal of Asian Studies* vol.20, pt.3, 1961:353-62

Sleen, W.G.N. van der, *A Handbook of Beads*, Liege, Musée du Verre 1967

Snook, B., *Embroidery Stitches*, London, B.T. Batsford 1972

Soh Eng Lim, 'Tan Cheng Lock', *JSEAH* vol.1, 1960:29-55

Somers Heidhues, M.F., *Southeast Asia's Chinese Minorities*, Longman 1974

Song Ong Siang, *One Hundred Years' History of the Chinese in Singapore*, London, John Murray 1902, University of Malaya Press 1967, repr. Singapore, Oxford University Press 1984, 1985

Sopiee, Mohd. Noordin, 'The Penang Secession Movement 1948-51', *JSEAS* vol.4, 1973:52-71

South China in the Sixteenth Century, C.R. Boxer (ed.), London University for the Hakluyt Society 1953

Spencer, J.E., 'The Houses of the Chinese', *Geographical Review* No.37, 1947:254-73

Spiegel, H., 'Soul-boats in Melanesia: a Study in Diffusion', *Archaeology and Physical Anthropology of Oceania* vol.6, pt.1, 1971:34-43

Stalberg, R.H. and R. Nesi, *China's Crafts*, London, George Allen and Unwin 1981

Steensgaard, N., *The Asian Trade Revolution of the Seventeenth Century: the East India Companies and the Decline of the Caravan Trade*, University of Chicago Press 1974

Stirling, W.G., 'Chinese Exorcists', *JMBRAS* vol.2, 1924:41-7

Straits Affairs: the Malay World and Singapore, compiled by D.J.M. Tate, Hong Kong, John Nicholson 1989

Stubbs-Brown, M.L., 'Trade and Shipping in Early Penang', *Malaysia in History* vol.21, 1978:17-35

Swann, N.L., *Food and Money in Ancient China*, Princeton University Press 1950

Swift, A., *The Larousse Encyclopedia of Embroidery Techniques*, New York, Larousse 1984

Symposium on Historical, Archaeological and Linguistic Studies on Southern China, South-East Asia and the Hong Kong Region, Hong Kong University Press 1967

Tan, C., *Penang Nyonya Cooking*, Singapore, Eastern Universities Press 1983

Tan Chee Beng, 'Baba Chinese, Non-Baba Chinese and Malays: a Note on Ethnic Interaction in Malacca', *Southeast Asian Journal of Social Science* vol.7, pts.1-2, 1979:20-29

Tan Chee Beng, 'Baba Chinese Publication in Romanised Malay', *Journal Asian and African Studies*, no.22, 1981:158-93

Tan Chee Beng, 'Mengenai sebuah pantun Baba dan perkahwinan dulu-kala orang Cina', *Jurnal Sejarah Melaka* Bil.7, 1982:42-53

Tan Chee Beng, *The Baba of Melaka: Culture and Identity of a Chinese Peranakan Community in Malaysia*, Petaling Jaya, Pelanduk Publications 1988

Tan, D., 'Some Activities of the Straits Chinese British Association, Penang 1920-1939', *Peninjau Sejarah* vol.2, pt.2, 1967:30-40

Tan Eng Seong, 'Culture-bound Syndromes Among Overseas Chinese', Normal and Abnormal Behaviour in Chinese Culture, A. Kleinman and Lin Tsung-Yi (eds.), Dordrecht, D. Reidel Pub. 1981:371-86

Tan Giok Lan, *The Chinese of Sukabumi: a Study in Social and Cultural Accomodation*, Cornell University Press 1963

Tan Kok Seng, *Son of Singapore: Autobiography of a Coolie*, Singapore, Heinemann 1972

Tan Pek Leng, *Chinese Secret Societies and Labour Control in the Straits Settlements*, MA thesis, Columbia University 1979

Tan Sooi Beng, 'An Introduction to the Chinese Glove Puppet Theatre in Malaysia', *JMBRAS* vol.57, pt.1, 1984:40-55

Tan Sooi Beng, *Bangsawan: a Social and Stylistic History of Popular Malay Opera*, Kuala Lumpur, Oxford University Press 1993

Tan, T., *Straits Chinese Cookbook*, Singapore, Times Books International 1981

Tan T.W., *Your Chinese Roots: The Overseas Chinese Story*, Singapore, Times Books International 1986

Tarling, N., *The Fall of Imperial Britain in South-East Asia*, Kuala Lumpur, Oxford University Press 1993

Teo Lay Teen, *A Study of the Malay Translation of Chinese Popular Fiction by the Baba Chinese: with Special Reference to Khian Leong Koon Yew Kang Lam*, unpub. MA thesis, Kuala Lumpur, University of Malaya 1980

Teo, M., *Nineteenth Century Prints of Singapore*, Singapore National Museum 1987

Tham Seong Chee, *Religion and Modernization: a Study of Changing Rituals Among Singapore's Chinese, Malays and Indians*, Singapore Graham Brash 1985

The Siauw Giap, 'Religion and Overseas Chinese Assimilation in Southeast Asian Countries', *Revue de Sud-est Asiatique* 2, 1965:67-83

Thierry, S., *Le betel: I. Inde et Asie du Sud-est*, Paris, Musée de l'homme 1969

Thomas, P.L., *Like Tigers Around a Piece of Meat: the Baba Style of Dondang Sayang*, ISEAS 1986

Till, B., *Porcelain of the High Qing: the Brian S. Mcelney Collection*, Art Gallery of Greater Victoria, British Columbia, 1983

Topley, M., 'Chinese Rites for the Repose of the Soul: with Special Reference to Cantonese Custom', *JMBRAS* vol.25, pt.1, 1952:149-60

Topsfield, A., *An Introduction to Indian Court Painting*, London, Victoria and Albert Museum 1984

Travellers' Tales of Old Singapore, compiled by M. Wise, Singapore, Times Books International 1985

Travellers' Tales of the South China Coast, Hong Kong, Canton, Macao, Singapore, Times Books International 1986

Treasures from the National Museum, Singapore National Museum 1987

Tregonning, K.G., 'Penang and the Old China Trade', *Malaya in History* vol.5, pt.1, 1959:2-12

Turnbull, C.M., 'Communal Disturbances in the Straits Settlements in 1857', *JMBRAS* vol.31, pt.1, May 1958:94-144

Turnbull, C.M., 'Convicts in the Straits Settlements 1826-1867', *JMBRAS* vol.43, pt.1, July 1970:87-103

Turnbull, C.M., *A History of Singapore: 1819-1975*, Kuala Lumpur, Oxford University Press 1977

Twentieth Century Impressions of British Malaya, A. Wright and H.A. Cartwright (eds.), London, Lloyds Greater Britain Pub. 1908

Vaughan, J.D., 'Notes on the Chinese of Penang', *JIAEA* vol.8, 1854:1-27

Vaughan, J.D., *The Manners and Customs of the Chinese of the Straits Settlements*, Singapore, Mission Press 1879, repr. Kuala Lumpur, Oxford University Press 1971, 1974

Vente, I., *Wayang:Chinese Street Opera in Singapore*, Singapore, Malaya Publishing House 1984

Viraphol, Sarasin, *The Nanyang Chinese*, Bangkok, Chulalongkorn University Press 1972

Vis, L., *The Stadhuys of Malacca*, Kuala Lumpur, National Museum 1982

Vlatseas, S., *A History of Malaysian Architecture*, Singapore, Longman 1990

Vollmer, J.E., *Five Colours of the Universe: Symbolism in Clothes and Fabrics of the Ch'ing Dynasty (1644-1911)*, Hong Kong, Edmonton Art Gallery 1980

Wakeman, F.E., *Strangers at the Gate: Social Disorder in South China 1839-1861*, Ph.D. thesis, University of California 1966

Wang Gungwu, *The Nanhai Trade: a Study of the Early History of Chinese Trade in the South China Sea*, JMBRAS vol.31, pt.2, 1958

Wang Gungwu, *Chinese Reformists and Revolutionaries in the Straits Settlements 1900-1911*, JSSS vol.15, pt.2, 1959

Wang Gungwu, *A Short History of the Nanyang Chinese*, Singapore, Eastern Universities Press 1959

Wang Gungwu, 'Early Ming Relations with Southeast Asia', *The Chinese World Order*, J.K. Fairbank (ed.), Cambridge, Mass. 1968-34-62

Wang Shi-Xiang, *Classic Chinese Furniture, Ming and Early Qing Dynasties*, London, Han-Shan Tang 1986

Wang Tai-peng, *The Origins of Chinese Kongsi, with Special Reference to West Borneo*, unpub. MA thesis, Canberra, Australian National University 1977

Wang Yarong, *Chinese Folk Embroidery*, London, Thames and Hudson 1987

Ward, B., 'A Hakka Kongsi in Borneo', *Hong Kong Journal of Oriental Studies* vol. 1, pt.s, 1954:358-70

Warisan Baba/The Baba Heritage, Kuala Lumpur National Museum 1983

Warren, J.F., *Ah Ku and Karayuki-san: Prostitution in Singapore 1870-1940*, Singapore, Oxford University Press 1993

Watson, W., *Cultural Frontiers in Ancient East Asia*, Edinburgh University Press 1971

Werner, E.T.C., *Myths and Legends of China*, London, George Harrap 1922, repr. Singapore, Graham Brash 1984

Westerhaut, J.B., 'Notes on the Chinese of Penang', *JIAEA* vol.8, 1854:1-27

Wheatley, P. *The Golden Khersonese*, Kuala Lumpur, University of Malaya Press 1961, repr. Pustaka Ilmu 1966

Whitmore, J.K., 'The Opening of Southeast Asia: Trading Patterns through the Centuries', *Economic Exchange and Social Interaction in Southeast Asia*, K. Hutterer (ed.), Michigan University 1977:139-53

Wiens, H.J., *China's March Toward the Tropics*, Connecticut, The Shoe String Press 1954

Wiens, H.J., *Han Chinese Expansion in South China*, Connecticut, The Shoe String Press 1967

Wilbur, M.E., *The East India Company and the British Empire in the Far East*, London, Russell and Russell 1970

Williams, C.A.S., *Outlines of Chinese Symbolism and Art Motives*, Shanghai, Kelly and Walsh 1932, 1941, repr. New York, Dover 1976

Williamson, G.C., *The Book of Famille Rose*, London, Kegan Paul, Trench, Trubner, 1927, repr. Tokyo 1970

Willmott, D.E., *The Chinese of Semarang*, Ithaca, Cornell University Press 1960

Wolf, M., *Women and the Family in Rural Taiwan*, Stanford University Press 1972

Wong, C.S., *A Gallery of Chinese Kapitans*, Singapore Ministry of Culture 1963

Wong, C.S., *'Kek Lok Si': Temple of Paradise*, Singapore, Malaysian Sociological Research Inst., 1963

Wong, C.S., *An Illustrated Cycle of Chinese Festivities in Malaysia and Singapore*, Singapore, Jack Chia 1987

Woo Keng Thye, *Web of Tradition*, Singapore, Heinemann 1986

Wood, V., *Victoriana: a Collector's Guide*, London, G. Bell 1960

Woods, W.W., *Report on the Commission on Mui Tsai in Hong Kong*, London, His Majesty's Stationery Office, col.no.125, 1937

Wu Lien Teh and Ng Yok Hing, *The Queen's Scholarships of Malaya 1885-1948*, Penang, Premier Press 1949

Yamawaki, Teijiro, 'The Great Trading Merchants, Cocksinja and His Son', *Acta Asiatica* no.30, 1976:106-16

Yap Pheng Geck, *Scholar, Banker, Gentleman, Soldier: the Reminiscences of Dr. Yap Pheng Geck*, Singapore, Times Books International 1982

Yeang, K., *The Architecture of Malaysia*, Kuala Lumpur, The Pepin Press 1992

Yeap Joo Kim, *The Patriarch*, the author 1975

Yen Ching-hwang, *The Overseas Chinese and the 1911 Revolution*, Singapore, Oxford University Press 1976

Yen Ching-hwang, *Class Structure and Social Mobility in the Chinese Community in Singapore and Malaya 1800-1911*, University of Adelaide 1983

Yen Ching-hwang, *A Social History of the Chinese in Singapore and Malaya 1800-1911*, Singapore, Oxford University Press 1986

Yetts, W.P., 'Notes on Chinese Roof-tiles', *Transactions of the Oriental Ceramic Society* vol.7, 1927-28:13-44

Yip Yat Hoong, *The Development of the Tin Mining Industry of Malaya*, Kuala Lumpur, University of Malaya Press 1969

Yong, K.P., 'Chinese Buildings in Malaya', *Peta* 1/3, June 1956:1-12

Anglo-Indian architecture
Palladian buildings in British India of the seventeenth and eighteenth centuries, characterized by white stucco on exterior and interior walls, high ceilings and neoclassical decoration.

Arcade
A row of arches supported by columns or piers.

Arita
Name of a kiln site in Hizen province, Japan which flourished in the seventeenth and eighteenth centuries; its polychrome wares include the Imari and Kakiemon types.

Art Deco
A style of design popular in the 1920s and 1930s. The name originated as the sub-title of an exhibition catalogue of *Arts Decoratifs* held in Paris in 1925; also called *Art Moderne, Modernistic, La Mode, Les Années 25* and others. It is classical inasmuch as it is symmetrical and rectilinear.

Art Nouveau
The name of a shop that opened in Paris in 1895 with objects that did not imitate the style of the past. This was part of a movement that had begun with production of books and textiles in England in the 1880s. By c.1890 it had influenced furniture and other furnishings. The origins of the style were in the designs of William Morris and English arts and crafts of the time. From 1892 onwards this movement spread to Brussels and France, where it centred on Nancy and Paris. Art Nouveau is characterized by the pervading use of undulating lines which conjure up images of sinuous flower stalks, flowing hair, waves and flames.

Baroque
Ornate, lavishly ornamented. The Baroque period of European history, c.1600-1750, applies especially to Italy, Spain, Germany and Austria, France and England. The term Baroque Classicism means Baroque tempered by classical elements. This is especially so in England.

Chinoiserie
A style and period of Chinese influence in Europe, beginning in the seventeenth century and culminating in the eighteenth century.

Classical
The style and motifs of the ancient Athenian Greek and Imperial Roman civilization (c.500 BC-395 AD), which were later emulated in the European Renaissance (c.1300-1500 AD) and neoclassical revivals. In architecture, there are five Orders of which three are Greek (Doric, Ionic and Corinthian) while the other two are Roman (Tuscan and Corinthian).

Cornice
The finishing or crowning protecting moulding along the top of a wall.

Corinthian Order
The third Order of Greek architecture in the fifth century BC. This Athenian column and façade design is characterized by the stylised acanthus leaves in the capital.

Crane
Regarded as the patriarch of birds and the messenger of immortals; a common symbol of longevity. Placed on a coffin, it is the vehicle carrying the soul to paradise.

Doric Order
The first and simplest order of Greek architecture.

Dutch gable
A raised façade of a pedimented central panel with symmetrically curving sides.

Dvaravati
A pre-Thai state of Mon peoples roughly coinciding with modern Bangkok from around the sixth to thirteenth centuries, with offshoots in the north around Chiang Mai.

Eaves
The lower, projecting portion of the roof.

Eclectic
In architecture and art, the collective combination of varied and often unrelated styles and motifs into a single work.

Entablature
The upper portion of an Order.

Enamel
In ceramics, a transparent or opaque pigment that is vitreous and is coloured with metallic oxides. As a decoration over the glaze it is fired at a low temperature. Such enamel colours on ceramic ware are of a wider range than those used under the glaze. See also Famille rose.

Epergne
Derived from the French *épargner*, to save. As a space saver at a dining table, it is an elaborate stand with several branching arms which support smaller detachable receptacles. This composite server also saves the trouble of passing many serving dishes at the dinner table. While mostly of glass, some epergne are of silver. The same principle of multiple receptacles is also applied to epergne serving as composite flower vases.

Famille rose
French for 'pink family'. The phrase was invented by A. Jacquemart in the second half of the nineteenth century. It is not a type of ceramic but a method of decoration just as its predecessors famille verte and famille noir (green and black family respectively) are. The 'family' of pinks can range from very pale pink to ruby red which are all opaque enamel colours (as opposed to transparent famille verte and famille noir enamels). These enamel colours, similar to those applied on metals, are painted on already fired ceramics which are then fired a second time, the enamels maturing at a lower temperature than the colours of the first firing. The pinks of famille rose are derived from salts of gold and this mode of decoration was especially popular during the reigns of Yong Zheng (1723-35) and Qian Long (1736-95).

Fanlight
The semi-circle, often with bars arranged like the ribs of a fan, atop a window.

Fascia
A horizontal board attached under the eaves; usually carved.

Fluting
Shallow concave grooves running vertically on a surface.

Frieze
The ornamented horizontal band immediately below the cornice along the upper part of an internal wall.

Gothic style
West European Medieval pointed architecture of the thirteenth to fifteenth century.

Granulation
A decorative technique whereby tiny granules of molten metal are soldered onto a surface to form patterns; such granules can at the same time be a means of soldering applique pieces.

Greek Revival
— see Neoclassical.

Imari
Name of a port near the kiln site of Arita in Hizen province, Japan, which gives its name to the type of porcelain exported through it from the beginning of the eighteenth century. Its decoration is reminiscent of brocades and textiles.

Ionic Order
The second Order of Greek architecture, where the capital has volutes or spiral scrolls.

Kakiemon

A type of decorative pattern which takes the name of a Japanese potter, Sakaida Kakiemon, who worked at Arita in the seventeenth century. From Kakiemon, who was noted for his simple and elegant style of decoration, a line of Japanese potters painted with much delicacy simple motifs of blossoms, twigs with birds, children at play etc.

Neoclassical

Severe and restrained late eighteenth century architectural style reviving motifs from classical Greek and Roman civilizations; a 'Greek Revival' being popular throughout the nineteenth century in Europe, America, and European colonies in Asia and Africa, it had a strong influence on the Anglo-Indian style. It is the last phase of classicism with monumentality and calm grandeur.

Order

The entablature and its supporting column in classical European architecture.

Overglaze

Decoration on the surface of ceramic ware after it has been glazed; also called on-glaze. Such colours are termed enamels.

Palladian, Palladianism

A building style following works and publications of Andrea Palladio (1508-80).

Pier

The mass of stonework or masonry support of an arch, etc., a buttress.

Plinth

The lowest square section of the base of a column.

Portico

An entrance or vestibule with colonnaded roof.

Qilin

Sometimes called the Chinese unicorn. There are many variations of this creature which can be leonine, with or without scales, horns, bushy mane and tail. The animal is a good omen, among several other auspicious attributes.

Renaissance

French for 'rebirth' of classical architecture in fifteenth and sixteenth century Europe.

Repousse

A refinement of simple embossed decoration.

Rococo

A term derived from motifs based on rocks (Fr. *rocaille*) and shells (Fr. *coquille*). In fact actually the last phase of Baroque, it is not a style in its own right. The new decoration is light in weight and colour, often asymmetrical with shell-like and coral-like forms in curves, somtimes with an introduction of Indian and Chinese motifs. The Louis XV (or Regency) period is characterized by this almost playful grace, lightness and 'arabesque'. The Rococo manner is linked to the neoclassical period by the transitional Louis XV and XVI period.

Ruyi

While the name itself means 'in accordance with your heart's desire', it is an object in the shape of a stretched out S-shape which has become a symbol of prosperity, being held as a sceptre and an attribute of Buddhism. The head of the object is trefoil or heart-shaped and is conventionally called *ruyi* lappet or *ruyi* head and used widely as a decorative element.

Satin stitch

Emulates the material satin, which is a closely woven fabric with a lustrous and unbroken surface.

Stucco

Plasterwork.

Tekat

A form of embroidery with a raised surface produced by a template covered with satin stitch.

Tapestry

A decorative fabric, usually pictorial. With a plain warp (the verticle yarns), thick weft (horizontal) threads are inter-woven to form patterns.

Underglaze

Colours on ceramic ware applied before glazing. They 'mature' about the same temperature as that for fusing the glaze. Blue from cobalt is the commonest underglaze colour.

Victorian style

Eclectic revivalist architecture in nineteenth century Britain; Queen Victoria 1837-1901.

Villa

Roman and Renaissance spacious home with gardens and outbuildings.